Heinz-Dietrich Fischer

American Journalists Cover U.S. Neighbor Countries

Pulitzer Prize Panorama

edited by

Prof. Dr. Heinz-Dietrich Fischer
(Bochum)

Volume 20

LIT

Heinz-Dietrich Fischer

American Journalists Cover U.S. Neighbor Countries

Pulitzer Prize Winning Materials about the Bahamas, Canada, Cuba, Haiti and Mexico

The drawing on the front-cover by British cartoonist Leslie Gilbert Illingworth was published in the *Daily Mail* on October 29, 1962. The drawing on the back-cover by Hispanic-American cartoonist Lalo Alcaraz was published on August 24, 2017.

Gefördert durch Mittel der Pressestiftung RWV, Essen

This book is printed on acid-free paper.

Bibliographic information published by the Deutsche Nationalbibliothek
The Deutsche Nationalbibliothek lists this publication in the Deutsche Nationalbibliografie; detailed bibliographic data are available on the Internet at http://dnb.d-nb.de.

ISBN 978-3-643-91162-9 (pb)
ISBN 978-3-643-96162-4 (PDF)

A catalogue record for this book is available from the British Library.

© LIT VERLAG GmbH & Co. KG Wien,
Zweigniederlassung Zürich 2020
Klosbachstr. 107
CH-8032 Zürich
Tel. +41 (0) 44-251 75 05
E-Mail: zuerich@lit-verlag.ch   http://www.lit-verlag.ch
Distribution:
In the UK: Global Book Marketing, e-mail: mo@centralbooks.com
In North America: Independent Publishers Group, e-mail: orders@ipgbook.com
In Germany: LIT Verlag Fresnostr. 2, D-48159 Münster
Tel. +49 (0) 2 51-620 32 22, Fax +49 (0) 2 51-922 60 99, e-mail: vertrieb@lit-verlag.de
e-books are available at www.litwebshop.de

Preface

In the plan of the awards named after Joseph Pulitzer (1847-1911), the Reporting Category since 1917 embraced all fields - local, national and international coverage. In 1929, a separate prize group called 'Correspondence' was set up for Washington and Foreign reports, followed by 'Telegraphic Reporting International' in 1942. Both award categories were merged in 1948 to 'International Reporting'. All prize groups relating to foreign press coverage of American newspapers and news agencies included reporting about all countries outside the United States.

This book concentrates on coverage of U.S. neighbor countries. During the early years of the Pulitzer Prizes, for example, press reportings on Cuba or Canada seldom came to the attention of the Pulitzer Prize jurors; only in a few cases they made it to the list of finalists but did not win an award. The first time dispatches from Havana, Cuba, were mentioned in an jury report dated from March, 1929, covering the Pan American Conference of the previous year. The first reports about Canada that made it to the list of finalists, could be found in an jury report of March 1932, covering the parliamentary sessions at Ottawa in the year before.

Why are Pulitzer Prize-winning reports about U.S. neighbor countries that rare, are they not relevant to American newspaper readers? Relating to U.S. press coverage of Canada, the editor of an American newspaper decades ago stated: „Canadians are much more aware of us than we are of them ... Yet many Americans still think there is nothing in Canada except mountains, ducks and fish ... Canadians often say that Americans don't know there are big Canadian cities, and think the 'natives' live like Eskimos ... Now a better understanding between Americans and Canadians is needed" to avoid stereotypes.

The book at hand presents small parts of all Pulitzer Prize-winning exhibits about U.S. neighbor countries, published between 1952 and 2016. The sources and the jury reports came from the Pulitzer Prize Collection at New York's Columbia University. They are reprinted with reference to the „Doctrine of Fair Use" as embodied in the United States Copyright Act. According to that doctrine, excerpts of copyrighted works for scholarly publications may be reprinted when their use does not encompass a substantial portion of these works. To realize this volume, I am very much indebted to Dana Canedy and Edward M. Kliment of the Pulitzer Prize Office at Columbia University, and to Dr. Jörg Kurzeja, Essen.

Ruhr University of Bochum, Germany,
October 2019

Heinz-D. Fischer

*This Volume
is dedicated
to*

Prof. Dr. Arnulf Kutsch

*- Distinguished Media and
Communication Historian -
on his 70th Birthday*

Contents

IV

Bahamas

CRIMINALS AND GAMBLERS
Stanley Penn/Monroe Karmin, *Wall Street Journal*

When the Pulitzer Prize juries assembled in March 1967 to filter out winners in all journalism award categories, they had a problem to find the right prize group for an specific entry. The *Wall Street Journal* had submitted an exhibit containing an international topic but entered it in the Local Reporting category. From there it was moved to the International Reporting group,but the jurors there thought it would fit better into the National Reporting category. The National Reporting jury, according to their report, had on their list of finalists reporters from the *Washington Evening Star*, *Chicago Daily News*, *Des Moines Register* and the *National Observer* but not the *Wall Street Journal*'s exhibit. The Pulitzer Prize Board did not accept any of the jury's favorites but gave the Pulitzer award to Stanley Penn and Monroe Karmin of the *Wall Street Journal* „for their investigative reporting of the connection between Arnerican crime and gambling in the Bahamas" in 1966.

Monroe William Karmin, born on September 2, 1929, in Mineola, New York, is a graduate of the Graduate School of Journalism at Columbia University and the University of Illinois. In 1953 he became a member of the *Wall Street Journal* news staff, mostly in the Washington bureau. In his early years in Washington he covered a wide variety of topics ranging from high finance at the U. S. Treasury to high legal doctrine at the Supreme Court. Later on, Karmin became a special writer concerned with urban affairs and civil rights as well as special investigatory projects. He also became a member of the National Press Club and of Sigma Delta Chi.

Stanley William Penn, born on January 12,1928, in New York City, went to New York Public Schools. He attended Brooklyn College for two years and spent the last two years at the University of Missouri in Columbia, Mo., where he was graduated with a Bachelor of Journalism degree. Penn joined the *Wall Street Journal* in 1952. He was a reporter in the *Journal*'s Chicago and Detroit offices before joining the New York staff in 1957. Karmin and Penn cooperated in several cases since that time. In 1967 the Pulitzer Prize for National Reporting was shared between the two reporters for the following article, published in the preceding year on October 5, 1966:

»Freeport, Grand Bahama Island - Scene: the gold-papered, crystal-chandeliered Monte Carlo room of the luxurious Lucayan Beach Hotel. Roulette wheels spin their reds and blacks. Crap shooters roll their sevens and elevens, Blackjack dealers turn their aces and kings. Slot machines whirl their lemons and plums.

Surveying the quick play and quiet players is the affable but cold-eyed man in charge, a runaway New Yorker wanted by American authorities. He is balding, 61-year-old Frank Ritter, alias „Red" Reed, whose natty appearance (mustard sports jacket with double vents,tapered beige slacks, brown suede shoes) fails to dispel the impression that he's familiar with the grime of the underworld.

Ritter's presence, and his suspected links with the U.S. crime syndicate, cast a pall over this „island in the sun" just 70 miles off the Florida coast. Grand Bahama, largely barren a few years ago, today attracts hundreds of millions of dollars from U.S. tourists and investors. A big magnet: Gambling.

THE ETHICAL CLIMATE

Now, newly discovered secret documents provide insight into how gambling came to Grand Bahama. The docurnents also tell a good deal about the ethical climate prevailing in the Bahamas, the multi-island British Colony.

The entrepreneurs on Grand Bahama, conforming to custom, did business in the early 1960s with the renowned „Bay Street Boys," the powerful group of merchant-politicians who dominate the colony from Nassau, the capital on New Providence Island, some 120 miles to the south of Grand Bahama.

To grasp the significance of these business dealings, a bit of background is necessary. Gambling is illegal in the Bahamas. Thus, to open casinos in Freeport took some doing - a special exemption from the colony's penal code. This exemption was granted in April 1963, not by the legislature, but by the governor's select, nine-member Executive Council which at that time was the most powerful arm of the government and pretty well ran the colony.

Executive Council deliberations are secret, and to this day there is no record of which members voted for or against gambling. But the result of the vote is no secret. The Council awarded a casino monopoly to Wallace Groves, a former Virginian who reigns as the „monarch" of Grand Bahama. He controls about one-half the total acreage on the island, is the dominant figure in Grand Bahama Development Co., Grand Bahama Port Authority and Bahamas Amusements, Ltd. The three companies comprise the major commercial interests responsible for developing the island.

MAIL FRAUD IN BACKGROUND

Mr. Groves has a blemish in his background. He's an old Wall Street operator who was convicted of mail fraud in 1941 and sentenced to two years in prison. Now, a quarter of a century later, Mr. Groves has wound up with the right to open any number of casinos on his island fiefdom.

But - on to the Bay Street Boys. The most powerful is Sir Stafford Sands, the Minister of Finance and Tourism (a post equivalent to the U.S. Secretary of the Treasury). Sir Stafford also is the most respected corporation lawyer in Nassau. As such, he represented the Groves group in its quest for a gambling license at the same time that he was a member of the Executive Council that granted the license.

Corporate records indicate Sir Stafford received for his services more than $1 million from a Groves-controlled company. This handsome fee was divided into several payments. Records of the company for 1964 show payment to Sir Stafford of $515,000 for legal services and also legal retainer payments of $10,000 per month.

Sir Stafford flatly denies payments of any such magnitude, although he does confirm he has done a good deal of legal work for Mr. Groves and his companies.

CONSULTING AGREEMENTS

But the corporate records, disputed though they may be by Sir Stafford, also show consulting agreements with him and two other members of the Executive Council - Sir Roland Symonette, the Premier, and Dr. Raymond Sawyer, a dentist. Besides Messrs. Sands, Symonette and Sawyer, still a fourth member of the Executive Council had personal business dealings with the Groves group - C. Trevor Kelly, the Minister for Maritime Affairs, who fittingly enough leased boats to a Groves company.

But business ties between the Grand Bahama entrepreneurs and the Nassau politicians weren't confined to members of the powerful Executive Council. Two other important political figures were quietly taken aboard as consultants. „Bobby" Symonette, the Premier's son and Speaker of the House of Assembly, was one. The other: Sir Etienne Dupuch, a member of the Senate and the editor-publisher of the *Nassau Tribune*.

Sir Stafford, according to a former official of one of Groves' Bahamian corporations, was to receive, under his consulting agreement, nearly $50,000 a year for 10 years, or as long as the Groves gambling license remained in effect. The official says the consulting fees were on top of the Sands legal fees. Again Sir Stafford denies he accepted any consulting fees.

Premier Symonette was to receive $16,800 a year for five years for his advice, the one-time Groves executive says. Not so, replies the Premier. Though a member of the Executive Council at the time of the gambling decision, it's reported the Premier voted „no." Besides being the head of government, Sir

Roland holds extensive shipping, real estate, liquor and other business interests, and is regarded as the second most important figure in the Bahamas.

Dr. Sawyer, the dentist, again according to a former Groves executive, was to receive $5,600 a year for five years as a consultant. The dentist, who has since left goverment, denies any knowledge of the agreement. He says he was forced to give up his publie duties because of the press of private business. Besides pulling teeth, Dr. Sawyer operates Nassau's Hobby Horse Hall racetrack. „Dentists don't make much money," he explains.

„Bobby" Symonette, the Premier's son, confirms that he was under contract to Grand Bahama Development, one of the Groves-controlled companies, at $14,000 a year, but says he ended the agreement some months back. Besides being a man of rising influence, the House Speaker also is an accomplished yachtsman whose picture has appeared on the cover of *Sports Illustrated*. The 40-year-old sailor explains that, because of his experience at sea, he was retained by the Groves group to advise on marina construction to earn his $14,000 a year.

„ MY PRIVATE BUSINESS "

Mr. Kelly, the maritime minister, is a wealthy businessman (some say he's among the wealthiest in the Bahamas) whose widespread interests include lumber, hardware and shipping. A series of his ships are named Betty K., after his daughter. Mr. Kelly confirms he's done a continuing business, through the Betty Ks, with the Groves group. An ex-Groves executive says the terms have been highly generous to Mr. Kelly, but the maritime minister will only reply, „that's my private business."

Sir Etienne Dupuch, in a February 1964 letter to Mr. Sands, acknowledged receipt from Grand Bahama Development of „a cheque for one thousand pounds ($2,800) in payment of consultant services for January and February." Both Sir Etienne and his newspaper had opposed Grand Bahama gambling, and his letter said the consulting fee would be turned over to charity. It is understood that, before too long, Sir Etienne had second thoughts - and stopped accepting the fees.

Sir Etienne's doubts were not shared by some of the other Bay Street consultants. A former Groves official recalls the company received „letters of complaint" from at least one consultant when his checks did not arrive within „two or three days after the first of the month."

Premier Symonette, while denying any consulting agreement, does say he had a road-building contract with Grand Bahama Development Co. years ago.

MAP LOCATION THE LUCAYAN BEACH HOTEL AND CASINO

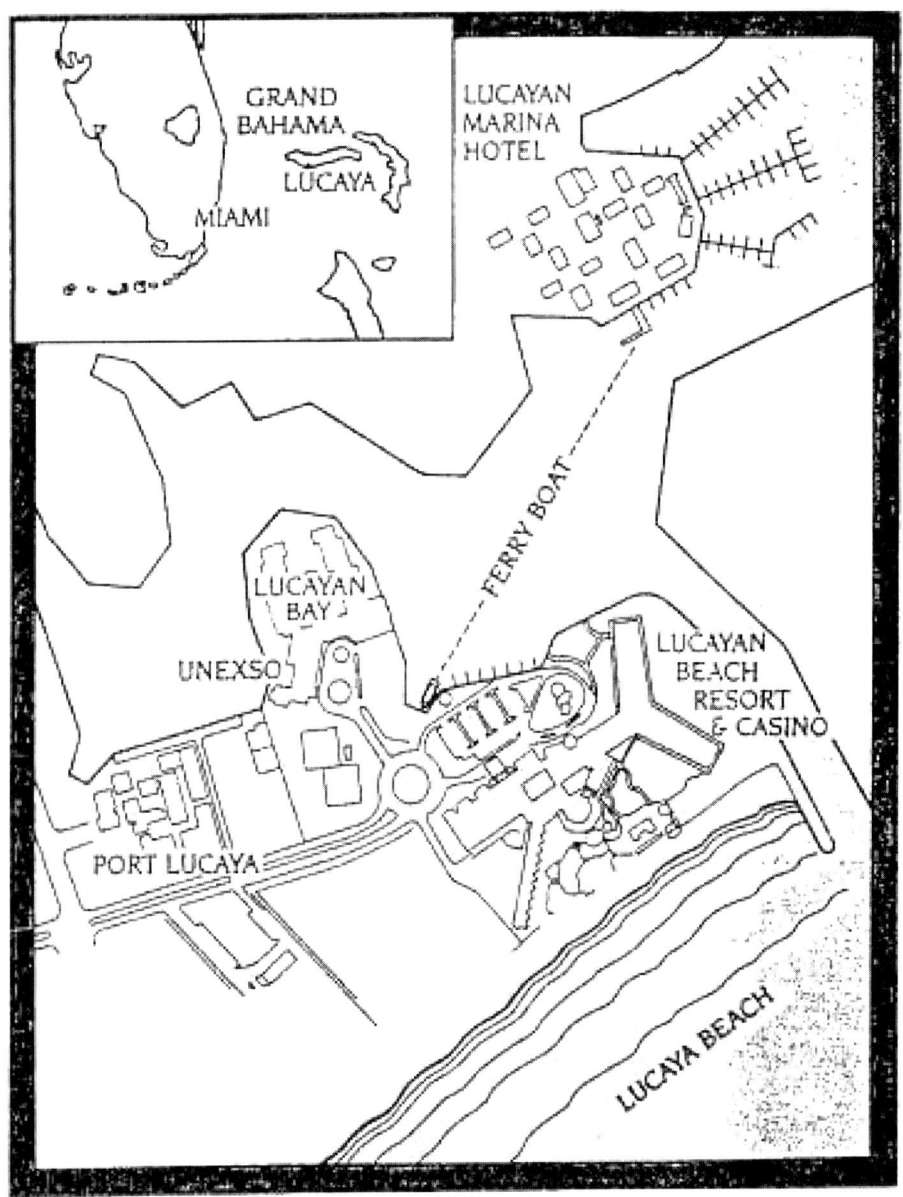

But he adds he gave it up in early 1964 when a new constitution took effect. The Premier says his contract with the development company „was nothing like" the reported $16,800 a year.

Sir Stafford Sands, vacationing in Europe, says he has acted professionally for Wallace Groves, president of the Grand Bahama Port Authority, since the late 1940s. But he adds: „In more than 15 years of this association, I have not collected a total of $1 million in fees from him or from the Port Authority, or from any other business with which we are jointly affiliated, or from all of them in the aggregate. Moreover, my records show that no checks approximating $500,000 were received for any purpose in the period you refer to."

Sir Stafford charges that his political enemies have falsely accused him in the past of accepting excessive legal fees. He notes that some of his income is in the form of a retainer, „which you have termed a consultant fee." Sir Stafford adds that his expenses include a legal office in Freeport, Grand Bahama, mainly serving the Port Authority and its associated companies. Also, much of his own time, as well as that of his staff in Nassau, is devoted to business for the same clients, he asserts.

„A SHARE OF PROSPERITY"

Earlier this year, Sir Stafford unburdened himself to an English journalist about his double duty as lawyer and public minister: „Ministers here are unpaid. As to the idea that I get a good share of the country's prosperity, of course I do. I would anyway since my family came over here 350 years ago, and I've been working here during the boom years. Anybody would come in for a share. I can't stop charging legal fees can I? But it's worth remembering that I've been a part of making all the islands a lot more prosperous."

This line of reasoning is echoed by many others. „We take the view that we should have unpaid government," explains Bobby Symonette, „because we couldn't afford to pay people in the government what they would earn privately." Indeed, the holding of public office by those possessing the greatest wealth has been the predominant style of government here since the beginning. This reflects the large educational and economic gulf that separates the ruling whites (20% of the population) from the colored majority. It also reflects the past ineffectiveness of the political opposition.

But it is getting harder to keep the lid on. Consider this episode, which has involved the highly regarded New York public relations firm of Hill and Knowlton, Inc., in what surely is one of the more curious arrangements in the history of publishing.

Hill and Knowlton operates the public relations department of the Bahamas' Ministry of Tourism under Sir Stafford. And it is a considerable operation: Last year the ministry spent $4.1 million, or 10% of the colony's revenues, to entice Americans and other tourists.

„THE UGLY BAHAMIANS"

In the process of serving the interests of Bahamian tourism, Hill and Knowlton recently arranged for Exposition Press of New York to buy a manuscript entitled The Ugly Bahamians. Exposition Press apparently thought highly of it - enough to pay the author $50,000 for the manuscript. Now, strange to say, Exposition Press has not the slightest intention of publishing its $50,000 property. It is safe to conclude, moreover, that the book will never be published. Hill and Knowlton has „no comment" on the incident.

Whether or not „The Ugly Bahamians" would have constituted an embarrassment to Sir Stafford and his ruling party, the United Bahamian Party, the winds of change are beginning to waft through the Bahamas. Slowly the opposition Progressive Liberal Party is gaining strength, though probably not enough to come to power in the next election which must be called by the end of 1967. Nevertheless, the PLP's Negro leader, 36-year-old Lynden Pindling, is putting the pressure on the controlling party.

Last year Mr. Pindling, who knows a good political issue when he sees one, brought conflict-of-interest charges before the United Nations in New York. „The ministers in the Bahamas Government today own large shares in nearly every major local enterprise," he told the UN, „and are allowed to award themselves Government contracts and they do unlimited business with the Government they themselves control."

Last July, the Bahamian Government made public a code of ethics that requires a minister to withdraw from any case in which he has a private interest. Government officials contend they have followed this practice at least since a new Bahamian constitution took effect in early 1964. The decision to publicize the code in July may have been prompted by the conflict-of-interest charges raised by the opposition party.

Mr. Pindling's most potent political weapon is the Grand Bahama gambling, with its potential benefits of Government tax revenue and its potential dangers of mobster infiltration. A few weeks ago, Mr. Pindling journeyed to the UN again to charge that the 140,000 Bahamian people were being sold out to „gangsterism" by his political opponents.

That's why Frank Ritter, in the Lucayan Beach Casino, is such a focal point of attention. Along with two casino helpers - Max Courtney, real name

Morris Schmertzler, and Charlie Brud, real name Charles Brudner - Ritter has been indicted three times in the U.S. for tax evasion and other offenses. Allegedly the three men operated a nationwide bookrnaking business from New York before they skipped town.

Robert Morgenthau, the U.S. Attorney for the Southern District of New York, wants Ritter, Courtney and Brudner back, but the U.S. has no extradition treaty with the Bahamas. Trevor Kelly, acting Premier one day recently when he was interviewed, dismisses the thought: „The only charges the (U.S.) Government has on them is tax evasion," a crime that is not taken seriously by Bahamians who don't have to pay income taxes.

But U.S. Authorities are after bigger fish - Meyer Lansky, the notorious Florida mobster who ranks high in the U.S. crime syndicate. The Lansky reputation is so black that the Nevada Gaming Control board bars him from Las Vegas casinos. U.S. officials suspect that Lansky controls or gets a piece of the profits of the Lucayan Beach casino. One bit of evidence: For many months, until Bahamian government officials invited them to leave the islands, Dino Cellini and George Sadlo were prominent figures at the Lucayan Beach casino. Both are known Lansky cronies.

ROLES DESCRIBED

One man in a position to know many of the intimate details of the casino operation describes the role of Cellini and Sadlo this way: „Cellini and Sadlo were Lansky's men. At the closing of the casino each night, all of the boxes were taken from the tables and brought into the counting room. There were three sets of keys to the boxes, but it was very important that either Cellini or Sadlo be present before a box was opened."

If indeed George Sadlo journeyed to the Lucayan Beach counting room on many a night to see to Meyer Lansky's interests, he was bringing with him a good deal of previous experience. Testimony before the Kefauver Committee in 1950 showed that Meyer Lansky and his brother Jake, along with George Sadlo, operated illegally the Club Boheme gambling casino in Florida. An accountant for the casino testified that, „At the end of the night ... after they close each table, they take the money and put it in the cashier's cage and they count it down."

„Who counts it?" asked a committee investigator. „Mr. Lansky," replied the witness. „Personally?" „Yes; or Mr. Sadlo, or whoever is there with him." If some of the Lucayan Beach casino's profits are, in fact, being „skimmed off the top" by the Lansky crowd, U.S. authorities suspect they are being used to finance the activities of American hoodlums.

LETTERS TO THE EDITOR

Churches Protest Casinos

Editor, The Tribune.

Very grave dangers from foreign organized gambling interests are threatening the security, prosperity and morality of the Bahamas. I therefore beg you to publish the following letter, dated 8th June from the Bahamas Christian Council to the Premier on this subject. A parallel letter strongly supporting the Christian Council's protest was also sent to the Premier by the Roman Catholic Bishop.

When the vast majority of Bahamian Christians, the Hotel-Owners Association and the undisputed opinion of the non-parliamentary meeting of the U.B.P. are all opposed to casinos being developed, it is difficult to understand why the Government should allow such a peril to spread to Paradise Island — and possibly to Cat Cay and other parts of the Bahamas.

Yours faithfully,

(Rev.) PHILIP BLACKBURN
Chairman,
Bahamas Christian Council

Nassau, July 10, 1965.

* * *

COPY of the letter sent to —
The Hon. Sir Roland T. Symonette,
Premier of the Bahamas.

8th June, 1965

Dear Sir Roland,

This petition is sent to you on behalf of the Bahamas Christian Council, which represents the majority of Bahamian Christians.

It has been brought to our notice that there is imminent danger of gambling interests being granted licences to operate a casino on Paradise Island. Eleven years ago the protests of the Christian Churches were effective in preventing the spread of organized gambling, but the recent licence granted at Freeport, Grand Bahama, was quickly done without regard for public opinion and the national well-being. The Colony was presented with a "fait accompli". We therefore earnestly and respectfully request the Cabinet, through you, to refuse the granting of any new gambling licence or the transfer of any existing licence for the operation of organized gambling.

Apart from our religious objections, on the grounds that gambling panders to the weakness of many people, is based fundamentally on greed and constantly causes the transgression of the Tenth Commandment, "Thou shalt not covet", we beg you to consider seriously that the establishment of a casino on Paradise Island would

(a) keep away a large number of decent tourists,

(b) bring in, as casinos have elsewhere, undesirable immigrants from the foreign underworld, crou-piers, pimps, prostitutes, narcotics pedlars etc.,

(c) create innumerable problems for the Criminal Investigation Department of our Police Force,

(d) bring in easy money but demoralize our people

— a long term irretrievable loss,

(e) cause widespread uneasiness among Bahamian people and especially among those who have confidence in your Government,

(f) be contrary to the traditions and moral standards of the Bahamian people.

May the blessing of Almighty God rest upon your deliberations.

I remain,

Yours faithfully,

(Signed) PHILIP BLACKBURN
Chairman
Bahamas Christian Council

(Signed) + Bernard, Nassau and the Bahamas
Harold Slater, Methodist Church,
Bahamas District
Talmage Sands, Supt.
Bahamas United Baptist Mission
James H. McIan Jack,
St. Andrew's Presbyterian Kirk, Nassau

The Tribune (Nassau, Bah.), July 12, 1965, p. 3.

Such suggestions draw staunch denials from the Nassau police. Sitting in his office in the police barracks, S. R. Moir, assistant commissioner, is every inch the stiff, proper, tight-lipped Britisher. „No evidence," he replies to inquiries concerning mob infiltration of the casino and the possibility of skimming profits off the top.

MOB INFILTRATION DENIED

The president of the company that operates the Lucayan Beach casino rejects reports of mob infiltration as „completely untrue." He is Keith Gonsalves, a former employe of Barclays Bank, and his company is Bahamas Amusements, Ltd., which is apart of the Groves group. Bahamas Amusements is required to pay all profits to the Grand Bahama Development Co., a land development firm, which is controlled by the Grand Bahama Port Authority, in turn controlled by Mr. Groves.

To confirm the integrity of the casino's operation, Mr. Gonsalves has ready a lengthy position paper. It mentions the presence of two security officers, hired on the recommendation of the police, who „have access at all times to all casino operations, including access to the countinghouse and records." Yet, the fact remains that the security officers are not policemen, are not employed by the government, but are employed by the company that runs the casino.

The Gonsalves paper also notes that the casino's books are audited by the accounting firm of Peat, Marwick, Mitchell & Co. Despite Mr. Gonsalves' assurances, suspicion persists, favored by the presence of Ritter, Courtney and Brudner in the Lucayan Beach casino. Just when this presence began is not clear, but it certainly dates back to the spring of 1963.

Then the Lucayan Beach hotel was in an early construction stage. When the gambling license was issued in April 1963, meetings were arranged to convert a planned convention hall into the casino. Someone who attended a session in Miami recalls that Ritter and Courtney were brought in to help with the designing. „They were experts on casinos," he remembers. There are those unkind enough to suspect the convention hall was intended to be a casino all along.

Ritter and Courtney - along with Lansky crony Dino Cellini - were especially important in setting up the casino. To remove any taint of Las Vegas and to give the Lucayan Beach casino „class" it was publicized widely that only European croupiers would be employed. Accordingly, a school was set up in London in early 1963 to train the European croupiers (they are not especially adept at the American game of craps). Apparently no effort was spared. The finishing school cost the casino $250,000.

„Cellini, Courtney and Ritter were sent over to start the school and to instruct the people," an insider recalls. „They returned to the Bahamas with 100 croupiers." Ritter, Courtney and Brudner were allowed to remain on Grand Bahama, after Cellini and Sadlo departed. Mr. Gonsalves explains why: „It was necessary to have Americans in some key positions because more than 90% of the patrons of the (Lucayan Beach) casino are United States citizens; and Messrs. Ritter, Courtney and Brudner and other professionals were employed because of their previous professional experience in gambling in the United States."

Ritter bears the title of credit manager; Courtney, chief supervisor; and Brudner, casino floorman. But Ritter is obviously the key man. Credit is vital to casino profits. Most gamblers come to win, not lose, so they don't bring all their money. When the luck runs bad, the trick is to know just how much credit to extend to whom. That's where Frank Ritter shines. His knowledge of the financial status of American gamblers, plus his contacts with the Las Vegas casinos, make him an expert on „instant credit" - and where to draw the line.

This talent was observed at the Lucayan Beach casino recently. It was late, and only a handful of hard-core gamblers remained. Among them were two brothers from the States. One was playing with $100 chips in a closed game at the blackjack table. He was losing heavily; his brother already had lost quite a bit. They both came to Frank Ritter for credit. „You're all right," barked Frank to one, „but not him," jabbing his finger at the other.

The incident raises an interesting, but unanswered, question. Granting Frank Ritter's expertise at his job, he's still human. Suppose he makes a mistake. Suppose a borrower fails to pay up after he returns to the States. Who duns hirn for the debt? The mob? That's what U.S. investigators want to find out. The casino is a sore point with many Bahamians. Mr. Pindling of the opposition party whose distress doesn't extend to favoring a shutdown of the casino, pledges: „If we came into power, we would renegotiate the entire casino license. Our concern is to eliminate all possible gangster influence."

Also distressed is the upper crust of Nassau society. Dining on the veranda of their spacious home, a banker and his wife view the distant Lucayan Beach casino as an „error of taste and judgment." They refuse to believe that American mobsters have infiltrated, but they fear the „potential" is there. The thought of an „offshore Las Vergas," as they term it, horrifies them.

And the man they blame for the mistake is Sir Stafford Sands, a huge man who, according to an acquaintance, „lives like an emperor." His Nassau estate, „Waterloo," comes complete with private lake. Sir Stafford has a penchant for expensive lounging jackets and elaborate paperweights. He's addicted to the grand gesture too. „At a dinner for four, he'll have caviar for a hundred," says one friend.

Friend and foe alike regard Sir Stafford as the mastermind behind the Bahamas' tourist boom (this year a record 800,000 visitors are anticipated). And all descriptions of him, sooner or later, converge on the words „brilliant" and „genius." Even Mr. Pindling, who seeks to oust the United Bahamians, admits that, if successful, he'd like Sir Stafford to remain as minister of finance and tourism.

A tiny glimpse of the man's power, and the way he uses it, is provided by the letter that Sir Etienne Dupuch, the Senator and *Tribune* editor-publisher, wrote to him acknowledging receipt of his consultant's fee from the Groves-controlled Grand Bahama Development Co.

The letter would seem to suggest Sir Stafford shoved Sir Etienne, who had criticized gambling editorially, into accepting money from the casino crowd. Read: „You had talked with me briefly on this proposal but I did not realize that it had been finalized. I am sure you know that I am not happy about having casinos in the islands but since a casino has been established at Grand Bahama, I am concerned to see that a high standard is maintained. If you think that my services in this way might be helpful, I shall do my best but I want you to feel that it is an arrangement that can be terminated at any time by either side."

„I told you at the time that this arrangement roust not in any way be considered as influencing my decision in the Senate or the policy of the *Tribune*. You agreed to this condition. I would have readily given my services free of charge but since you insist on paying what you say is the normal fee for this kind of service I shall deposit the money to a special account I have in the Royal Bank of Canada for helping children and for other charitable purposes."«

OFFSHORE TAX PARADISES

Bastian Obermayer, *Miami Herald/Süddeutsche Zeitung*

When the 2017 Pulitzer Prize International Reporting jurors had done their work they placed four entries on their shortlist, one of them coming from an „International Consortium of Investigative Journalists, McClatchy and The Miami Herald". The Pulitzer Prize Board moved that exhibit to another award category, called „Explanatory Reporting," where the Board lauded the year-long investigation on the so-called *Panama Papers* for „using a collaboration of more than 300 reporters on six continents to expose the hidden infrastructure and global scale of offshore tax havens."

The *Panama Papers* investigation grew out of a five-year reporting push by numerous journalists, including reporters of the German *Süddeutsche Zeitung* from Munich. They dug into dark corners of financial secrecy havens, including the British Virgin Islands, Luxembourg,Switzerland and also the Bahamas. The P*anama Papers* investigation exposed offshore companies linked to more than 140 politicians in more than 50 countries - including 14 current or former world leaders. It also uncovered offshore hideaways tied to mega-banks, corporate bribery scandals, drug kingpins, etc.

It was noted that the investigation would not have been possible without the collaborative spirit of Bastian Obermayer and Frederik Obermaier, two German journalists who received the original leak from a confidential source. Instead of hoarding the trove of 11.5 million secret documents for themselves and their newspaper, S*üddeutsche Zeitung*, they shared them with others. This allowed the Washington-based International Consortium of Investigative Journalists to pull together a cross-border partnership and join forces with *SZ*, McClatchy Company, the *Miami Herald, Fusion* and more than 100 news organizations to investigate the explosive documents.

The *Panama Papers* investigation has prompted police raids, arrests and resignations of high-profile figures. Reporting by ICIJ and its pertners has sparked more than 150 inquiries, audits and investigations in many countries and has driven new legislation and financial rules in the United States and abroad.

The following story, first part of the Pulitzer Prize-winning disclosures and dated April 3, 2016, was reported and written by Bastian Obermayer, Gerard Ryle, Marina Walker Guevara, Michael Hudson, Jake Bernstein, Will Fitzgibbon, Mar Cabra, Martha M. Hamilton, Frederik Obermaier, Ryan Chittum, Emilia Diaz-Struck, Rigoberto Carvajal, Cécile Schilis-Gallego,

16

Marcos Garcia Rey, Delphine Reuter, Matthew Caruana Galizia, Hamish Boland-Rudder, Miguel Fiandor and Mago Torres:

»The files expose offshore companies controlled by the prime minister of Iceland, the king of Saudi Arabia and the children of the president of Azerbaijan and the prime minister of Pakistan. They also include at least 33 people and companies blacklisted by the U.S. government because of evidence that they'd been involved in wrongdoing, such as doing business with Mexican drug lords, terrorist organizations like Hezbollah or rogue nations like North Korea and Iran. One of those companies supplied fuel for the aircraft that the Syrian government used to bomb and kill thousands of its own citizens, U.S. authorities have charged.

„These findings show how deeply ingrained harmful practices and criminality are in the offshore world," said Gabriel Zucman, an economist at the University of California, Berkeley and author of "The Hidden Wealth of Nations: The Scourge of Tax Havens." Zucman, who was briefed on the media partners' investigation, said the release of the leaked documents should prompt govern-ments to seek „concrete sanctions" against jurisdictions and institutions that peddle offshore secrecy. World leaders who have embraced anticorruption platforms feature in the leaked documents. The files reveal offshore companies linked to the family of China's top leader, Xi Jinping, who has vowed to fight „armies of corruption," as well as Ukrainian President Petro Poroshenko, who has positioned himself as a reformer in a country shaken by corruption scandals. The files also contain new details of offshore dealings by the late father of British Prime Minister David Cameron, a leader in the push for tax-haven reform.

The leaked data covers nearly 40 years, from 1977 through the end of 2015. It allows a never-before-seen view inside the offshore world - providing a day-to-day, decade-by-decade look at how dark money flows through the global financial system, breeding crime and stripping national treasuries of tax revenues. Most of the services the offshore industry provides are legal if used by the law abiding. But the documents show that banks, law firms and other offshore players have often failed to follow legal requirements that they make sure their clients are not involved in criminal enterprises, tax dodging or political corruption. In some instances, the files show, offshore middlemen have protected themselves and their clients by concealing suspect transactions or manipulating official records.

The documents make it clear that major banks are big drivers behind the creation of hard-to-trace companies in the British Virgin Islands, Panama and other offshore havens. The files list nearly 15,600 paper companies that banks set up for clients who want keep their finances under wraps, including thousands created by international giants UBS and HSBC. The records reveal a pattern of covert maneuvers by banks, companies and people tied to Russian leader Putin. The records show offshore companies linked to this network moving money in transactions as large as $200 million at a time. Putin associates disguised payments, backdated documents and gained hidden influence within the country's media and automotive industries, the leaked files show. A Kremlin spokesman did not answer questions for this story, but instead went public March 28 with charges that ICIJ and its media partners were preparing a misleading „information attack" on Putin and people close to him.

The leaked records - which were reviewed by a team of rnore than 370 journalists from 76 countries - come from a little-known but powerful law firm based in Panama, Mossack Fonseca, that has branches in Hong Kong, Miami, Zurich and more than 35 other places around the globe. The firm is one of the world's top creators of shell companies, corporate structures that can be used to hide ownership of assets. The law firm's leaked internal files contain information on 214,488 offshore entities connected to people in more than 200 countries and territories. ICIJ will release the full list of companies and peonle linked to them in early May.

The data includes emails, financial spreadsheets, passports and corporate records revealing the secret owners of bank accounts and companies in 21 offshore jurisdictions, from Nevada to Singapore to the British Virgin Islands. Mossack Fonseca's fingers are in Africa's diamond trade, the international art market and other businesses that thrive on secrecy. The firm has serviced enough Middle East royalty to fill a palace. It's helped two kings, Mohammed VI of Morocco and King Salman of Saudi Arabia, take to the sea on luxury yachts. In Iceland, the leaked files show how Prime Minister Sigmundur David Gunnlaugsson and his wife secretly owned an offshore firm that held millions of dollars in Icelandic bank bonds during that country's financial crisis. The files include a convicted money launderer who claimed he'd arranged a $50,000 illegal campaign eontribution used to pay the Watergate burglars, 29 billionaires featured in *Forbes* Magazine's list of the world's 500 richest people and movie star Jackie Chan, who has at least six companies managed through the law firm.

As with many of Mossack Fonseca's clients, there is no evidence that Chan used his companies for improper purposes. Having an offshore company isn't illegal. For some international business transactions, it's a logical choice. The Mossack Fonseca documents indicate, however, that the firrn's customers have included Ponzi schemers, drug kingpins, tax evaders and at least one jailed sex offender. A U.S. businessman convicted of traveling to Russia to have sex with underage orphans signed papers for an offshore company while he was serving his prison sentence in New Jersey, the records show. The files contain new details about major scandals ranging from England's most infamous gold heist to the bribery allegations convulsing FIFA, the body that rules international soccer.

The leaked documents reveal that the law firm of Juan Pedro Damiani, a member of FIFA's ethics committee, had business relationships with three men who have been indicted in the FIFA scandal - former FIFA vice president Eugenio Figueredo and Hugo and Mariano Jinkis, the father-son team accused of paying bribes to win broadcast rights to Latin American soccer events. The records show that Damiani's law firm in Uruguay represented an offshore company linked to the Jinkises and seven companies linked to Figueredo. In response to the reporting by ICIJ and its media partners, FIFA's ethics panel has launched a preliminary investigation into Damiani's relationship to Figueredo. A spokesman for the committee said Damiani first informed the panel about his business ties to Figueredo on March 18. That was one day after the reporting team sent questions to Damiani about his law firm's work for companies tied to the former FIFA vice president.

The world's best soccer player, Lionel Messi, is also found in the documents. The records show Messi and his father were owners of a Panama company: Mega Star Enterprises Inc. This adds a new name to the list of shell companies known to be linked to Messi. His offshore dealings are currently the target of a tax evasion case in Spain. Whether they're famous or unknown, Mossack Fonseca works aggressively to protect its clients' secrets. In Nevada, the records show, the law firm tried to shield itself and its clients from the fallout from a legal action in U.S. District Court by removing paper records from its Las Vegas branch and having its tech gurus wipe electronic records from phones and computers. The leaked files show the firm regularly offered to backdate documents to help its clients gain advantage in their financial affairs. It was so common that in 2007 an email exchange shows firm employees talking about establishing a price structure - clients would pay $8.75 for each month farther back in time that a corporate document would be backdated.

In a written response to questions from ICIJ and its media partners, the firm said it „does not foster or promote illegal acts. Your allegations that we provide shareholders with structures supposedly designed to hide the identity of the real owners are completely unsupported and false." The firm added that the backdating of documents „is a well-founded and accepted practice" that is „common in our industry and its aim is not to cover up or hide unlawful acts."

THE INTERNATIONAL BESTSELLER

THE

PANAMA

PAPERS

Breaking the Story of

How the Rich & Powerful

Hide Their Money

'This decade's most important book'
Times Literary Supplement

BASTIAN OBERMAYER AND FREDERIK OBERMAIER

Winners of the 2017 PULITZER PRIZE for Explanatory Reporting

The firm said it couldn't answer questions about specific customers because of its obligation to maintain client confidentiality.

The law firm's co-founder, Ramon Fonseca, said in a recent interview on Panamanian television that the firm has no responsibility for what clients do with the offshore companies that the firm sells. He compared the firm to a „car factory" whose liability ends once the car is produced. Blaming Mossack Fonseca for what people do with their companies would be like blaming a carmaker „if the car was used in a robbery," he said.

UNDER SCRUTINY

Until recently, Mossack Fonseca has largely operated in the shadows. But it has come under growing scrutiny as governments have obtained partial leaks of the firm's files and authorities in Germany and Brazil began probing its practices. In February 2015, *Süddeutsche Zeitung* reported that German law-enforcement agencies had launehed a series of raids targeting one of the country's biggest banks, Commerzbank, in a tax-fraud investigation that authorities said could lead to criminal charges against Mossack Fonseca employees. In Brazil, the law firm has become a target in a bribery and money laundering investigation dubbed „Operation Car Wash" („Lava Jato," in Portuguese),which has led to criminal charges against leading politicians and an investigation of popular former president Luiz Inacio Lula da Silva. The scandal threatens to unseat current President Dilma Rousseff.

In January, Brazilian prosecutors labeled Mossack Fonseca as a „big money launderer" and announced they had filed criminal charges against five employees of the firm's Brazilian office for their role in the scandal. Mossack Fonseca denies any wrongdoing in Brazil. The disclosures found inside the law firm's leaked files dramatically expand on previous leaks of offshore records that ICIJ and its reporting partners have revealed in the past four years.

In the largest media collaboration ever undertaken, journalists working in more than 25 languages dug into Mossack Fonseca's inner workings and traced the secret dealings of the law firm's customers around the world. They shared information and hunted down leads generated by the leaked files using corporate filings, property records, financial disclosures, court documents and interviews with money laundering experts and law-enforcement officials. Reporters at *Süddeutsche Zeitung* obtained millions of records from a confidential source and shared them with ICIJ and other media partners. The news outlets involved in the collaboration did not pay for the documents.

Before *Süddeutsche Zeitung* obtained the leak, German tax authorities bought a smaller set of Mossack Fonseca documents from a whistleblower, a move that triggered the raids in Germany in early 2015. This smaller set of files has since been offered to tax authorities in the United Kingdom, the United States and other countries, according to sources with knowledge of the matter. The larger set of files obtained by the news organizations offers more than a snapshot of one law firm's business methods or a catalog of its more unsavory customers. It allows a far-reaching view into an industry that has worked to keep its practices hidden - and offers clues as to why efforts to reform the system have faltered. The story of Mossack Fonseca is, in many ways, the story of the offshore system itself.

CRIME OF THE CENTURY

Before dawn on Nov. 26, 1983, six robbers slipped into the Brink's-Mat warehouse at London's Heathrow Airport. The thugs tied up the security guards, doused them in gasoline, lit a match and threatened to set them afire unless they opened the warehouse's vault. Inside, the thieves found nearly 7,000 gold bars, diamonds and cash. „Thanks ever so much for your help. Have a nice Christmas," one of the crooks said as they departed. British media dubbed the heist the „Crime of the Century." Much of the loot - including the cash reaped by melting the gold and selling it - was never recovered. Where the missing money went is a mystery that continues to fascinate students of England's underworld.

Now documents within Mossack Fonseca's files reveal that the law firm and its cofounder, Jürgen Mossack, may have helped the conspirators keep the spoils out of the hands of authorities by protecting a company tied to Gordon Parry, a London wheeler-dealer who laundered money for the Brink's-Mat plotters. Sixteen months after the robbery, the records show, Mossack Fonseca set up a Panama shell company called Feberion Inc. Jürgen Mossack was one the company's three „nominee" directors, a term used in the business for stand-ins who control a company on paper but exercise no real authority over its activities. An internal memo written by Mossack shows he was aware in 1986 that the company was „apparently involved in the management of money from the famous theft from Brink's-Mat in Landon. The company itself has not been used illegally, but it could be that the company invested money through bank accounts and properties that was illegitimately sourced." Mossack Fonseca records from 1987 make it clear that Parry was behind Feberion. Rather than help authorities gain access to Feberion's assets, the law firm took steps that prevented U.K. police from gaining control of the company, the records show.

After police obtained the two certificates that controlled the company's ownership, Mossack Fonseca arranged for Feberion to issue 98 new shares, a move that appears to have effectively wrested control away from investigators, the leaked records show. It was not until 1995 - three years after Parry was sent to prison for his role in the gold caper - that Mossack Fonseca ended its business relationship with Feberion. A spokesman for the law firm said any allegations the firm helped shield the proceeds of the Brink's-Mat robbery „are entirely false." The spokesman said Jürgen Mossack „never had any dealings" with Parry and was never contacted by police about the case. Mossack Fonseca's defense of the dodgy company illustrates how far many offshore operatives will go to serve their customers' interests.

The offshore system relies on a sprawling global industry of bankers, lawyers, accountants and go-betweens who work tagether to protect their clients' secrets. These secrecy experts use anonymaus companies, trusts and other paper entities to create complex structures that can be used to disguise the origins of dirty money. „They are the gasoline that runs the engine," says Robert Mazur, a former U.S. drug agent and author of The Infiltrator: My Secret Life Inside the Dirty Banks Behind Pablo Escobar's Medellin Cartel. „They're an extraordinarily important piece of the formula of success for criminal organizations." Mossack Fonseca told ICIJ that it follows „both the letter and spirit of the law. Because we do, we have not once in nearly 40 years of operation been charged with criminal wrongdoing."

The men who founded the firm decades ago - and continue today as its rnain partners - are well-known figures in Panamanian society and politics. Jürgen Mossack is a German immigrant whose father sought a new life in Panama for his family after serving in Hitler's Waffen-SS during World War 11. Ramón Fonseca is an award-winning novelist who has worked in recent years as an adviser to Panama's president. He took a leave of absence as presidential adviser in March after his firm was implicated in the Brazil scandal and ICIJ and its partners began to ask questions about the law firm's practices. From its base in Panama, one of the world's top financial secrecy zones, Mossack Fonseca seeds anonymous companies in Panama, the British Virgin Islands and other financial havens. The law firm has worked closely with big banks and big law firms in places like The Netherlands, Mexico, the United States and Switzerland, helping clients move money or slash their tax bills, the secret records show.

An ICIJ analysis of the leaked files found that more than 500 banks, their subsidiaries and branches have worked with Mossack Fonseca since the 1970s to help clients manage offshore companies. UBS set up .mare than 1,100 offshore companies through Mossack Fonseca. HSBC and its affiliates created more than 2,300. In all, the files indicate Mossack Fonseca worked with more than 14,000 banks, law firms, company incorporators and other middlemen to set up companies, foundations and trusts for customers, the records show.

Mossack Fonseca says these middlemen are its true clients, not the eventual customers who use offshore companies. The firm says these middlemen provide additional layers of oversight for reviewing new customers. As far its own procedures, Mossack Fonseca says they often exceed „the existing rules and standards to whieh we and others are bound."

In its efforts to protect Feberion Inc., the shell company linked to the Brink's-Mat gold heist, Mossack Fonseca used the services of a Panama-based firm, Chartered Management Company, run by Gilbert R.J. Straub, an American expatriate who played a cameo role in the Watergate scandal. In 1987, as U.K. police were investigating the shell company, Jürgen Mossack and Feberion's other paper directors resigned, with the understanding they'd be replaced by new directors appointed by Straub's Chartered Management, the secret files show. Straub was eventually caught in a U.S. Drug Enforcement Administration sting that was unrelated to the Brink's-Mat case, according to Mazur, the former undercover agent. During one of his deep-cover stints, Mazur built the case that led Straub to plead guilty to money laundering in 1995. Believing Mazur was a well-connected money launderer, Straub tried to establish his own criminal bona fides, Mazur says, by describing how he'd illegally channeled cash to President Nixon's 1972 re-election campaign.

SECRETS AND VICTIMS

Nick Kgopa's father died when Nick was 14. His father's workmates at a gold mine in northern South Africa said Nick's dad had been killed by chemical exposure. Nick and his mother and his younger brother, who is deaf, survived thanks to monthly checks from a fund for widows and orphans of mineworkers. One day the payments stopped. His family was one of many that lost out because of a $60 million investment fraud pulled off by South African businessmen. Prosecutors alleged that a group of individuals connected to an asset management company, Fidentia, had schemed to loot millions from investment funds - including the mineworkers' death benefits pool that was supporting some 46,000 widows and orphans. Mossack Fonseca's leaked documents show that at least two of the men involved in the fraud used the Panama-based law firm to create offshore companies - and that Mossack Fonseca was willing to help one of the fraudsters protect his money even after authorities publicly linked him to the scandal.

Ponzi schemers and other fraudsters who bilk large numbers of victims often use offshore structures to pull of their schemes or hide the proceeds. The

Fidentia case isn't the only big-ticket fraud that appears in the files of Mossack Fonseca's clients. In Indonesia, for example, small investors claim a company incorporated by Mossack Fonseca in the British Virgin Islands was used to scam 3,500 people out of at least $150 million. „We really need that money for our son's education fee this April," one Indonesian investor emailed Mossack Fonseca in April 2007 after payouts had stopped. „You can give us any suggestion something we can do," the investor asked in broken English after seeing Mossack Fonseca's name on the investment fund's advertising leaflet. In the Fidentia case, Mossack Fonseca's records show that one of the men later jailed in South Africa for his role in the fraud, Graham Maddock, paid Mossack Fonseca $59,000 in 2005 and 2006 to create two sets of offshore companies, including one called Fidentia North America. The law firm's records say it gave him „the VIP service."

Mossack Fonseca also created offshore structures for Steven Goodwin, a man that prosecutors later claimed had played an „instrumental role" within the Fidentia swindle. As the scandal broke in 2007, Goodwin flew to Australia, then to the U.S., where a Mossack Fonseca lawyer met with him at a luxury hotel in Manhattan to discuss his offshore holdings, the firm's internal records show. The firm official later wrote that he and Goodwin „spoke deeply" about the Fidentia scandal and that he had „convinced Goodwin to better protect" his offshore company's assets by passing them to a third party. In his memo, the firm official told colleagues that Goodwin wasn't involved in the scandal „in any way whatsoever" - he was just „a victim of the circumstances." In April 2008, the FBI arrested Goodwin in Los Angeles and sent him back to South Africa, where he pleaded guilty to fraud and money laundering. He was sentenced to 10 years in prison.

A month after Goodwin's sentencing, an employee at Mossack Fonseca suggested a plan for frustrating South African prosecutors who were expected to start digging into assets linked to Goodwin's offshore company, Hamlyn Property LLP, which had been set up to buy real estate in South Africa. The employee proposed having an accountant „prepare" audits for 2006 and 2007 „to try to prevent the prosecutor from taking actions against the entities behind Hamlyn." He set off „prepare" in quote marks in his email. It's unclear whether the proposal was adopted. Mossack Fonseca did not answer questions from ICU about its relationship with Goodwin. A representative for Goodwin told ICIJ that Goodwin „had nothing whatsoever" to do Fidentia's collapse „or anything directly or indirectly to do with the 46,000 widows and orphans."

POLITICALLY EXPOSED

On Feb. 10, 2011, an anonymous company in the British Virgin Islands named Sandalwood Continental Ltd. loaned $200 million to an equally shadowy firm based in Cyprus called Horwich Trading Ltd. The following day, Sandalwood assigned the rights to collect payments on the loan - including interest - to Ove Financial Corp., a mysterious company in the British Virgin Islands. For those rights, Ove paid $1. But the money trail didn't end there. The same day, Ove reassigned its rights to collect on the loan to a Panama company called International Media Overseas. It too paid $1. In the space of 24 hours the loan had, on paper, traversed three countries, two banks and four companies, making the money all but untraceable in the process.

There were plenty of reasons why the men behind the transaction might want it disguised, not least of all because the money trail came uncomfortably close to Russian leader Vladimir Putin. St. Petersburg-based Bank Rossiya, an institution whose majority owner and chairman has been called one of Putin's „cashiers," established Sandalwood Continental and directed the money flow. International Media Overseas, where rights to the interest payments from the $200 million appear to have landed, was controlled, on paper, by one of Putin's oldest friends, Sergey Roldugin, a classical cellist who is godfather to Putin's eldest daughter.

The $200 million loan was one of dozens of transactions totaling at least $2 billion found in the Mossack Fonseca files involving people or companies linked to Putin. They formed part of a Bank Rossiya enterprise that gained indirect influence over a major shareholder in Russia's biggest truck maker and amassed secret stakes in a key Russian media property. Suspicious payments made by Putin's cronies may have in some cases been designed as payoffs, possibly in exchange for Russian government aid or contracts. The secret documents suggest that much of the loan money originally came from a bank in Cyprus that at the time was majority owned by the Russian state-controlled VTB Bank. In a media conference call last week, Putin spokesman Dmitry Peskov said the government wouldn't reply to „honey-worded queries" from ICIJ or its reporting partners, because they contain questions that „have been asked hundreds of times and answered hundreds of times." Peskov added that Russia has „available the full arsenal of legal means in the national and international arena to protect the honor and dignity of our president."

Under national laws and international agreements, firms like Mossack Fonseca that help create companies and bank accounts are supposed to be on the lookout for clients who may be involved in money laundering, tax evasion or other wrongdoing. They are required to pay special attention to „politically exposed persons" - government officials or their family members or associates. If someone is a „PEP," the middlemen creating their companies are expected to review their activities carefully to make sure they are not engaging in corruption. Mossack Fonseca told ICIJ that it has „duly established policies and procedures to identify and handle those cases where individuals" qualify as PEPs. Often, Mossack Fonseca appeared not to realize who its customers were. A 2015 internal audit found that the law firm knew the identities of the real owners of just 204 of 14,086 companies it had incorporated in Seychelles, a tax haven in the Indian Ocean. British Virgin Islands authorities fined Mossack Fonseca $37,500 for violating anti-money-laundering rules because the firm incorporated a company for the son of former Egyptian President Hosni Mubarak but failed to identify the connection, even after the father and son were charged with corruption in Egypt. An internal review by the law firm concluded, „our risk assessment formula is seriously flawed."

In all, an ICIJ analysis of the Mossack Fonseca files identified 61 family members and associates of prime ministers, presidents or kings. The records show, for example, that the family of Azerbaijan President Ilham Aliyev used foundations and companies in Panama to hold secret stakes in gold mines and London real estate. The children of Pakistani Prime Minister Nawaz Sharif also owned London real estate through companies created by Mossack Fonseca, the law firm's records show. Family members of at least eight current or former members of China's Politburo Standing Committee, the country's main ruling body, have offshore companies arranged though Mossack Fonseca. They include President Xi's brother-in-law, who set up two British Virgin Islands companies in 2009. Representatives for the Azeri, Pakistani and Chinese leaders did not respond to requests for comment.

The list of world leaders who used Mossack Fonseca to set up offshore entities includes the current president of Argentina, Mauricio Macri, who was director and vice president of a Bahamas company managed by Mossack Fonseca when he was a businessman and the mayor of Argentina's capital, Buenos Aires. A spokesman for Macri said the president never personally owned shares in the firm, which was part of his family's business. During the bloodiest days of Russia's 2014 invasion of the Ukraine's Donbas region, the documents show, representatives of Ukrainian leader Petro Poroshenko scrambled to find a copy of a home utility bill for him to complete the paperwork to create a holding company in the British Virgin Islands. A spokesperson for Poroshenko said the creation of the company had nothing to do with „any political and military events in Ukraine." Poroshenko's financial advisers said the president didn't include the BVI firm in his 2014 financial disclosures because neither the holding company nor two related companies in Cyprus and the Netherlands have any assets. They said that the companies were part of a corporate restructuring to help sell Poroshenko's confectionery business.

When Sigmundur David Gunnlaugsson became Iceland's prime minister in 2013 he concealed a secret that could have damaged his political career. He and his wife shared ownership in an offshore company in the British Virgin Islands when he entered parliament in 2009. He sold his stake in the company months later to his wife for $1. The company held bonds originally worth millions of dollars in three giant Icelandic banks that failed during the 2008 global financial crash, making it a creditor in their bankruptcies. Gunnlaugsson's government negotiated a deal with creditors last year without disclosing his family's financial stake in the outcome. Gunnlaugsson has denied in recent days that his family's financial interests influenced his stances. The leaked records do not make it clear whether Gunnlaugsson's political positions benefited or hurt the value of the bonds held through the offshore company. In an interview with an ICIJ media partners, Reykjavik Media and SVT, Gunnlaugsson denied hiding assets. When he was confronted with the name of the offshore company linked to him - Wintris Inc. - the prime minister said „I'm starting to feel a bit strange about these questions because it's like you are accusing me of something."

Soon after, he ended the interview. Four days later, his wife took the matter public, posting a note on Facebook asserting that the company was hers, not his, and that she had paid all taxes on it. Since then, members of Iceland's parliament have questioned why Gunnlaugsson never disclosed the offshore company, with one lawmaker calling for the prime minister and his government to resign. The prime minister has fought back, putting out an eight-page statement arguing he wasn't required to publicly report his connection to Wintris because it was really owned by his wife and because it was „merely a holding company, not a company engaged in commercial activities."

OFFSHORE COVER-UPS

In 2005, a tour boat called the Ethan Allen sank in New York's Lake George, drowing 20 elderly tourists. After the survivors and families of the dead sued they learned the tour company had no insurance because fraudsters had sold it a fake policy. Malchus Irvin Boncamper, an accountant on the Caribbean island of St. Kitts, pleaded guilty in a U.S. court in 2011.to helping the con artists launder proceeds of their frauds. This created a problem for Mossack Fonseca, because Boncamper had served as the front man - a „nominee" director - for 30 companies created by the law firm. Once it learned of Boncamper's criminal conviction, Mossack Fonseca took quick action. It told its offices to replace Boncamper as director of the companies - and to backdate the records in a way that made it appear the changes had taken place, in some cases, a decade earlier. The Boncamper case is one of the examples in the leaked files showing the law firm using questionable tactics to hide its own methods or its customers' activities from legal authorities.

In the „Operation Car Wash" case in Brazil, prosecutors allege that Mossack Fonseca employees destroyed and hid documents to mask the law firm's involvement in money laundering. A police document says that, in one instance, an employee of the firm's Brazil branch sent an email instructing co-workers to hide records involving a client who may have been the target of a police investigation: „Do not leave anything. I will save them in my car or at my house." In Nevada, the leaked files show, Mossack Fonseca employees worked in late 2014 to obscure the links between the law firm's Las Vegas branch and its headquarters in Panama in anticipation of a U.S. court order requiring it to turn over information on 123 companies incorporated by the law firm. Argentine prosecutors had linked those Nevada-based companies to a corruption scandal involving an associate of former presidents Nestor Kirchner and Cristina Fernandez de Kirchner.

In an effort to free itself from the American court's jurisdiction, Mossack Fonseca claimed that its Las Vegas office, MF Nevada, wasn't in fact a branch office at all. It said it had no control over the office. The firm's internal records show the opposite. They indicate that the firm controlled MF Nevada's bank account and the firm's co-founders and another Mossack Fonseca official owned 100 percent of MF Nevada. To erase evidence of the connection, the law firm arranged to remove paper documents from the branch and worked to delete computer traces of the link between the Nevada and the Panama ope-rations, internal emails show. One big worry, an internal email said, was that the branch's manager might be too „nervous" to carry out the effort, making it easy for investigators to discover „that we are hiding something." Mossack Fonseca declined to answer questions about the Brazil and Nevada affairs, but denied generally that it had obstructed investigations or covered up improper activities. „It is not our policy to hide or destroy documentation that may be of use in any ongoing investigation or proceeding," the firm said.

REFORMING THE SECRET WORLD

In 2013, U.K. leader David Cameron urged his country's overseas territories - including the British Virgin Islands - to work with him to „get our own houses in order" and join the fight against tax evasion and offshore secrecy. He could have looked no further than his late father to see how challenging that would be. Ian Cameron, a stockbroker and multimillionaire, was a Mossack Fonseca client who used the law firm to shield his investment fund, Blairmore Holdings, Inc., from U.K. taxes. The fund's name came from Blairmore House, his family's ancestral country estate. Mossack Fonseca registered the investment fund in Panama even though many of its key investors were British. Ian Cameron controlled the fund from its birth in 1982 until his death in 2010.

A prospectus for investors said the fund „should be managed and conducted so that it does not become resident in the United Kingdom for United Kingdom taxation purposes." The fund did this by using untraceable certificates of ownership known as „bearer shares" and by employing „nominee" company officers based in the Bahamas, the law firm's leaked records show. Ian Cameron's tax-haven history is an example of how deeply offshore secrecy is woven into the lives of political and financial elites around the world. It's also an important economic engine for many countries. The weight of that self-interest has made reform difficult. In the U.S., for example, states like Delaware and Nevada, which have allowed company owners to remain anonymous, continue to fight against efforts to require greater corporate transparency. Mossack Fonseca's home country, Panama, has refused to embrace a plan for worldwide exchange of information about bank accounts - out of concern that its offshore industry could be left at a competitive disadvantage. Panama officials say they will exchange information, but on a more modest scale.

The challenge that reformers and law enforcers face is how to find and stop criminal behavior when it's buried beneath layers of secrecy. The most effective tool for breaking through this secrecy has been leaks of offshore documents that have dragged hidden dealings into the open. Document leaks uncovered by ICIJ and its media partners have prompted legislation and official investigations in dozens of countries - and fanned fears among offshore customers who worry their secrets will be revealed. In April 2013, after ICIJ released its „Offshore Leaks" stories based on confidential documents from the British Virgin Islands and Singapore, some Mossack Fonseca customers emailed the firm looking for reassurance that their offshore holdings were safe from scrutiny, Mossack Fonseca told customers not to worry. It said its commitment to its clients' privacy „has always been paramount, and in this regard your confidential information is stored in our state-of-the-art data center, and any communication within our global network is handled through an encryption algorithm that complies with the highest world-class standards.«

Canada

SOCIAL-ECONOMICAL SYSTEM

Austin C. Wehrwein, *Milwaukee Journal*

It was really a surprise when, while the Korean War was straining the nerves of the American public, the 1953 Pulitzer Prize for International Reporting was awarded for the coverage of a subject totally unconnected with one of the major international crisis. The jury had named six finalists on their report of March 1953, starting with Austin C. Wehrwein of the *Milwaukee Journal*. „Here... is the most outstanding work submitted," one juror stated, „twenty-six related stories about Canada. I have read many articles about Canada, magazines, press services and special pieces. This writer's leg work, plus good writing and know-how, brings our neighbor on the north into the house. Economics, politics, finance, moose pasture stockateers, the St. Lawrence seaway, Canada's need for more people, aluminium - all these and more subjects are brightly written and outlined. Austin C. Wehrwein of the *Milwaukee Journal* is easy to read and easy to understand. His work is distinctive." The Pulitzer Prize Board shared that praise and honored Wehrwein „for a series of articles on Canada." It was the first award for reporting about a country which because of its geographical neighborhood with the U.S.A. had hardly been covered by American foreign correspondents so far.

Austin Carl Wehrwein was born on January 12,1916, in Austin, Texas. He was educated in the public schools of Madison, Wisconsin, and graduated from the University of Wisconsin in 1937 with a B.A. degree in economics. He became a reporter of the *Milwaukee Journal* after graduation until he entered the Columbia University Law School, from which he graduated in 1940 with an LL.B. degree. Afterwards he became a member of the Wisconsin Bar, but instead of practicing law he returned to newspaper work. Between 1940 and 1943 when he volunteered for the army he worked for the *Associated Press* and the *Milwaukee Journal* in Madison Wisconsin, and in the Washington, D. C., bureau of the *United Press* news agency. Next he was on the Shanghai edition of *Stars and Stripes*, and after the war he returned to the *United Press* in Washington, resigning in 1948 to go to England where he attended the London School of Economics. He subsequently joined the Economic Co-operation Administration (ECA), working on the ECA information staff in London, Copenhagen, and Oslo. Wehrwein resigned from ECA in 1951 and joined the *Milwaukee Journal* as a reporter, assigned to the financial page of that newspaper. His series of articles written for the newspaper in 1952 about the economic, political, and cultural aspects of Canada was published as a booklet entitled, „Canada's New Century." Following now are several of

Wehrwein's Pulitzer Prize-winning articles, published in the *Milwaukee Journal* from October 12 - October 29, 1952:

ECONOMIC FRONT

»"The 20th Century belongs to Canada." That prophecy was made about 50 years ago by one of Canada' s great statesmen, Sir Wilfrid Laurier. Today as the world plods wearily into the second half of the century it is coming true. Not in the sense that Canada expects to become a great military conqueror, with its tiny population of 14 million now and perhaps 40 million in the year 2000. Rather in the sense that she commands the economic resources that are essential to the United States and the free world in war or peace.

Equally as important, Canada shares our belief in freedom and will use her power as a decent neighbor and partner on this continent. But we must face the fact that while we grow poorer by the hour in natural resources Canada grows richer. Although we use up half of the world's production of raw materials we produce only a fraction of what we need. We totally lack some of the most vital materials, and even import iron ore and oil. But here is Canada, with a population not much bigger than that of New York city and its metropolitan districts, on an area one-third bigger than the United States, with this record:

Supplying 90% of the free world's nickel and 70% of the asbestos; leading in production of uranium and platinum and nonferrous metals; ranking second in gold, zinc and in other mysterious metals that are the key to modern industry. Her iron ore deposits are probably the world's largest and her crude oil reserves, also among the biggest, increased 34 times in the last six years. Yet, the potential is still virtually untapped. Nor should it be forgotten that Canadian wheat feeds 100 million mouths, nor that her forests supply the paper on which nine out of ten American - and three out of five world - newspapers are printed - including the one you hold in your hand at this moment.

Just as sure as the Canadian winter winds that sweep down over Milwaukee, our country must depend upon Canada. And by the same token, Canada needs us. We are wedded, for better or for worse, for richer or for poorer, in sickness and in health. Yet, Canada's mushrooming progress is not confined to basic commodities. Although the government refused to encourage „hothouse" industries that need tariff protection, Canada has in the last three decades become a highly industrialized nation, tripling manufacturing volume. Here, too, we have a tremendous stake, perhaps more than Canadians would like, although the government welcomes our participation. There are more than 3,000 branches of United States firms here, double the number in 1939, of which 347 entered since 1946. Among the new arrivals are 13 which have their home offices in Wisconsin, including three from Milwaukee. They are Automatic Products Co., Ladish Co., and Globe-Union Corp.

The branch plants do a quarter to a third of Canada's manufacturing business. From January, 1950, to mid-1952, Americans invested nearly one and one-half billion dollars here, and it is estimated that reinvestment of Canadian profits added a sum equal to more than one-half of that figure. Americans have invested close to eight billion dollars all-told in Canada. Our people own one-eighth of all the government and corporate bonds, a quarter of all the business capital and 37 % of the manufacturing. In 1950 American investment in all branches of the oil industry was 54% of the total book value, and is undoubtedly higher now. Last year, 378 million dollars went out of Canada for interest and dividends to Americans.

At the same time, since 1946, Canadians themselves have set aside some 20 billion dollars for new investment, or more than one-fifth of their total production. Government economists here point out that large as it is, American investment is only about 10% of the total, with perhaps another 5% coming from Europe, the remainder being home grown. Just as important as our money is American willingness to go into risky fields and bring in experts to help speed development. A case in point is oil. Another bonus that comes with American investment is the assurance that the Canadians will have a market. Case in point: Iron ore mined for our steel mills. No doubt, the oil and natural gas discoveries in western Canada, the opening up of the high grade iron ore reserves on the Quebec - Labrador border and in northern Ontario, and the big aluminum projects both in Quebec and British Columbia have been the most spectacular. Capital investment in such projects alone is expected to be a billion dollars in the next three years.

But nearly every industry and region has been touched with the magic wand. No longer is Canada confined to the area which lies 100 miles north of the 3,000 mile border. Many of the projects are in the northern frontier country, and the boom has given new depth to Canada, both in geography and diversification of industry. Steel production, for example, is triple prewar and the country is on the road to self-sufficiency. With but a fifth of the potential harnessed, hydroelectric production is half of ours. And a host of new industries is growing up around the oil discoveries on the prairies. Although the economies of the United States and Canada are complementary, Canadians are willing to compete with us when they can. At Malton, Ont., near Toronto, the Avro Canada Co. is building one of the world's most powerful jet engines and is laying the groundwork for the capture of the jet air liner market across the border.

The firm has already built its first commercial jet aircraft and when its defense output eases off will be ready to supply them in volume to our air lines. Of interest to Americans in the market for stocks is the fact that the Toronto Stock Exchange is now the biggest on the continent in volume. On Bay St., Canada's Wall Street, they joke that the day the volume hit the record of 7,500,000 shares (Oct. 19, 1951) was the day that „America discovered Canada." In the past American-Canadian relations have been strained by the „stockateers" and „moose pasture" salesmen who worked out of Bay St., selling Americans millions of dollars worth of worthless stocks by mail and telephone. Now, however, the brokers' association and the Ontario authorities are working closely with our securities and exchange commission to stamp out the evil.

As far as the individual coming into Canada is concerned, this country's coming of age is immediately brought home as soon as he changes his American money into Canadian. The American dollar, once the undisputed champion of the world, no longer weighs in at 100c or more in Canadian money. Today a visitor gets but 95c for each buck. „It's too bad we don't call our dollar a 'sheaf' or a 'shoat' or something," one economist remarked. „Then our American friends who do not understand why their money isn't 'just as good' as ours wouldn't be so put out about it."

Another statistic must be cited to complete the picture. We are each other's best customers. Last year Canadians bought goods from us worth more than 2.3 billion dollars, and we sold them even more, or 2.8 billion dollars worth. „It might not be too far fetched to compare Canada today to that stock character in fiction - the young girl who for years tries vainly to attract the attention of the big boy next door," Finance Minister Douglas Abbott commented. „When he suddenly becomes aware that she has grown into a beautiful young woman and begins to pay her a lot of attention, she doesn't quite know how to handle the situation. But of course she enjoys it, and like most young girls today, learns pretty quickly how to take it in her stride. „So do we!"

BUDGET BALANCES

The Liberal party, which has been in power in Canada for 17 years, is giving Canada a „businessman's government." Canada is riding one of the biggest booms in economic history and financing a rearmament program on the side without price or wage controls, without an excess profits tax and with a bare minimum of curbs on materials and scattered rent controls. And observers here say that despite some complaints from organized labor the system is working. They point out that the cost of living index, pulled down by falling food prices, is below that of a year ago. Generally speaking, rents are comparable to ours, and prices, if you allow for special taxes and costs added because many goods must be imported, are on a par with those in the United States.

What's more, the budget has been balanced every year since the end of the war and the national debt has been reduced out of surplus. Economists say our growing deficit, on the other hand, can breed inflation. Despite an increase of 150 million dollars in defense spending, Canada had a 262 million dollar surplus in the first three months of this fiscal year. There is talk now of a tax cut, what with an election due next year. There is no capital gains tax levied on profits from the sale of securities or property, except in the case of professional speculators. The top federal income tax on corporations is 47.6%. Ours is 52%, plus the excess profits tax if it applies to a given case. But individual income taxes are about the same as ours in the lower brackets, and higher in the upper. A 20% surcharge was slapped on when the Korean war started.

And there are stiff sales taxes. A 23c levy brings the cost of American cigarets to 45c a pack and Canadian brands to 39c. The general 10% sales tax at the wholesale level applies to all goods except fuels, building materials and most foods. There is a 25 % tax on automobiles, radios, cameras and household and electrical appliances. Two words are the key to the government's policy: „Flexibility" and „indirect." The aim has been the same as that of the American government: To encourage defense production, to conserve scarce materials and to combat inflation. But the weapon here has been the use of restrictions on credit, rather than on prices, be they for things or labor. After the Korean war started, Canada was faced with a situation similar to ours. There was scarce buying and the prospect of shortages that would send up prices. Like us, Canada has participated in NATO and has a defense program of her own.

Although they are now off (as are ours), Canada put curbs on consumer credit and housing loans. And most important, commercial banks agreed to limit the aggregate of their lending to a figure similar to that of the pre-Korean period. This, too, has been eased now. Although the government did not tell banks what loans to make, they agreed, in effect, to refuse „nonessential loans." Our banks, too, had a voluntary restraint program, but it was not related to a specific volume. Right after the end of World War II, the government encouraged reconversion by easing up on taxes on business through a liberalization of the depreciation allowances. Now the government has reversed the process, and has worked out an ingenious system of „deferred depreciation." Even before deferred depreciation Canada tax laws were more generous than ours in allowing a businessman to claim depreciation on his equipment and plant. And while there are some accelerated tax write-offs, similar to those our government grants to defense goods producers, they are not dished out as often.

But this deferred depreciation is the other side of the coin. If the government doesn't approve of a proposed expansion it doesn't deny materials or try to halt the job - although it should be added that there is some control on steel and a few other very scarce materials. What happens is a warning that the company can't start depreciating its investment for four years. If this sounds complicated, it can be summed up by saying that it means higher taxes on nonessential expansion. But a stubborn businessman can often go ahead if he doesn't care. „In dealing with the inflationary pressures arising out of Korea and rearmament, we based our policies on three broad principles," explained Finance Minister Douglas Abbott. „In the first place we were determined to follow a pay as you go policy. The second principle was to devise measures which strike at the root causes of inflation. Thirdly, since increased production is vital, we sought to encourage output and to avoid measures whieh blunt the incentives of our people."

How much of the lesson can be applied in the United States? In the first place, there are wide grounds for valid comparisons. No two countries have as many cultural, geographic and industrial factors in common. After all, the border is largely an artificial one, and what goes on in our northern tier of states is the same as what goes on up here. In fact, Canada's major trade lines run south, rather than east and west. But in other respects there are major differences whieh make direct comparison misleading. For one thing, the banking system is more closely influenced - if not regulated - by the central government bank than ours is by the federal reserve system. The government is on more intimate terms with business leaders, simply because the population is so small, and personal persuasion is easier. Contrawise, no businessman needs to hire a „5 per center." He can have lunch with the official he wants to see almost any time.

And while there is a strong urge to keep private enterprise free, the government historically has been in control of major sectors of the economy - though not in a monopoly position - such as transportation and power, the latter on the provincial level. While there has been a tremendous boom - government officials prefer to call its „expansion" or something else because „boom" suggests a later „bust"-it has been in terms of capital investment that encourages more production. And increased production is a cure for inflation. Labor has not, until recently, demanded higher wages, which is a source of inflationary pressure in the United States. Wages are from 25 to 30c an hour lower than in the United States, and although the Canadian affiliate of the CIO United Steel-workers recently won „wage parity" with their American brothers, the $1.43½ an hour figure is a basic rate, and the United States differentials are higher. In May, 1952, the United States labor department said the hourly wage for factory workers generally was $1.66, adding that there were wide variations.

However, the victory has spurred other unions to make a similar „parity" demand, and businessmen naturally take a dim view. They argue that Canadian industry isn't yet big enough to absorb the cost of higher wages by increasing productivity. An intangible factor some economists cite is the tendency for Canadian businessmen to be more conservative than their American colleagues, even in this period of rapid growth. This keeps them from trying to expand as rapidly as they might, thus avoiding a scramble for goods which bids up prices. Then, too, the arms program here is proportionately smaller than ours, which means that it takes a smaller chunk out of the materials supply and labor market and thus generates less inflationary steam.

CANADIAN DOLLAR

As you have probably noticed, the United States greenback has shriveled somewhat the last few years. Up here it's even shorter. That our dollar is worth less than the Canadian may not be news to international bankers. But many American visitors seemingly don't know or can't believe it. It doesn't seem right somehow. „How much more is my money worth up here?" a surprising number ask as soon as they set foot on Canadian soil. The reply, given with a cross between a smirk and a smile, usually adds up to this: „It' s the other way round now, you know." Bypassing the whys for a moment, the situation is simply that our dollar usually „sells" at a 5% discount. For example, a $20 bill gets you only $19 in their black and green bills, which are printed in both English and French and which bear a likeness of the late King George of England and Canada.

Some hotels give you a bit extra. This works out to about 10c on the $20 exchange. If you are really loaded, a bank in dire need of a lot of our dollars might go as low as 3½%, which would work out to $19.30 (Canadian) on the deal. But the going rate is 5% „off." To avoid mental arithmetic some stores do accept American money at par on small purchases, but your change will probably be in American coins. Stores and hotels doing a lot of tourist business used to trade even on all transactions when the gap was narrower. But they can't afford a 5% loss just to be nice now. As for our silver and copper coins, which get hopelessly mixed with their Canadian cousins in a traveler's pocket,

the King Edward hotel cashier summed up the attitude with:
„We take them but we don't like them."

In other words, most business places don't have the time to pick the wheat from the chaff in the chicken feed, particularly as the two moneys are minted in the same denominations. But not a few change makers take sly pleasure in slipping an American a bit of his own small stuff in a handful. One reason is that, if they get stuck with a lot of American coins and have to take them to a bank, the bank will take an 8% bite. The additional discount is a handling charge. Now if all this sounds like a lot of rigmarole, remember that the shoe used to be on the other - the American - foot. There were times before World War II when an American could get $1.20 for every one of his dollars. During the war and after, the exchange rate was pegged to give us a 10c bonus on each dollar, which, of course, meant that a Canadian got only 90c in our money when he crossed the border - if he could find a taker.

But by September, 1950, the pegged price - set by law - had become a fantasy. The boom here had reached the hurricane stage. In New York and other financial centers speculators and investors were scrambling for Canadian funds, bidding up the unofficial price. So the Canadian government set their currency free to find its own level. By last March it was „even Stephen" with ours. It has since hopped past the tired old buck. The „why" can besummed up simply, It's the old law of supply and demand. And the demand is greater than supply because Canada sells more than it buys from other countries, because American and other investors are pouring money into the country and because the country has a strong fiscal position.

In the international money market, currencies fluctuate in value - that is, price - just like potatoes at the supermarket. The demand is enormous for Canadian dollars because an American - or any non-Canadian - must, in effect, first buy Canadian dollars before he can buy Canadian stocks or goods. He must, in other words, buy Canadian „poker chips" to sit in their game. Canadians are elated over this symbol of their new economic maturity, especially in view of the fact that their population is less than one-tenth of ours. The emotion is akin to that of a Marquette alumnus after the Hilltoppers beat the Badgers. But there are flies in the gravy. Many world prices are and will continue to be set in United States dollars. For example, Canadian wheat is sold by international agreement at $1.80 (our money), which means the grower will get only $1.71 in his money. The loss will come to about 50 million dollars this year.

Other exporters, not tied up by long term contracts or special agreements, are on a spot. If they hold the price line in terms of United States dollars they are automatically taking a 5% loss. If they up the price to cover the discount

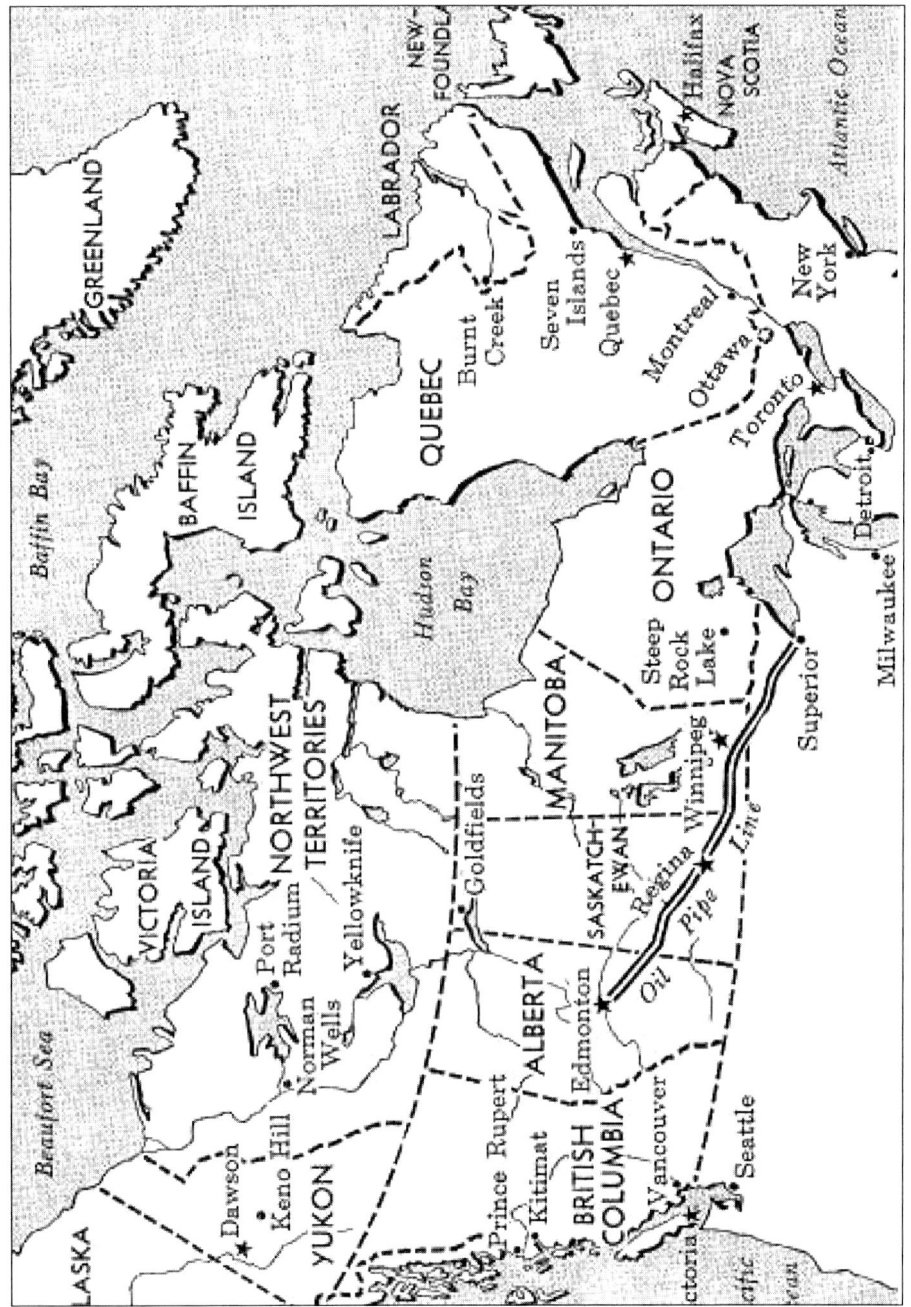

they get no extra profit here, but the buyer has to pay more - just as the tourist finds his Canadian vacation is 5 % more expensive. Importers, on the other hand, have been able to get what they buy at lower prices. But because many of the imports are semifinished goods or machines, the general consumer has not benefited much directly. When the rate began to go up there was some fear that it would hurt the tourist trade, which last year brought in 258 million American dollars, plus assorted other currencies. But the Ontario travel and publicity bureau expects 1952 to be another record year. Nevertheless, while they are tickled to be on the high side of the foreign exchange teeter-totter for once, many businessmen here say they'd like to see the rate at or near par.

The government has, however, turned a deaf ear to the few suggestions that it step in again and set the rate by fiat. Only if it should rise farther would the government take action, and then it would attempt to haul its free wheeling dollar back by unloading some government holdings (thus depressing the market) rather than by direct control. Meantime, the situation is giving American tourists a taste of international finance, although the lesson doesn't always take. There was a Chicago businessman, who arrived here this week, for example. When he bought a paper with a $10 (United States) bill at a newsstand, the vender said, apologetically, „I'm sorry, I'll have to give you a little less in change." „That's all right," answered the Chicagoan, „we've got a sales tax at home, too."

JETPLANE MARKET

Canada hopes to take the American commercial jet airplane market away from both British and American manufacturers. At its huge new 45 million dollar plant at the airport here, which serves Toronto, 20 miles away, the Avro Canada Co. has just begun production on one of the the most powerful jet engines in actual use. Today they are going into fighter planes of the Royal Canadian air force. But Avro already has turned out a commercial jet liner, capable of doing 450 m.p.h., reaching an altitude of six miles, and with a passenger capacity of 40 to 60. At present its four 3,500 pound thrust Rolls Royce jets limit it to „medium" ranges. But with the new Orenda power packages, with a thrust of about 6,500 pounds, it could be moved up a notch. There is only one now flying, but when the heat is off defense production Avro will make a quick transition. Howard Hughes, meanwhile, has had it in California for some hush hush radar tests and the United States air force is interested in a military model.

On the eve of the Korean war, National Airlines, which links New York and Florida, was dickering for 10. Because Capt. Eddie Rickenbacker, president of Eastern Air Lines, and other American air men have thrown up their hands over British dawdling, Avro has hopes of selling across the border. One American air line is reported to have booked an order already on an if and when basis. „After all we're on the same continent, and it is likely that American air lines will feel better dealing with somebody close to home," an Avro spokesman said. All this is still over the horizon. The big news now is that the official opening of the jet engine plant marks the coming of age of the aviation industry here and establishes Canada, despite its tiny population, as the third air power in the western world.

Coincident with the formal ribbon snipping ceremony was the announcement that the government had given the firm a 66 million dollar contract for Orendas - so called because the word in the Iroquois language means „the spirit that endows things with great power." These engines will power Sabre jets being made under United States license at Montreal. Souped up with the Orenda, these Canadian made fighters promise to be the fastest in general operation and will soon tangle with the Russian built MIG's in Korea. In time, they will be supplied to western Europe as part of Canada's contribution to NATO. More important, Avro also makes its own fighter, the CF-100 Canuck which is tailor made for arctic flying - for use over the north pole ice cap which will be the battle air of the future. Defense of this polar frontier is a joint job with our country, and while military security forbids discussion, Avro spokesmen hint that the American defense planners are interested in flying the Canuck too.

It is described as one of the world's most powerful, and the first long range, all-weather, day and night jet fighter. It, too, will havs the new Orendas. Performance details have not been disclosed. But it can probably make 700 miles per hour and operate at 40,000 feet. Eventually it will take the place of the Sabre jets as part of the country's two billion dollar air force expansion program. Whatever the ultima impact on the American industry, C. D. Howe, the defense minister, pointed out that the American government has encouraged Canada to grow its own industry both to make Canada independent and to give the United States an alternative source of supply. As part of this cooperation, Canada has standardized its military equipment with us, opening the door to two way trading. Avro is the short name for A. V. Roe-Canada, Ltd., a sister company of an English firm, whose parent is the British Hawker Siddeley Group Ltd. It is now the biggest unit in the family.

Avro stands on its own feet as far as the corporate relationship is concerned, although the government has put about 15 million dollars into the organization because of its importance to defense. This, by the way, is unusual. The „businessman's government" here has nothing like our Reconstruction Finance Corp., for defense plants. Only a few years ago Canada's aviation industry consisted of a few branch assembly plants, putting together components imported from the United States. Building an aviation industry over night has not been easy. For example, 2,000 skilled British technicians had to be imported for this plant alone. The top management is symbolic of Canada's position as a bridge between Britain and the United States. Kingpin is a Canadian, Crawford Gordon, jr., the president. Jim Floyd, the chief aircraft designer, is English, and Tom McCrae, who came from General Motors, is manager of the gas turbine division.

Men like these have the American industry worried. They were able to work out a commercial jet carrier for half the cost estimated for the job by our industry. And they have other plans locked in the safe. One is the production of the „flying triangle," which is one of Britain's most advanced designs and a product of the sister company there. Avro has also developed a new alloy which may solve some of the toughest problems in atom driven aircraft, according to industry reports. This, which the company will neither confirm nor deny, would make possible a light weight screen around the atomic reactor. At present it is understood that a lead shield - far too heavy for aircraft - is necessary. If this comes to fruition, authorities here estimate that four pounds of uranium would fuel an atom plane for several round the world nonstop flights.

STOCK EXCHANGE

The Toronto Stock Exchange celebrates its 100th birthday this month and an exhilarated clientele, which includes a lot of Americans, has given it a happy anniversary year. The daily volume of shares traded here frequently tops that of the New York Stock Exchange, and through September of this year the total was something like 492 million shares, compared to around 280 million on New York's „big board." Back in 1852 a seat on the baby exchange, set up because mother country England wouldn't invest in the raw colony, cost $5. Last month one sold for $90,000, more than double the price on the New York exchange. In short, like a number of things in this deep breathing, muscle flexing country, the Toronto exchange has grown up. And in a rush.

Prior to World War II, there were 312 stocks listed. Now there are 1,007, including 10 American issues. This is only about 500 fewer than the big board listings and includes all but 301 of the publicly owned companies of any size in Canada. In fact, the trading, which is mostly in oil and mine shares, is so furious that the statistical department has ordered an electric brain to help it keep abreast of the transactions. The exchange here now does 70% of all the stock market business in Canada, having shoved Montreal back into the shadows. This makes Toronto the financial center of the realm - realm being the term they use now instead of dominion. „In 1929 Montreal was the center," said an exchange official. „But Montreal money is static. Out here, money is more speculative. And the new oil and mineral developments need that kind of money."

At the same time, the Toronto exchange is still behind the big board and the New York Curb Exchange in the value - as opposed to the number - of traded shares. This reflects the low per share value of the mining shares, some of which are worth only a few cents and which average out to about $2. That is, until pay dirt is hit. And, of course, Canada has but one-tenth of our population. Mining and oil shares constitute 75% of the listings and about the same proportion of the trading. The quoted market value is about 19 billion dollars. Of that, 15 billion dollars is accounted for by the industrials. The modernistic building on Bay St., Canada's Wall Street, is supported by 106 active members. Of these, six are recognized as „American," although technically members are supposed to be Canadian citizens. Additionally, there is a handful of „hybrid" members who front - but not in the invidious sense - for Americans.

Unlike our exchanges, members do not go onto the floor. Instead they can send four representatives and spend their time back in their offices cooking up deals. But it is the member, rather than a junior partner, who votes on policy questions. Another difference is that the quotations are carried on the board and the tape as „bids" and „asks," rather than the price of the last sale. This gives a more realistic picture of the market, but it created a lot more work for the staff. „Because of the mining shares, this has always been a heavy trading exchange, and we've been forced to develop ways to handle it," one of the statistical staff explained. The exchange, therefore, has the most efficient gadgets in the world. Among them is a „dial ticker" device. By dialing a three digit code, a broker can get the current quotation on about half of the listed stocks. The quotation is typed off on a tape by a tiny, telegraphlike machine. The one-half limitation is only there because it covers just the active issues.

A visitor doesn't have to go far to see signs of public interest in the market. Bend an ear in any of the crowded cocktail lounges and you'll hear market gossip. You even hear it at drugstore lunch counters. Brokers and dealers are convinced that, despite heavy American investment, the bulk of the money flowing into the exchange is home grown. „There has been a wave of American money in the last two years," D'Arcy M. Doherty, exchange president, said in an interview. „It has been big, but not as big as many people think." „F day" - F for „foreign" - was Oct. 19, 1951. On that day the exchange had a record 7,500,000 share volume, and it was estimated that a quarter of the money was American. Additional money gushed in from Switzerland, which is a funnel not only for Swiss but all surplus European holdings looking for safe and lush pastures.

The record single day's volume in trading at New York was approximately 16 million shares during the 1929 market crash. The trading for the last few months has been about a million shares a day. „We know that American and other investment is attracted by our spectacular growth and by the soundness of our government's fiscal policy. But we realize that some of it is 'flight capital' and that the resulting rise in the value of our dollar may not last," an exchange authority said. „In any event, we joke up here that Oct. 19 was the day the Americans discovered Canada." And although they are exuberant, leading brokers here are still realistic. They recognize that New York is still the weather vane and, in fact, the market here follows trends there quite closely. When New York broke sharply not long ago, so did Toronto.

They also admit that some Canadian stocks have been overvalued. „I feel that there was too rapid a rise in speculative securities such as oils, and they are now going through a normal corrective period," Doherty said. He described the present state of the market as a „digestive period," observing that the „overall growth picture is good. The market ran ahead of development. Now development is catching up." Recession is not something that money men - particularly here - like to talk about. But both brokers and bankers here are far more optimistic about the future of business in Canada than many fiscal experts in the United States are about the United States' future. For one thing, the Canadian prosperity is based to a much smaller degree on direct government spending for defense items.

Yet, while even a short time visitor can smell the excitement in the air, observers here say that there is no hysteria on the 1929 scale. There isn't much heavy buying on shoestring margins, and even those who take a flier on „moose pasture" or „elephant country" issues usually know what they're doing. The public, no doubt about it, is interested. When the American firm of Merrill Lynch, Pierce, Fenner & Beane sponsored a lecture on what to do with your money, they had to hold two repeat sessions to take care of the crowd. Many persons, veteran observers report, who once regarded the market like a dressed up Irish sweepstakes now see it as an opportunity to have a stake in the vast national expansion. At the same time, Oswald E. Lennox, chairman of the Ontario securities commission, as cautious a man as you'll find north of the border, told the writer that even before the boom, it was not unusual for a modest income family to pick up some very dubious „moose pasture," often at 10 or 15c a share, more or less for the fun of it.

„If a Canadian puts $250 in such shares he thinks he's quite a fellow. But some of your people will put $10,000 into stock like that on the basis of a phone call, and then expect results overnight," he observed. It should be said at this point that „moose pasture" stocks are not necessarily outright gyps. In the jargon of the trade here, the term is used for almost any long shot and brokers insist that almost any mine or oil property is just that. That's why they warn again and again that even on the most likely proposition there's bound to be a wait while exploration and development go on. Canadians, men like Lennox observe, are patient. Americans aren't. Brokers can reel off story after story both about 10c stocks now selling for $20 and 20c stocks selling for nothing. The big profit, if any, is in the „growth" side, the increase in the value resulting from a rich strike. When it comes to yields, official stock market statistics show that earnings on stocks which are comparable to the normal run on the New York exchange are about the same.

Bank stocks pay an average of 4.4%. Preferred industrials about 5.14% and common 5.31 %, oil refineries (not wells) 5.31 % and mining stocks about 6.90%. Because most of the oil has been discovered only since the end of World War II, only about 20 of the 116 oil stocks on the board have paid any dividends. The exchange gets a special shot in the arm that dosen't exist in „the States," however. This is the fact that there is no capital gains tax - that is a tax on the money you make when you sell your holdings after a rise. Our federal government taxes such profits, but at a lower rate than on earned income. This applies only if the stock is held more than six months. But what about the perpetrators of the stock frauds on Americans - the high pressure boys who used to flood our mails with fictional claims? That's another story, and we'll get to it next.

STOCKATEERS' BUSINESS

Have the „moose pasture stockateers" gone the way of the dodo bird? The official story on Bay St., the Wall Street of Canada, is that the „buccaneers of Bay St.," who fleeced American suckers out of millions, are on the decline. Privately, brokers admit that some of the worst - many of them Americans - are still on the scene. But they haven't broken Canadian law, and if the American government has something on them for past performances it is up to the Yanks to extradite them, authorities here say. The extradition treaty was broadened last August to deal with the situation, but so far there has not been a single case brought under its provisions.

„Moose pasture stockateers," it should be explained, are rapid conversational types attracted to this financial center by the possibility of a fast buck from the country's big oil and mineral discoveries. Using long distance telephone calls and hyperthyroid literature they sold millions of dollars worth of low priced but worthless securi ties to Americans. How much is a matter of sheer guess. Our securities and exchange commission once estimated the loss at 10 to 50 million dollars a year. But Oswald E. Lennox, the mild mannered chairman of the Ontario securities commission who has two Bibles on his desk, estimated that the top was about 10 million dollars.

And Clarence H. Adams, one of the SEC commissioners, said last month that the swindle had „come to a virtual halt." This jibes with information from Wisconsin sourees. The Milwaukee Better Business Bureau has reported a sharp drop in complaints; in the period January to August, the Wisconsin department of securities issued only five stop orders, compared with 18 in the like period last year. Lennox said in an interview that he had canceled about 60 licenses in the last two years, a rate far exceeding any other period except for 1946, when there was a general cleanup. „I can truthfully say that to my knowledge there are no 'boiler rooms' operating," said John Rogers, chairman of the Ontario Broker-Dealers' association. He is a partner in one of the leading securities houses, Doherty, Roadhouse & Co., whose senior partner, D'Arcy M. Doherty, is president of the Toronto Stock Exchange.

In the language of the trade, „boiler rooms" are outright thieves' dens - crooks who do things like selling nonexistent stocks. Actually, the moose pastute boys have real live companies with land, but the prospects are usually imaginary. As for such remaining operators, Rogers said: „In all businesses there will be some crooks. We think we've made great strides in rectifying various evils which existed in the past." The problem is attacked on two fronts. Ultimate power is in Lennox's commission - there is no federal body, regulation being left to the provinces, which correspond roughly to our states. On the day to day policing level is the Broker-Dealers' association, which was given its powers by law about four years ago. Stock listed on the exchange must also meet that body's requirements. In general outline, the securities law follows our securities and exchange act and requires „full disclosure" of the facts surrounding a proposed stock offer.

The association requires salesmen to pass a written examination, has financial requirements for members, and audits their books. The commission also makes surprise audits. The association sets the ceiling profits a broker can make, judging each stock separately and allowing a wider spread on speculative issues than on industrials. It reviews all literature sent out by association members, and does its best, Rogers said, to cut out misleading and flamboyant statements. It often orders a rewrite job. This is probably its most important function as far as an American is concerned, because most of the suckers were caught on that kind of bait. The commission reviews the formal „prospectus" - but many stock buyers do not have sense enough to ask for one, and, anyhow, it takes an expert to understand what they say - like the fine print on an insurance policy.

In general, the association can keep shady characters out of the brokerage business, fine erring members up to $1,000, or kick them out. It can also ask the commission to cancel their license to do business. But there are loopholes. One is the fact that Canadian law does not permit tapping telephones, and while Rogers said that flamboyant telephone conversations have been the grounds for discipline, such cases are hard to get evidence on. That goes right to the heart of the matter because the telephone was the chief „gimmick" in the wholesale frauds. „The vicious thing is the reported telephoning," Lennox admitted. „It's something we don't understand in this country. People here don't buy that way." The stockateers operated mostly on Americans.

Lennox recalled a case of a salesman who sold some stock one day and then called the American customer again the next day to say the mine had „come in" - a manifest impossibility - and sold $10,000 more of the stock. „But we can't prove the calls," he said. Another difficulty is that the commission does not have a staff big enough to make spot checks on properties, some of which may be as far away as the Yukon. Commission approval of a prospectus is not, therefore, a guarantee of its accuracy, as it would be with the SEC. However, if lies were discovered, the guilty would be prosecuted. And in fact, authorities say, most of the prospectuses are accurate because they are gotten up with the aid of reputable engineering firms. And not even the SEC will guarantee the merit of a stock or promise that it will make money.

Another loophole is that there is a whole group beyond the reach of both the commission and the association. They are what is known as „promoters." They buy stock directly from the treasury of a company. Because they are the owners of the stock - just as John Jones could own stock - and not brokers, who act as agents buying and selling for others - they do not have to register or be members of the association. The theory is that a man can do as he likes with his own property. Thus, their literature is not subject to review, nor are their ethics scrutinized. However, if they tie up with a broker, asking him to sell their stock, that broker must be a member. If there is a skulduggery, the „front" man may get caught, but the promoter behind is safe. He has no license to lose.

The prospectus is supposed to list everyone with a 5% or more interest in an offering. But by simply creating a second front company, the identity of the real owner can be concealed. Thus, some of the most notorious characters are still in business. There are at least four or five promoters who have been the subject of a number of exposes in the United States still doing business, often through reputable firms. Bay St. brokers shrug their shoulders, observing that the stockateers' current operations may be on the level. Then add that it is, anyhow, very hard to trace ownership. Unmasking the source of a buck, they say, is hard any place. And they say that the commission, if it can, will force the promoter's names to be made public. One of these is Albert Edward De Palma, who started his career as a St. Louis necktie salesman, a bail jumper on a United States mail fraud indictment and reportedly on the SEC's most wanted list. He is said to be one of the richest men in town. Any broker here can mention others.

Canadian susceptibilities were deeply wounded by „unfavorable" publicity when the swindles were at their height. Observers contend that when the SEC was most critical not a single concrete instance of fraud was called to the attention of the government here. Now, however, Lennox said that the SEC has sent him information on about a dozen complaints in the last year. „We are working in close co-operation with the SEC-hand in glove," he said. „And we are working with the other provinces." This intra-Canadian co-operation may be very important for us, because the word in Bay St. is that some of the „bad boys" are setting up shop in Montreal, the No. 2 financial center.

Some brokers insist that rnany things labeled „fraud" are the result of a misunderstanding on the part of American customers. For example, the profit margin between what a promoter pays and what he sells the stock for may seem too high. But, authorities here argue, speculative oil and mineral stocks can't be marketed on the same basis as industrials. And, in fact, there have been almost no complaints about industrial offerings. Another technical difference that looks bad on paper is that a stock seller does not have to „stabilize the market." That is, he may sell you a stock for 30c a share, and then offer the next block at 40c. In the meantime, he will tell you that he still has some of the 30c stuff left, but that the „price is going up." Here's your chance to get some at the „old price," he says. Now, that is true in a sense - but not in the sense that the market price has gone up, because there is no market. He is not obligated to buy it back from you at his price - that is, to stabilize the market. And you may find that you can't sell it to anybody.

But, brokers here point out, many stocks offered by legitimate firms are like that. They are speculative, and in some cases they grow up to be big strapping $20 shares. „Where oil and minerals are involved, there is speculation,“ Rogers pointed out. „Nobody really knows what's in the ground. I think the public should realize that the odds are against any one property starting from scratch - from the green grass - and becoming a producing mine.... So if you buy a cheap stock and it does come in - you're well rewarded. But the odds are against you.“ But Rogers added he did not think that anybody in his association was „knowingly selling moose pasture.“ So an in all, the securities industry represented by men like Rogers and Lennox feel that there are real opportunities in Canada, and that the American purchaser who uses common sense should be able to buy stocks without tears. But they counsel patience because even projects that appear to have excellent prospects won't pay off overnight. And if a salesman on the telephone tells you otherwise, hang up.

Finally, Canadian securities men and the commissioners in the various provinces are ready to take a step which is unprecedented, according to the SEC. Although Canadians don't like to put it this way, it boils down to an agreement to enforce the laws of the United States in Canada. The SEC plans, after long discussions with Canadian authorities and the Broker-Dealers' association, to permit Canadians to file issues up to an aggregate of $300,000 a year under the so-called „short form,“ which means with a minimum of red tape. In return for this right, the provincial commissions will take action against any Canadian who does not avail himself of the privilege. This amounts to writing that SEC regulation into Canadian law. Issues of more than $300,000 would have to be registered under normal procedures. This goes a long way. A few years ago, all Canadians in the business, good and bad (plus the American fringe group), railed against the SEC for „expecting us to enforce your laws.“

But the problem isn't cleared up, because most states - including Wisconsin - also require registration. And in the past, the complaint has been made here that good stocks were labeled „fraudulent“ simply because they weren't registered with state securities agencies. The point Canadians make is that the use of that nasty word „fraud“ to describe „technical violation“ was too sweeping. In any event, this pending SEC action may prove far more important than the broadening of the extradition treaty, which so far has netted nothing, despite wide claims when it became effective. There is no magic about an extradition treaty. It does not mean that a Milwaukee policeman can fly up here and make a pinch if he thinks he's got the goods on a stockateer.

What actually happens is that our law enforcement officials ask Canada to send a man back. But - and here's the catch - the accused is entitled to a hearing, and the judge has to be satisfied that the alleged crime fits the Canadian interpretation of the fraud provision in the treaty. Nor does he find the man guilty - he only decides where there is a prima facie (at first sight) case. The Milwaukee cops might think it is fraud on Wisconsin Av., but the judge here will ask himself whether it is fraud on Bay St.

SMALL POPULATION

What this country needs is more Canadians. Here is a great continental ex-panse, one-third greater than the United States, with a population of only 14 million persons, less than a tenth of ours. Most of the population today is strung along the 3,000 mile border, roughly within 100 miles of that unfortified line. This is natural, because the north is still largely wilderness and is not an inviting area for settlement. But if Canada is to consolidate her current economic expansion, she must be willing to pioneer into the bleak north where much of her new mineral wealth has been found. As Canada enters her new century, she has more than enough agricultural lands to feed a bigger population and some rich soil still unbroken. Her natural resourees are vital to the United States and the rest of the free world. Her rushing streams promise more and more hydroelectric power, and when the atomic power age dawns she'll be there, too, with the world's biggest supply of uranium.

But she needs people to continue her expansion. Already labor is scarce on her big construction projects, with more - such as the St. Lawrenee seaway - to come. And she must „import" experts, engineers and supervisors from the United States and Britain. And while her boom is real and her economy sound, the country has a very tender Achilles heel: To thrive, Canada needs an expanding market in the United States and the rest of the world. Canada is free - and dependent. So, aside from the brain and muscle new residents would provide, they would also help build up a bigger internal market. This would diversify the economy, provide new opportunities for individuals, and cushion business against the ups and downs of the world market. Even allowing for the difficulties in settling the north, which is akin to our difficulties in „planting" a population in Alaska, the disparity between our internal market and Canada's can be seen in the fact that Canada has hardly four persons a square mile on the average, compared to our 50. And we, too, have some wide open spaces.

Prime Minister Louis St. Laurent said last week that the country needs 40 million persons by the year 2000. Other leaders have spoken of doubling the present population within a generation. Last year 194,000 immigrants arrived, the most since 1914. This year, because of a cutback which has been fiercely criticized in the press, the total will be between 150,000 and 165,000. To reach the 40 million goal, Canada would have to have at least 225,000 immigrants annually for the next 48 years. This takes into account the annual baby crop and is based on the fond hope that only 10,000 Canadians will leave. Actually, some authorities think that at least 240,000 immigrants would be needed each year. Using the larger figure, that would mean something more than 11 million foreigners, which is only three million fewer than the present population. The United States, by comparison, welcomed 39 million immigrants in the 174 years between 1776 and 1950. In 1950, the last year for which figures are available, our intake was 249,000. The biggest immigration year was 1914, when we got 1,218,000.

So Canada faces a tremendous digestive process in the years ahead. It is complicated by the tacit official policy favoring British, Irish and (to a lesser extent) north European peoples, where as Italy, for example, has the biggest and most anxious to move surplus population. The official policy has been to attempt to preserve the "fundamental character" of the country, which means, to some extent, the hope that the bulk of the new citizens will come from the British isles. But often the „citified" British make poor immigrants; sometimes they're too „smart aleek," regarding the proud Canadians as „colonials." Because of the French speaking third of the population, largely concentrated in Quebee, French immigrants also are welcomed, but they are not numerous and are not popular with the French Canadians, whose traditions date back to the 17th century.

Although they have clung to their own culture, they have been out of direct contact with France and, among other things, they dislike the modern French attitude toward the Catholic church, which is the root of life here in Quebec province but is not in France itself. Too, their language is a patois - a corruption of the original tongue. Another factor is that Canadians have only recently „discovered" themselves. Nationalism is growing now, but the country wasn't really unified until 1867, and Newfoundland broke away from England only in 1949, creating for the first time a confederation „from sea to sea." The lack of good roads and thin population tended to make each province, which has far more „state rights" than our states, somewhat „insular." Canadians go south to the United States more often than they go east or west.

All this has added up to a feeling in the past that an individual is „French" or „Scottish" or „English," rather than „Canadian." Such awareness of race, intensified by a lack of intermarriage (partly because of religious differences) between the French and the other groups, has made many Canadians a bit uneasy about foreigners or „new Canadians," as the government propaganda calls them. This is less true in the west, where the population is generally like that of our middle west, with many persons of (for example) German, Polish, Swiss, Lithuanian, Dutch and Croatian descent. There are also many Ukrainians and some Russians whose numbers include the Doukhobors, a few of whom belong to the weird sect which sometimes parades in the nude. But while the French Canadians are making rapid progress, the dominant influence in Canada is still British, and with that there is often a touch of snobbishness.

As a representative citizen of Toronto, which prides itself on being one of the „most British" of Canadian cities, told the writer: „We still raise our eyebrows when we hear a non-Anglo-Saxon name." Canadians lack - even now - the counterpart of what we call „Americanization." While the concept has sometimes been abused in the United States, it has provided a driving force which has speeded up assimilation and made an immigrant want, often desperately, to „become Americanized." As explained to the writer, the Canadian theory is „integration" rather than „melting pot." This is based on the idea that foreign cultures often have value, which, preserved, can enrich the society. But it has tended to segregate some groups. In practice, the mechanics of their immigration policy is much like ours. While there are no set quotas, a „selective screening" process to eliminate paupers, undesirables, and subversives and otherwise to pick and choose has resulted in the same thing. Asiatics, except for a token allowance of 150 from Indian, Pakistan and Ceylon (which are in the British Commonwealth), are excluded.

That our system is similar to Canada's does not tell the whole story. For one thing, there is less than total agreement in the United States as to the desirability of our policy, and second, Canada needs population to keep her date with destiny, while we have met and married that allegorical young lady. The more advanced thinking about „new Canadians" was expressed last week by Rene B. Perrault of Montreal, president of the Canadian Chamber of Commerce. „With a wealth of virtually every vital resource, Canada is short of the most important resource-people," he told the annual chamber convention at Toronto. „The answer is immigration, more immigrants - many more!"

More people, he told the assembled businessmen, are necessary for defense and will raise the standard of living. „We should be aware of the danger of trying to keep so rich a land all to ourselves," he said. „Our moral sense urges us to provide sanctuary and opportunity. The advisability of continued immigration has been challenged in recent months and the government a few months ago tightened up its selective program. But I believe, and the Canadian chamber believes, that the needs outweigh the difficulties foreseen in immigration at the rate of the last year." When Premier St. Laurent suggested the year 2000 goal as 40 million, which was five million more than the previous target, it was assumed that a new policy was being worked out.

The point is that starting last July, the brakes were put on immigration from Italy, Germany, Austria, Greece and Finland. Labor union pressure, caused by the fear of job competition in some areas, was believed to be one of the factors. But in the press, at least, the policy was roundly criticized and the door is expected to open again next year. As part of the policy, set in 1947, of increasing the population „with due regard to the absorbtive capacity and the fundamental character" of the country, most immigrants are either placed in jobs before they leave Europe, or are required to work a year on farms. This is often a waste of skill, but, on the other hand, if an immigrant breaks his agreement, nothing is done to penalize him. Yet this points up another problem. Today's immigrants are usually city people. Everywhere there is a trend away from the land, and if Canada is to open up her north, she needs men and women willing to live close to the land, just as did the Europeans who hacked away our wilderness during the last century.

Even native Canadians are slow to plunge into the north, and Canadians joke that the country needs a modern Horace Greeley, saying, „GO north, young man, go north." Closely related to this is the fact that perhaps the most important long range problem Canada has faced in trying to fill up her vast space is the steady drain of her best brains and most ambitious youth south to the United States. Up to now the country simply hasn't offered the opportunities available in the United States. And even today wages and professional salaries are often as much as 30% below ours. Contrawise, today Canada draws heavily on our industrial and business manpower to help „staff" her boom. „Let's Stop Exporting Canadians," was the heading on a recent editorial in the *Montreal Gazette*.

Since 1945, Canada admitted 582700 immigrants, but in the same period it lost 314,600 persons for a total net gain of only 268,100. The total net loss of immigrants and native Canadians runs about 1,000 a month, according to immigration minister W. E. Harris. Canadians like to reel off the names of America leaders who originated here. Right in Wisconsin, our lieutenant governor, Georgs Smith, is an ex-Canadian. This correspondent met a German youth who arrived recently and after he said that he was glad he had a job in an Ottawa department store stockroom rather than working in the „bush," he asked eagerly, „Don't you think I should go to the States? I hear you can make a lot of money there."

But Canadians hope that the tide is turning. Said Harris: „I do not want to minimize the loss. It is a regrettable one - but far less serious than some would have us believe. And to offset it, over the last seven years, our intake from the United States has been at an average of about 8,500 a year or a total of almost 60,000. Returning Canadians have added another 25,000 to this total so that the traffic north across the border has been at the rate of about 12,000 a year." Canadians hope that this will increase. They are particularly happy to see the prodigal sons return, and they point out that some of the big expansion - particularly in the western oil fields - has been manned by Americans on the top executive level. The welcome mat is out for the Yanks, and Canadians hope they'll stay.«

RESOURCES AND INDUSTRIES
Austin C. Wehrwein, *Milwaukee Journal*

This second part of Wehrwein's Pulitzer Prize-winning articles on Canada contains stories published in the last two months of 1952. By that time, as the publisher of the *Milwaukee Journal* expressed in a statement, „Canadians are much more aware of us than we are of them ... Yet many Americans still think there is nothing in Canada except mountains, ducks and fish. Canadians are not too touchy about our ignorance of their country, but once in a while they get it a bit „cheesed off" - as they say. Millions of Americans cross the border every year on vacations. None, Canadians are convinced, know anything about Canada before they arrive. Canadians often say, rather palintively, that Americans don't know there are big Canadian cities, and think the 'natives' live like Eskimos."

„Now a better understanding between Americans and Canadians is needed," the publisher of the *Milwaukee Journal* added, „for a new economic era is bursting forth in Canada, stirring up new American interest in our northern neighbor and its financial, industrial and business development... To accurately report the story of 'Canada's New Century', the *Milwaukee Journal* sent Austin C. Wehrwein, a member of the *Journal* staff and an experienced business reporter, to Canada for on the ground observation and reports. His travels took his from one end of Canada to the other, and, in a series of more than twenty articles, he made his report to readers of the *Milwaukee Journal*. So much interest has been shown in these articles and so many requests have been received for copies that we decided to reprint this material in book form." Following now are several of Wehrwein's Pulitzer Prize-winning articles, taken from that publication, covering the time of November and December 1952:

ALUMINUM PRODUCTION

»You can't talk about Canada's boom without talking about aluminum. The story starts in this „model" planned community reminiscent of Kohler, Wis. Arvida is about 100 miles west of Maine's northern tip and 250 miles northeast of Montreal. Its sole reason for being is aluminum. Arvida is the aluminum capital of the world. And in Canada, aluminum means Aluminium Limited, the sole Canadian producer of raw aluminum. It is also an international holding company. Its operating subsidiary is the Alurninum Company of Canada - „Alcan" for short. [That extra „i" in Aluminium Limited is correct. That's the British spelling. The „limited" means limited liability, that is, a corporate organization.] In 24 years the holding company has grown 10 times, boasting today of 800 million dollars in gross assets. Its current expansion program,based on the faith that the demand for aluminum will rise like a rocket, is conservatively set at 300 million dollars.

That brings us back to Arvida, with its big smelter, the world's largest. Production here is more than double the biggest single United States plant. To appreciate what's happened, it must be remembered that while Canada produces a fourth of the free world's aluminum, it has not a single ounce of the bauxite ore from which the silvery metal is extracted. The crumbly ore, the color of light chocolate, must be hauled by ship from French West Africa and British Guiana in South America. So why in the world do they bother to make it up here, thousands of miles away? The answer is one word: Power. Alcan likes to say that it really sells „packaged power" - electricity in solid form.

Indeed they do, for the electricity needed to make one ton of aluminum would supply all the electrical needs of the average Milwaukee home for more than 10 years. Cheap power equals cheap aluminum, and Alcan is the largest and lowest cost producer of primary ingots, the chunks of metal fabricated later into pots, pans, airplanes and a host of other products. To get power, and to get it cheaply, Arvida was founded in the mid-1920's here in the valley of the wild Saguenay river. Today the 400 million dollar, privately financed development produces two million horse-power in electrical energy, and the expansion program will add half a million more. By comparison, Hoover dam in Nevada produces 1.4 million horsepower.

The river development project along the Saguenay and its tributaries is the second largest in this hemisphere, ranking next to the Grand Coulee system in the United States Pacific northwest. Center of the Saguenay valley system is the two Shipshaw powerhouses, which are equipped with turbines (water wheels) made by the Allis-Chalmers Manufacturing Co.'s Canadian company. By next year the 120 million dollar growth program is geared to increase ingot capacity in Alcan's various Quebec works (including one at Beauharnois near Montreal) by 44,000 tons to 540,000 tons annually. Now, to complete the „big picture," we must go to British Columbia, the Pacific coast province where Alcan is building, at Kitimat, the biggest hydro project ever paid for by private capital.

Much has already been written about this development, 450 miles northwest of Vancouver. But it can be said again that it is one of the most breathtaking jobs in the history of engineering. River dams will raise the elevation of lakes for 100 miles. One of two water tunnels 10 miles long is already being bored through the coastal range, and an entire power plant will be built inside a mountain. There will be a town, like Arvida, whose population is expected to reach 50,000. At first only 450,000 horsepower will be generated, but eventually two million may be produced. Even in the early stages it will generate more power than Grand Coulee. The latter, however, is primarily a flood control and irrigation project, with power of secondary importance. Eventual output is set at something like 550,000 tons of aluminum, doubling the holding company's present world-wide production. The final cost may be 600 million dollars.

These projects are only part of the expansion job. New storage and dock space will be provided; 40 million dollars is going into the island of Jamaica, where the ore for Kitimat will be mined, and new facilities are going ahead in French West Africa. A long range plan for a hydro development in the Gold Coast, in west Africa, which would be close to bauxite deposits, is in the planning, but hush hush, stage. In addition, the holding company already has small smelters in Norway, Sweden, Italy, Brazil and India; four fabricating plants in Canada, three in Britain and others in 12 countries. Alcan's history goes back to 1902, and that of the holding company to 1928. Briefly, it can be summed up by saying that originally the Canadian operation was a little brother of the Aluminum Company of America, or „Alcoa," in which the Mellon family of Pittsburgh had a substantial interest.

Today, however, Alcan and the holding company are independent, and, company spokesmen say, a strong competitor of its relative south of the border. While it is true that the first 943 shareholders in the holding company were identical with Alcoa's, today there are 11,000 shareholders. And, partly as the result of an antitrust suit in 1950, only 32% of the stock is owned by Alcoa stockholders, with the voting rights held by trustees. Nevertheless, the company has a strong American coloration, although its policy is to become more and more identified with Canada. While 65 % of the shareholders are Canadian, 70% of the stock itself is held by Americans, including that held by the trustees. Of the 12 directors, nine are American, including the president-director, 37 year old Nathanael Davis, who succeeded his father in 1947. President of Alcan and a director of the holding company is Ray E. Powell, who started his business career in Wisconsin. Below the top management level, more and more Canadians are coming up. But financially it is evident that Aluminium Limited will, like other Canadian firms, have to continue to tap American capital for expansion. Canada, with a population of 14 million, compared to our 150 million, does not have the reservoirs of money to feed its growth.

But these financial and management ties aside, what does this mean for the United States? Simply, the significance lies in the fact that our government estimates that within 20 years this country will need three times as much aluminum as we are using now. And the rest of the free world will be using four times the current consumption. To Aluminum Limited these estimates are timid. „In a conservative estimate we calculate world demand in 1960 at 3.3 million tons, of which 1.8 million would be taken by the United States," Edwin J. Mejia, vice-president of the holding ccmpany, said. „To meet this estimated demand of 3.3 million tons, there will be a world production of 2.7 million tons - 600,000 short, even if all announced expansion plans are completed and even if all high cost plants continue to operate What is the demand for Houses, ships, teapots, skyscrapers, stepladders, automobiles, planes, containers, pipe, horne appliances, hardware, and a thousand other useful articles."

Already Canada (the United States' only outside source) supplies 15% of United States consumption, and while bauxite is almost unlimited, the pinch is in cheap power. The United States is running out of sites for low cost hydroelectricity, and many industries compete for those locations which are available. Already our aluminum producers are using natural gas and steam plants. Alcoa has plans for an Alaskan plant, along the lines of Kitimat, but Canada's consent will be needed because some of the water supply is within Canada's territory. There is evidence this may not be easy to get. As matters now stand, Canada still has plenty of unharnessed power sites, away from industries which would want a share.

The manpower needs are small compared with similar industries, because the process is largely automatic. Aluminum experts say it takes seven men to semifabricate the amount of aluminum one man can manufacture. So the Canadians, and Americans on the job here, argue that the sensible thing is for Canada to produce the raw aluminum at a cost below ours, and let our factories work the metal in to its final form. Closer to home is the stake Milwaukee industry has in „big aluminum." A. O. Smith Corp. supplied 1,175 tons of fabricated steel for Kitimat. Nordberg Manufacturing Co. provided screening equipment, and the Le Roi Co. compressor equipment. The Harnischfeger Corp. supplied hoists for the works at Kingston, Ont., and shovels for the project in French West Africa.

Other Milwaukee firms selling large amounts of products to this company were Trico Fuse Manufacturing Co., Allen-Bradley Co., and Chain Belt Co. The Racine Tool & Machine Co. has also sold products here. Canadian Allis-Chalmers is a major supplier, and has also sold tractors made in Milwaukee to the company. Ray E. Powell, the American president of the Aluminum Company of Canada, got his start selling pots and pans in Waukesha, Pewaukee, Oconomowoc, Hartford, West Bend and points in between. A native of Table Grove,

III., Powell, who today is one of the biggest men in the international aluminum business, 45 years ago, was a student at Monmouth college, Monmouth, III., working his way through school. In 1907 he answered an advertisement to help „advertise" a new fangled metal. He soon found that this meant he was to be a house to house salesman working on commission.

Headquarters of his territory was Waukesha, where he and his partner, Frank G. James, now a retired Cleveland (Ohio) advertising man, lived in the Carroll college women's dormitories. „Of course," explained Powell, „the girls were away for the summer." Making his rounds in a horse and buggy, Powell would stop overnight at little German hotels (with restaurant and beer garden attached). Often he'd barter pots and pans for a night's lodging. During the day he'd lug his big suit- case of utensils to farmhouses, demonstrating his wares in the kitchens. „Not one woman in a hundred had heard of the stuff," he recalled. „Some of them thought it would burn up, confusing aluminum with celluloid. So I would go in and make pancakes' to prove it wouldn't." Powell remembers Waukesha as a „quite good summer resort" and while the salesmen partners worked all day, they often danced late into the night. „But life was simple then," he said. „When we had saved up a little money, we'd go to a show in Milwaukee. And that was a big evening. Why, until I embarked on that summer I had never tasted beer."

Powell can still reel off the prices of the items he sold, and he thinks that his first taste of the aluminum business was a „wonderful experience." Door to door selling, he said, forces a young man to „be resourceful and get a thick skin." „In some ways, I think a young man who has to paddle his own canoe is fortunate," he observed. When he was forced to leave college in 1909 for lack of funds, the utensil firm offered Powell a salaried job organizing college student salesmen. He worked out of Dallas, Tex., and later New Orleans, La., where one of his star salesmen was Huey Long, who later sold the voters a different bill of goods. Powell's company was the Pittsburgh Reduction Co., which later grew into the giant Aluminum Company of America (Alcoa) , Alcoa started the Aluminum Company of Canada, and Powell has been in Canada since 1929. A lot has happened during his 42 years in the business, but Powell looks back on those Waukesha days as one of the high spots of his career.

IRON ORE

The snow is two feet thick here. They're digging in for the long, dark winter, watehing the thermometer for the first morning it will sink to 60 below. This cold, cold corner of Canada is a thousand flight miles northeast of Milwaukee, directly north of New England and on the same la titude as the Alaskan panhandle. It is the uppermost outpost of the Iron Ore Co. of Canada. It is the „edge of the spade" which will open up the vast, rich iron ore deposits - small mountains of it - in Labrador and Quebec. The ore is destined for American steel mills, ore we need desperately to feed our steel furnaces as our own reserves dwindle away. Burnt Creek, so called because the forests on the rocky ridges have been burned out, so that only scrub second growth is left, is a huddle of log buildings and steel quonset huts on each side of the stream that gave the place its name.

It is reminiscent of the Wisconsin lumber camps of earlier days, but it is the germ of a community, too. Besides the 130 single men there are 11 families, with nine children among them, who live in small, company built houses at the edge of the camp. The fathers are mostly supervisors, some of whom expect to stay and settle when the mine is open two years hence. By then a new community of some 2,000 will be established on the shores of Knoblake, 10 miles distant. Burnt Creek itself, perched on a ridge of the richest ore in the area, will be but a hole in the ground because the ore is so close to the surface that it will be scooped up as it has been in the Minnesota Mesabi range. But today the area, hundreds of miles from „civilization," is, outside of the camp, no different than it was a few years ago when it was known only to an occasional Montagnais (meaning mountaineer) Indian trapper.

By the end of next year the 360 mile railway being smashed up from the town of Seven Islands on the St. Lawrence gulf will reach here. But until then, the only transportation is that provided by the company air line, an around the clock air lift which is the biggest air cargo haul in Canada, When the planes are earth bound by bad weather, if you're in Burnt Creek, you're nowhere. No better symbol of Canada's new century can be found than this 200 million dollar project. A joint Canadian-American enterprise supported entirely by private capital, it is staffed on the operating and construction and largely by Canadians. It is a product of the air age - virtually all supplies, even heavy equipment, has been flown to the construction camps along the line the railroad will take. And, like other developments in the Canadian boom, it is of tremendous importance to the United States.

Besides the mine, the dock facilities at Seven Islands and the railroad and air line, the project includes two hydroelectric installations, one of which will serve the Burnt Creek-Knob lake area and the other Seven Islands. Over an area half as big as the state of Wisconsin, the company has „proved" close to half a billion tons of high grade ore. Hawever, the American and Canadian companies teamed up in the Iron Ore Co. must reduce their holdings in Labrador and Quebec to a mere 500 square miles in each province by the end of 1953. The railroad, which is now past the 70 mile mark, will be hauling out annually five million tons of ore, 55 to 65% iron, by 1955 and 10 million tons annually by 1956,. more than double Canada's entire 1951 production. Heavy, diesel drawn trains, guided by the most modern of control systems, will rumble day and night to get the ore to the dockside at Seven Islands before winter freeze-up.

Winter, however, will not be idle time. It will be the time for repair, maintenance and stock taking, as it is now up here at Burnt Creek, where the log storehouses are crammed with 10,000 different kinds of supplies, from candy bars to bulldozer spare parts. The whole development will not reach fruition until the St. Lawrence seaway is completed - Canadians hope that will be in five years. The big ore ships which will load up at the extensive dock facilities now building at Seven Islands can't get through the present shallow bottleneck below Montreal. Until the seaway is built - by Canada, it now seems certain - the ore will have to reach our mills by rail from Montreal. When the lake ports are accessible, it is possible that production will be doubled to 20 million tons a year.

What does this new supply of iron ore mean to American industry? To answer that, it must be remembered that this is only one of the new developments coming along in Canada, although Canada's own steel industry, Great Britain and Germany are already nailing down a share of the additional ore. New workings are in process in Newfoundland, Ontario and British Columbia. For example, the Steep Rock project, 150 miles due north of Superior, Wis., is expected to produce four million tons a year by 1956. To get at the ore, a wilderness lake had to be drained - the ore was at the bottom! A second point to be kept in mind is that, in effect, one ton of ore equals one ton of steel. Steel also includes a percentage of junk metal, which covers the shrinkage. But the rule of thumb ratio provides a workable concept in judging the industry's ore needs. Our annual steel production is now at a rate exceeding 100 million tons.

To maintain that production, our mills have had to import more and more ore. In 1949, for example, this country produced 85 million tons of iron ore and imported seven million tons. The Lake Superior area accounted for 68 million tons, compared with 82 the year before. Between 1892, when the Minnesota Mesabi range was opened, and 1937, it produced just over a billion tons, only twice the known reserves up here. Some experts think the recoverable ore in the Mesabi will be gone by 1975. Although progress has been made in the „beneficiating" of low grade iron ores, the cost of processing them to a point where they approach the quality of the higher grade stuff is still high. Mining men here believe that even if the low grade ores do get to market from the Mesabi and the upper Michigan mines - and from some Wisconsin mines, too - there will be no lack of demand for the „juicy" ore from up here and other parts of Canada. And, too, some authorities state that all together, Canada's iron ore potential is the world's greatest.

So we take comfort in reports that the deposits up here in the „Labrador trough" are hardly nicked so far. This is true in other ore bearing areas. Explorations north of Burnt Creek are already being made; United States Steel is mentioned as one of the interested parties. What is the future of this country in human terms? Will these modern pioneers, who go forth in airplanes instead of wagons, establish a new land which will flourish as did our west a century ago? The old-timers up here, who remember when there were more Indians than whites in Seven Islands, shake their heads. These engineers, supply clerks, bulldozer drivers and laborers are not lone pioneers, staking out individual plots. They work for „the company," which provides them with camps now and planned towns tomorrow, with fresh milk at only 30c a quart even after it is flown 400 miles, meat at 85c apound and innerspring mattresses.

„Pioneering" in Canada is big business-private enterprise, it is true, but on a corporate scale, not an individual. The accountants and purchasing agents from the company headquarters in Montreal fly in, put parkas over their business suits, look things over and fly out again in business suits. Too, even though Seven Islands is a boom town, sprawling into the scrub spruce behind the old fishing village while the company town is being built a distance away, everything feeds at the company's breast. There is no farming, no industry except the fringe service industries - hotels, beauty shops, restaurants and stores, all dependent on the „IOC" pay roll. Still, at any time, Seven Islands is as busy as State St. in Madison on homecoming night. The big red and yellow construction trucks roar over the potted sand streets. The narrow sidewalks are thronged with men just arrived - from „up the line" - booted, bearded, often a bit loaded. But for a boom town, it is not unusually wild - there is a dance hall, but several raids have put the brakes on prostitution and there is no wide open gambling.

The local girls often wear nylon stockings, and pick their way over the rutted streets in high heel shoes, while the wives of the company engineers wear slacks. The older French Canadians, whose forebears founded the town more than 300 years ago aren't too happy, but the younger generation is in on a good thing. There are, for example, 70 cabs in the place, and plenty of jobs in the two hotels, the four banks and the stores which are mushrooming all over. On a clear day the sound of hammers building new houses to supplement the old weather stained fishermen's shacks - nobody goes fishing now - sounds like the rattle of gun fire. A rented room costs $100 a month. And just this month they started a Lions club. This, together with the shiny new signs, „Buvez Coca-Cola Glace" (drink ice cold you know what) , are the crowning touches which have made Seven Islands a „modern" up to the minute community. Even the CIO is on hand to organize the construction workers - and later the miners and railroad men into unions.

One hope for a diversified economy is that Seven Islands may become a wheat elevator port, if the ore boats, returning empty from the mills can pick up grain cargoes. The wheat would be unloaded here for shipment to Europe. But that's only a guess right now. Other than that, the old-timers don't see much broad development. But more optimistic observers point out that even though the area will ship its wealth away instead of fabricating it here, the development has already increased Seven Islands' population from 800 to more than 3,000 - in a few years the community grew more than in its previous 300 years of existence. There are people like Walter Balke, a 25 year old electrical engineer here at Burnt Creek, who plan to make this outpost ahorne. They like the freedom, the space and the sense of doing. Balke has his wife here - she teaches the seven children of school age. „I wanted a job just like this," he said. „I like the rough atmosphere. I worked in industry, but I don't think I'd go back. You don't feel as though you're working on piece rates here."

Down in Seven lslands, 36 year old Mrs. Harold Irwin, who is a teletype operator and whose husband works in the railway supply section, said she has not regretted leaving Toronto, where her husband worked for the Massey-Harris Co. In the summer the wind whips the sand - Seven Islands has nothing underfoot except sand - into her two bedroom company house. In the winter the sand mixes with the snow, which often covers the house. But she said, „It's really not a hardship." There is an active, constant, social life. „People are very, very friendly, and only too willing to share," she said. The stores in Seven lslands are stuffed with furniture, refrigerators, electrical appliances and clothing. What they don't have, Mrs. Irwin can order by mail from Montreal. „We felt this would be a great opportunity - something new was starting up. We hated to think that things were being built and we wouldn't be part of it. I've never regretted coming. This will be rny life."

The optimists expect more mines to open up north of Burnt Creek and perhaps minerals other than iron will be found. Obviously, the land won't support a heavy population, but it has been finally won, and people like Balke and Mrs. Irwin will stay as long as there's a living. It has meant a change, too, for the Montagnais tribe. The government has built real homes for them on a nearby reservation, although a few still live in a slumlike patch on the edge of Seven Islands. Their log huts there are worse than a southern Negro shanty town. Some families still live in tents - although they have radios inside! Bob Ross, a veteran fur buyer who can remember when there were 750 Indians to 350 whites (almost all French Canadians) in the town, isn't so sure whether the project has been good for the Indian. It hasn't been good for the fur business, in any event.

„This mine outfit has ruined my business," he said with a laugh. „This year 10 families are trapping. Before the railroad came there were a hundred. Now they're making $10 a day and are as happy as larks." He said that a few of the Indians want to go back to trapping, but he added: „The real Indian would rather go hunting. Then he's free to live." But Ross, who speaks both French and the Indian language, pointed out that the Indians are multiplying under the government's care, especially since steps were taken to stamp out TB - the scourge of Indians everywhere. But „Outi Moss," which means „Young Boss" as the Montagnais still call Bob, shrugged. „There'll be damn few hunters in 10 years."

OIL BOOM

Though the big oil fields are several hundred miles north, Calgary is the financial and bookkeeping center of Canada's petroleum boom. What's happened can be summed up in a joke the oilmen have. They say they have two calendars. One is the Gregorian. On it, this is 1952 A.D. The other is the oil calendar. On this one, this is 5 A.L.-"After Leduc." The new oil empire was born on Feb. 13, 1947, in the Leduc field south of Edmonton. On that day, after 11 years of drilling, 133 dry holes and 23 million dollars down the drain, a crew working for Imperial Oil Co., a Standard Oil of New Jersey subsidiary, brought in Leduc No. 1. That day turned the course of history, both in Canada and the United States. For oil is to national security and industry what water is to the human body. Canada had limited oil production before Leduc No. 1; even a boom or two many years ago. But the 1947 discovery opened a new era in Canada which will shift the whole foundation of the economy. Even with a tremendous expansion already accomplished, oilmen say that future prospects barely have been tasted.

The figures to date are impressive enough: Since Leduc No. 1, known oil reserves have been multiplied about 34 times. Money has poured in like - well, like oil - with 1.2 billion dollars invested, more than half of it from American pockets. And another billion is expected within the next few years.

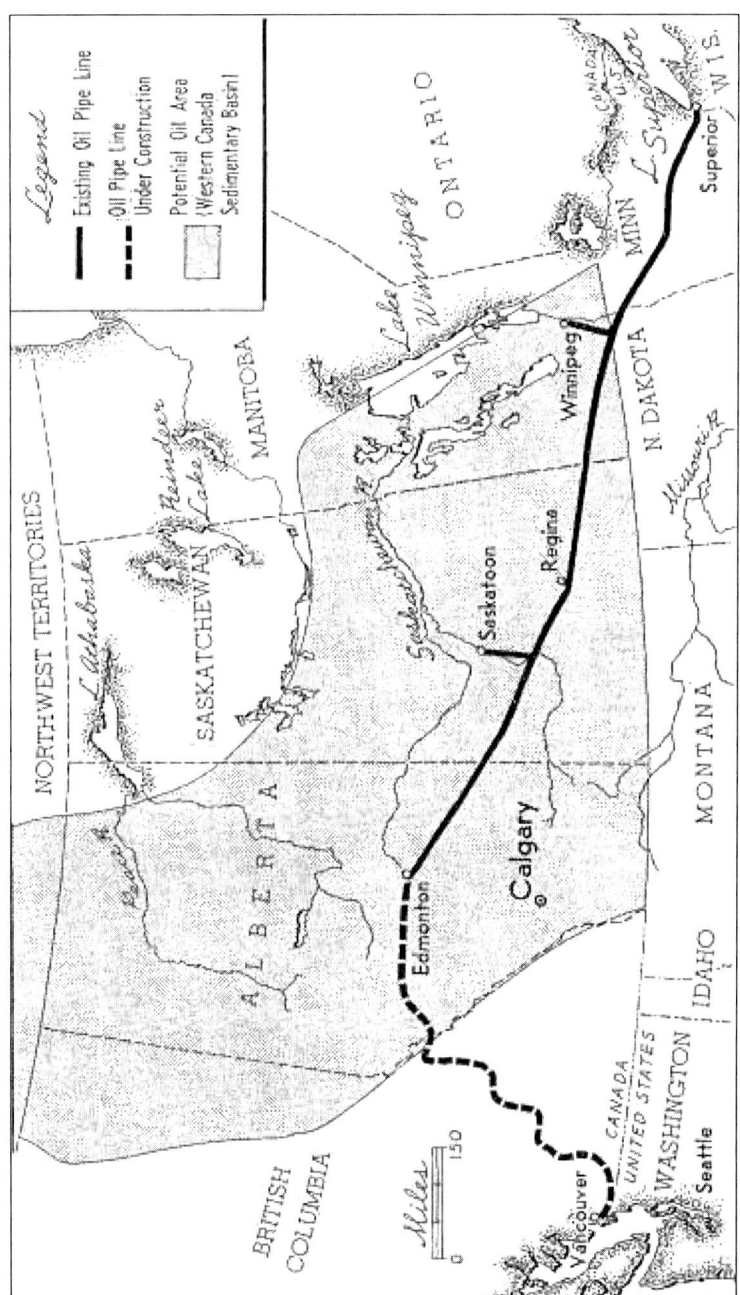

At the end of the long pipe line from the lush Canadian fields is Superior, Wis. From Superior, oil is shipped by water back to Canada for refineries in Ontario. Some Canadian oil, however, is refined at Superior. The westward pipe line to Vancouver, now being built, will carry oil destined chiefly for new refineries in our northwestern states.

Three-quarters of a million dollars is spent every day on exploration for oil and natural gas, and a new well comes in on an average of every two and one-fourth days. On top of that are the millions being spent for pipe lines and the mush-rooming chemical industry at Edmonton. The search area is ever widening, like the ripples moving out from a stone dropped into a pool. There are drilling rigs in the subarctic north-west territories, northeastern British Columbia and in Saskatchewan and Manitoba. In fact, the country's potential oil and natural gas producing area is as big as all of the United States east of the Mississippi river.

Known reserves, most of which are in Alberta now, are 1.7 billion barrels and the figure is rising by about 300 million a year. Of the 27 states of the United States producing oil, only three are lusher than Alberta: California, Louisiana and Texas. But while United States fields are getting weaker, Alberta's are constantly expanding. And although Alberta is slightly smaller than Texas, its underground formations which are possible oil givers are three times larger than the Lone Star State's. There is a difference, of course, between „reserves" and „potential." The former is the bird in the hand, the latter is the two in the bush. Nobody knows exactly what the total Canadian potential is, but estimates range from 5 to 50 billion barrels, and tend to hover at about 20 billion. To the layman those figures are meaningless, so let's make some comparisons.

In 50 years of oil production, Texas has accounted for 14 billion barrels, with 14 or 15 in reserve. California's dwindling reserves are a little more than three billion and Louisiana's just under three billion barrels. These figures do not take into account the Athabasca tar sands in northeastern Alberta. There is so much of it that it hasn't all been seen yet, but it is estimated that there are 30,000 square miles of the black, oily sands. In this mass, as thick as molasses, Canada may have as much known oil as all the rest of the world, perhaps 250 billion barrels of it. But the catch is to divorce the oil from the sand, and while there is hope that the trick will be turned in 10 years, it is still in the laboratory stage today. Meantime, Socony-Vacuum, Sun Oil, five Canadian firms and a Swedish outfit have secured exploration permits.

The provincial government owns most of the oil, leasing the right to search for it and the right to take it out of the ground if it is found. So the oil companies, in most cases, rarely own the land they drill. So far the oil boom has, apart from heavy American financial interest, been largely a Canadian show. Canada has used most of the oil, saving half a billion dollars which would have otherwise been spent to import oil. Six years ago Canada produced only 9% of her needs. Today, even though Canadian use of oil has risen 86 % since 1946, the wells here in the west provide a third of the country's total needs. The wells Canada has right now could supply 70% of the requirements if they were turned on full, but the government of Alberta, by order, holds down production because there isn't adequate transportation to reach markets at either end of the „realm."

In short, it is cheaper to buy American or South American oil in the east coast and Pacific coast areas. Transportation is the crux of the oil business. It is a case of getting farthest with the cheapest as well as getting there firstest with the mostest, and for that reason Superior, Wis., has had a key role in the development of this western Canadian boom. Superior has been like the acrobat at the bottom of a human triangle, the support for the producers of the west and the refineries in the east. Here's why: To haul oil by rail from Alberta to the refineries in Ontario near Detroit would cost $3 a barrel, which would mean that producers would have to sell at below cost to compete. The answer was a pipe line to Lake Superior and then tankers to the Sarnia and Toronto refineries.

After settling on a pipe line terminal on Lake Superior's shore line, the question immediately arose: Where shall the pipe line end, at Fort William, Ont., or at Superior? Fort William is on the northern shore of the lake, and is surrounded by rugged country which would boost construction costs. So despite national pride and some strong political outcry, the line was run to Superior. Called the Interprovincial Pipe Line, it was completed in 1950 at a cost of 90 million dollars, and instead of $3 a barrel, western oil can travel the 1,900 miles to Ontario for 71c a barrel. Imperial Oil built three tankers, the world's largest fresh water oil carriers, to transport oil from Wisconsin. The British American Oil Co. also built a large tanker especially for the run. The Interprovincial line serves Saskatchewan and Manitoba refineries along the way and also provides oil to the Lake Superior Refining Co. at Superior. Thus Wisconsin was one of the first non-Canadian customers for Canadian prairie oil.

This exclusive customer rating will not last long, however. Our Pacific coast states are next on the list. California's needs have become so great that the state must bring oil across the American Rockies for her own use. Yet in the Pacific northwest there is a hunger for oil amounting to a quarter of a million barrels a day, which California is expected to supply. And there is a small Canadian market around Vancouver. Simple logic suggested that Alberta's oil be thrown into the breach, but there were mountains in the way. In spite of construction difficulties, however, the Trans Mountain Oil Pipe Line Co. has completed about half of the 711 mile line, which is scheduled to be in operation by next August. Final cost is estimated at 86 million dollars. All but about 190 miles of the route from Edmonton to Vancouver is in mountainous terrain; the continental divide is crossed at an altitude of 3,729 feet at Yellowhead pass, and the line later reached a 4,000 foot elevation in the Rockies. The men building it call it the „Ripley" line - the „roughest inch pipe line ever yet."

Oil pipe line construction in Canada has given the A. O. Smith Corp. of Milwaukee a substantial volume of pipe business. For the line between Edmonton and Superior, the firm supplied about 800 miles of pipe in diameters of 18 to 22 inches. For the Trans Mountain line from Edmonton to Vancouver, A. O. Smith supplied about 50 miles of 24 inch pipe. The company would not put a dollar value on the two orders. Northwestern Mutual Life Insurance Co. of Milwaukee has participated in financing of both of these pipe lines. It invested two million dollars in 3½ % first mortgage and collateral trust bonds, series E, due Jan. 1, 1970, of Interprovincial. It bought six million dollars worth of 41½ % first mortgage and collateral trust bonds, series A, due Apr. 1, 1972, of Trans Mountain. Northwestern Mutual also has invested two million dollars in Canadian Chemical Co., Ltd., a „petro chemical" plant development near Edmonton. The insurance firm purchased 4¾ % first mortgage bonds, series A, due Sept. 1, 1969, of this company.

Even as the Ripley line is being snaked over the mountains, work will be under way on the Pacific coast's first modern refinery. This is the 35 million dollar facility near Bellingham, Wash., 12 miles south of the Canadian-Washington border. It will be operated by General Petroleum Corp., west coast affiliate of Socony-Vacuum. Standard Oil of California, which has an interest in Trans Mountain, will build another refinery near Seattle. Other companies, on both side of the border, will also use the mountain climbing Alberta crude. Besides this, tankers will carry it to northern California refineries. It may seem like a modern version of carrying coals to Newcastle, but the stark fact is that the United States consumes 60% of the world's petroleum but has only 20% of world petroleum resources. There are as many ideas about how long America's oil reserves will last as there are American oilmen, and many laugh off fears of an oil famine, arguing that new sources are constantly being found. But Gov. Allan Shivers of Texas told an audience at Banff, Alta., not long ago that at the present rate of consumption American proved reserves would be gone in 12½ years, and gas in about 25.

Interior Secretary Oscar L. Chapman has estimated that the defense of the western hemisphere requires a million more barrels per day than we are now getting. It is impossible, therefore, to overstate the importance of Canada's oil both to the industry and to the military security of this continent. Many of our foreign sources belong to somewhat capricious governments - such as those in the middle east - and can reach us only by sea. Canada, however, is a torpedoproof source - and even if her own industrial expansion means that a good share of her oil will be used north of the border, it will be used in a common cause, and will mean that much less drain on our supply. „Until recently the continental oil supply was based on two great internal producing areas, one in the mid-continent, Texas-Gulf of Mexico area and the other in California," R. H. C. Harrison, president of the Western Canadian Petroleum association, said. „Now there is being formed a great triangle with one apex in the Texas-Gulf, one in California and the third in western Canada. In the interests of continental security, it is essential that these areas develop their potential oil production to the maximum so that continental needs can be met as fully as possible from internal sources."

The key word is „continental," because geography and finance have made western Canadian oil part of our system. The pattern of this spectacular new industry is being shaped by these forces. Harrison predicted that, within the next five years, Canada, a Cinderella less than six years old in oil resources, will be able within another five years to get oil equal to her requireinents from these prairies. But that is not to say that all Canadians will be using Canadian oil, because in areas far from the prairies it may still be eheaper to get it from the United States or other non-Canadian sources. Contrariwise, there will be areas like the Pacific northwest and Superior where Canadian oil will be more readily available. Thus, the pattern will be one of give and take, and it will provide a daily object lesson in how close these two countries are bound.

OIL INVADERS

This financial center of the Canadian oil boom, a buzzing but far from bolsterous city, was born 77 years ago. It was then a fort manned by the then new mounted police force - to repel an invasion of Americans from Montana who were making a fast buck selling whisky to the Blackfoot Indians. Today there is another „invasion" of Americans, several thousand of them, mostly from Texas, Oklahoma and California. They are the key men in the skyrocketing oil industry, which is dominated by American firms. Needless to say, they, too, are making a fast Canadian buck. But the Canadians aren't repelling this modern American „invasion" (the term is a sample of Canadian humor), which began in 1947 when the first well „came in." They are, in fact, part of the act. Calgary, now with a population of 140,000, compared to 95,000 before the boom, has more cars per capita than any North American city except Los Angeles.

Close to 3,000 new homes were built last year, but the housing shortage is acute, and the oil companies often build homes and rent them to their American employes who come here. Rents on the kind of places the company exeeutives expect - that is, something like they had at home - are usually at least $200 a month. Many of the numerous new residential areas look like Fox Point. Mayor Donald B. Mackay, who expects his city to grow to 300,000, said that there are 100 millionaires, nearly all of them new oil millionaires, in the community. Conservative bankers agree that he isn't far wrong. One of them, Eric Harvey, an extremely retiring lawyer in his fifties, is supposed to have made 200 million dollars on oil lease deals. If this is true - and he won't say - he may be one of the richest individuals in Canada. True or not, it is the kind of talk heard around town. The Calgary millionaires stay right here, the mayor went on. They don't splurge like the Texas variety. „It's not the Canadian way," the mayor said. Some, he added, do spend their winters in the Caribbean.

Calgary is the headquarters for the oil companies - 95% have their offices here - because it is closer to the United States than is Edmonton, about 190 miles north, around which the big fields are dustered. Calgary always has been the money mart of Alberta, and was the front office town for the relatively small oil industry to the south that existed before the big bonanza. Edmonton, too, has boomed. Perhaps more than Calgary. Its 82% increase in population to 170,000 in the last 10 years was the fastest in North America, and it expects to be a city of half a million. Between the two there is a rivalry as to which is the „oil capital" of Canada. „We like to say that Edmonton has the industry, but we have the brains," the mayor summed up. The new „oil settlers" have not made as much of an impression as one might think. For one thing Calgary has a permanent „American colony," now about 26,000 including the oil „invaders."

Many have been here 20 to 40 years. In the hinterland are a number of American farmers and ranchers, including some bearded, black clad Mennonites. Few of the Americans, reported the American consul, Cyrus B. Follmer, have become Canadian citizens. Too, this is a tourist center. It is the gateway to Banff, Jasper and other national parks in the near-by Rockies. 'Stampede week,' a super-rodeo show recalling Calgary's cowtown days, draws some 40,000 visitors, many of them Americans. So Yanks are no novelty here. „The Americans have fitted themselves remarkably well into the picture," Mayor Mackay said of the new arrivals. Almost all of the „invaders" are on the top shelf executive level here. At Edmonton there are more of the younger engineers, and some skilled rig workers are in the fields. But while the group is sizable, there never was an army of oil field workers - „roughnecks," as they are called in the business.

For one thing it is easier and cheaper (the fields are not unionized) to recruit and train Canadians. For another, the Canadian government put pressure on the American firms to hire Canadians, which is only right. The American companies are actually affiliates or subsidiaries; their public relations people pull pained expressions when asked about American connections. The attempt is to look as Canadian as possible. Neither Calgary or Edmonton are „boom towns" in the Hollywood western movie sense. Like other prairie provinces, Alberta has a strict and staid liquor control law, and enforces the federal Sunday blue laws. There are no cocktail bars; liquor is sold through a government store only (theoretically) for home guzzling, and while it is possible for a man or a woman to get a drink of beer in a „parlor" attached to a hotel, they can't drink together. The parlors in Calgary are segregated for men only and for women only!

You can't even get a beer with a sandwich in a restaurant. „Of course, it has some advantages," a plumber's helper remarked. „If a dame wants to have a drink with you she has to go with you in a car or to a hotel room. You've got an advantage from the start." The sale of spirits by the drink being prohibited, there are no night clubs. Still, the cities do not lack flavor. Cowboys in full rig push in and out of the parlors near the Alberta Canadian Pacific railway station. The white Stetson cowboy hat is worn, too, by many businessmen. Parkas with fur trimmed hoods are a common sight on the streets. Edmonton has a special color, being Canada's most northern city and the gateway to the Alaska highway and the far north. A new chemical industry is mushrooming up there as the result of the oil and natural gas discoveries. It is the jumping-off place not only for the oil seekers but for mineral prospectors and miners - and uranium bearing areas are found north of Edmonton.

But if Calgary and Edmonton have taken the American invasion in stride, what of the Yanks? The reaction is mixed, naturally. There are Americans who are incapable of liking any place but the home town, even among oil families, who are shipped all over the world by their companies. The Texans and the Californians find the winters hard. There are often three or four weeks when the temperature is 20 degrees below zero. There are no Sunday papers. The Texans and Oklahomans often telephone home long distance to get football scores. The women complain that the stores don't come up to American standards, and often send home for things. Then men complain that the Canadian income tax, to which they are liable after living here six months (thereafter being exempt for the United States income tax) is stiffer than ours on salaries over $5,000. And because of taxes and transportation, cars run high. A Buick here can cost what a Cadillac would cost at home.

„It isn't too rough. I suppose what we're most concerned with is the weather," said John Euston, an accountant for the Union Oil Company of California. „And they close everything down pretty tight on Sunday." Euston, who has a girl, 6, and a boy, 5, has been here three years. His home is in Pasadena, Calif. He said there wasn't enough competition in the economic life, and he complained that the publicly owned utilities don't give as good service as do privately owned utilities. Like other Americans here, he said the schools were good, but he was a bit perturbed, although amused, when his little girl came home and reported that every morning at school they said a prayer for Queen Elizabeth. Ben T. Routh, an engineer for the Canadian affiliate of Gulf Oil, found few adjustments to make because he had been in Calgary briefly during the war. He is a native of Oklahoma, and he, his wife and his children, boys, 3 and 5, have been in Calgary just over a year.

He's noticed minor differences in speech, which enable him to spot a Canadian „as fast as they spot us. When you drive home you do notice it is a long way to travel," he said. „And their roads are like those in the States 25 to 30 years ago." The women have a thriving chapter of the American Women's club, a standard fixture in American „colonies" in foreign lands, but it was here before oil was hit in a big way. The Petroleum club is the hub of the male social life. Americans find no lack of welcome in community activities, which seem to be well organized. The community organizations sponsor such things as dances and skating and hockey for children. Children, of course, provide a common ground the world over. „Some of the people with growing girls are getting a bit worried," said a top executive. „They are dating Canadian boys, and their folks fear they may want to get married and stay here." The oil companies have had a big import on the clerical professional labor market. One oil man said that he had to offer a young engineer more than he would in the United States. Secretaries are almost as scarce as palm trees. Of course the demand for housing has hurt the native salaried man. It is not uncommon to see a want ad reading: „House wanted - by American oil executive, price no object." It makes for some bitterness among the natives.

On the other hand, the American companies, along with the purely Canadian concerns, are opening up new opportunities. For example, some companies send trainees, in lots of 50, to their United States parent companies for special training. And the University of Alberta has worked out an arrangement with the University of Oklahoma, whereby students can study two years here and get their degree in oil engineering down there. One place oil has not yet penetrated, however, is the Ranchers' club, a sedate „ancient and honorable" institution resembling a London gentlemen's club. The old wealth here was in ranching, and the ranchers are still the elite. „I have no objection to oil men, mind you," said a Ranch club member over a glass of sherry, drinking being legal in a private club. „But at the Petroleum club they talk nothing but business. You'll see a group around a table with a map on it, their heads together. „We brought in gas in this section,' is the level of the conversation. No, I have no objection to oil people, but I don't want to talk oil all the bloody time."

NATURAL GAS

Oil and natural gas go together like beer and foam, being the product of the same natural causes. But while western Canada's oil bonanza has been roaring along since 1947, serious development of natural gas has lagged. The situation is as tangled as a ball of hair. There are competing private interests on both sides of the border. On top of that the Canadian federal and provincial governments and our own federal power commission all have a say in the debate. Unlike oil, which is free to move wherever it can find a market once it has been produced, the destination of natural gas is subject to close governmental control in both countries. Alberta has legislation on the books aimed at insuring an adequate supply for Canada before the gas is permitted over the border. This adds up to a political tug of war. Natural gas statistics run so long that only an astronomer, familiar with interplanetary distances, can comprehend them. They come in packages of trillions of cubic feet. A trillion is a one followed by 12 zeros: 1,000,000,000,000. A million million.

At present Canada's known natural gas reserves are small compared to ours. We have 194 trillion cubic feet, more than half of which is in Texas. But on the other hand, Canada's known reserves are growing rapidly. Of the 27 gas producing states, only Texas and New Mexico increased their net reserves faster than Canada did last year. The reserves up here are expected to increase by a trillion cubic feet a year for the next eight years. And only eight of the 27 states producing natural gas have more than Canada's present known reserves. The trillion a year increase estimate may be conservative, because the actual increase between 1950 and 1951 was more than double that figure. As against our 194 trillion cubic feet, however, the latest Canadian federal government estimate put the Alberta and British Columbia reserves at nine trillion. Reserves in the other provinces are tiny so far.

E. C. Manning, Alberta's premier, said this week that at the present rate of development, Alberta would have, within 10 years, enough gas to take care of the province's own needs for 60 years. Stepped up oil production will leave more residual gas, he pointed out. But lack of a ready market means that these gases must now be capped - stored in the ground. As it is, every community of more than 2,500 population in Alberta is served with natural gas. Natural gas has also brought in a "petro-chemical" industry. Canadian Chemical Co., a subsidiary of Celanese Corp., a synthetic fiber maker, is putting up a 55 million dollar plant near Edmonton and should be producing by next summer. Sherritt Grodon Mines is constructing a 17.5 million dollar refinery which will use natural gas to make ammonia that will be used in the recovery of nickel from the ore. It will turn out ammonia sulphate, useful for fertilizer, in the process. Shell Oil Co., primarily an oil producer, has plants at Jumping Pond, Alta., to extract sulphur from natural gas. Royalite Oil Co. also has a sulphur extraction plant south of Calgary.

As for the export of natural gas to the United States, the situation at the moment is this: 1. Export from the southern gas field near Pincher Creek, probably the richest single field in Canada, has been banned for the present. Canadian Gulf Oil Co., subsidiary of Gulf Oil Corp., Pittsburgh, controls most of it. 2. But the federal Canadian government has given the green light for export from the Peace River area, which laps over both Alberta and British Columbia. The line would start near the southern end of the Alaska highway close to Dawson Creek, B. C., and run south about 1,000 miles to the Vancouver area. In the United States another line operated by a subsidiary would run south to Portland, Ore. The estimated cost is 111 million dollars. It is called the Westcoast Transmission Co., and Sunray Oil of Tulsa, Okla., has a big interest in it.

But our federal power commission also must approve the project. The commission will resume hearings on the question Feb. 16. The Pacific northwest is the only part of the United States not now served by natural gas, but Henry Gellert, president of the Seattle Gas Co., the largest gas utility in the state of Washington, wants none from Canada. He prefers American gas on the grounds that the Peaco River supply would just not be enough. „We have been denied by the Canadian government entry into their lush fields in central and southern Alberta (Pincher Creek) and have been told that the only place we can get gas is from the sparse fields in distant northern Alberta and British Columbia," Gellert said. So that's one stumbling block. Chief rival of the Peace River to Vancouver line is the Pacific Northwest Pipe Line Co., which will ask the federal power commission for permission to pipe gas to Washington and Oregon from New Mexico, Arizona, Colorado and Utah.

On top of this, California utilities are demanding that gas from New Mexico should serve them, and not the northwest states. What our federal power commission decides will be of great importance to Canada, because the Canadian line will not pay without an American market. The Vancouver area could absorb only 14% of the „through put." On the other hand, American utility men fear that if supplies ran low, Canadians would have first choice, threatening American customers with a cut-off. American interests also argue that gas from the rich Pincher Creek field would be cheaper. At this time, the only Canadian natural gas going across the border is from another southern Alberta field, which is supplying Montana as an emergency defense measure.

As for the east, here's how the situation shapes up: Two pipe lines have been proposed. Western Pipe Lines wants to build an 833 mile connection from Pincher Creek to Winnipeg, Man. This, in turn, would tie up with the Northern Natural Gas Co. of Omaha (Neb.) system and would ultimately serve the Minneapolis-St. Paul market. This could be of benefit to western Wisconsin communities as well. The second proposal is to build an all-Canadian line from southern Alberta, running north of Lake Superior, to Montreal. It would be the longest in the world and would cost upward of a quarter of a billion dollars. This would be the Trans-Canada Pipe Lines Co., a creature of Delhi Oil Corp., Dallas, Tex. It would serve not only Montreal, but Ottawa, Toronto, Fort Williams and Port Arthur. Neither can get to first base until the lid is taken off the southern Alberta fields, of course.

Although it would be source of pride to have eastern Canada served by an all-Canadian route, the natural alternative is for the United States to send gas up there by way of Detroit. The Tennessee Gas Transmission Co. wants to do just that and has asked for federal power commission permission. This would provide a balance, with western Canadian natural gas going south to our coast states and our gas going north to the eastern Canadian markets. Meanwhile the Canadian reserves are building up, and there is no incentive to drill for gas because there is no big market. Gas drilling here has usually been only incidental to oil exploration. Oil and gas authorities here feel that in the end the question is „when." With the American demand rising faster every year, Canadian natural gas will become as big as oil, they are sure.

FARMING AREAS

Canada shares, and has shared, many things with the United States. One of them was the dust bowl - the drought years of the 1930' s when the prairies turned to desert. They still remember here how half a million head of cattle had to be thrown on the market because of badly overgrazed land that swirled dustily upward into the skies. Those cattle were bought for ½c to 1c a pound.

More than half a million tons of feed had to be shipped into the dry lands of Alberta and Saskatchewan and breeding herds were lost. Ghost farms appeared in the wake of the drought, forsaken land reverted back to the provincial governments. Then came the drought of 1949. That year, they say, was just as dry as 1937, but not a steer was put on the market, not a ton of feed was shipped in. In the meantime, Canada had done something about the problem - water was brought to the land.

Since the thirties, Canada has spent nearly 140 million dollars to revive and diversify the agriculture of the prairie provinces and British Columbia. On top of this, millions of dollars have been spent by the farmers themselves. More will be spent. It will take 25 years to complete the work, which, some experts think, will be even more important in terms of people than the oil boom in the long run. It will mean more family sized farms, engaged in diversified agriculture; flood control and cheap hydroelectric power; recreational facilities. The optimists call it the „green acre boom." True, oil is a wealth making natural resource, but it is not an industry that provides jobs in proportion to the wealth generated. But productive medium sized farms mean a direct, individual livelihood for thousands of people. The biggest project is still in the planning stage. It is the 104 million dollar, 10 year south Saskatchewan river development. It would involve a dam which would create a lake 140 miles long and 30 miles wide, doubling the number of farms and increasing production fourfold in a 500,000 acre area.

Already operating are two big projects in southern Alberta. One is the St. Mary river development, which is scheduled for completion in three years. Some 135,000 acres are under irrigation, and when it is finished it will spill water over 519,000 acres. Key to this development is Canada's largest earth dam, west of Lethbridge, the „irrigation capital." Nearly a half a mile long, it is higher than Niagara falls. The dam has created a huge lake. The water is stored in 10 reservoirs, connected by 220 miles of canals, which in turn spill water into 2,700 miles of farm irrigation ditches. The federal government is paying for the primary works, but the provincial government digs the ditches and turns them over to self-governing irrigation districts. A minor land boom has sprung up for this new land, sold at $8 an acre, plus $10 for the irrigation rights so the province can get its investment back.

There are three applicants for every farm available, and veterans get preference as new land is brought „under the ditch." Land is put on the market gradually at the rate of 50,000 acres a year, so that the growth will be even and steady. The other project in the early ditching stage is the Bow river development. Its immediate importance is that it offers new hope to thousands of farmers across the line in Saskatchewan's dust bowl area - an area where the soil is so sterile that more than 1,000 of its 8,000 families have left. The Bow river project has put 60,000 acres under the ditch, and in two years will water 250,000 acres of one of the driest parts of Canada. The first families settled last year. Average rainfall in the Bow and St. Mary areas is 10 to 12 inches, whereas it is 15 to 20 inches in Alberta as a whole. (Milwaukee's average annual rainfall is 30.8 inches.)

High winds and a scarcity of trees cause rapid evaporation, which makes the area even worse. Now, however, irrigation water is providing trees as well as prosperity. The green acres boom has set in motion a minor revolution in Canadian agriculture. Here has grown up the country's largest sugar beet industry, triple the prewar size. A vegetable canning industry has come in the wake of the new agriculture, supplying 60% of the country's frozen foods. The natives claim their summer sunshine is as good as California's. A new trend has started in cattle, too. Instead of shipping cattle to eastern Canada and the United States for fattening, cattlemen can now fatten them out here on waste sugar beet mash. And where it took 40 acres to pasture a cow under the preirrigation conditions, today two can thrive on that space. Dry land, formerly used only for grazing, is now raising grain. Corn and fruit are also coming along.

As the country grows, so do the towns - places with names like Medicine Hat, Brooks, Magrath and Lethbridge. A place called Tabed tripled in population - to 3,000 - in the last 10 years, for example. Lethbridge nearly doubled in size - to 25,000-in the last 10 years. They are becoming a market basket for oil booming Alberta, providing food that used to come long distances at high freight costs. These big projects are only part of the story. Well over a million acres of abandoned land - similar in status to northern Wisconsin's tax delinquent land - has been put back to work in a joint federal-provincial community pasture program.

The federal government fences the land, coaxes grass back, provides stock watering facilities. The federal government asks the provinces to clear up the titles. Saskatchewan turns such lands over to the federal government - to „Ottawa" as they say, as we say „Washington." Manitoba gives Ottawa the right to control the land, and Alberta has set up its own program. The federal government, or the province, in the case of Alberta, then administers the community tracts, charging the ranchers a grazing fee. There are 1.5 million acres of community pasture in Saskatchewan and 160,000 acres in Manitoba. In addition, with federal government assistance, prairie farmers have built themselves 40,000 water dug- outs, 6,000 stock watering dams and 2,500 small irrigation projects. The federal government, which runs this program through the prairie farm rehabilitation branch of the department of agriculture, is also interested in flood control, and has spent some $400,000 to tame the western rivers, a sum matched by the provinces.

The federal agency has also aided British Columbia, irrigating about 53,000 acres in that westernmost province. The long range south Saskatchewan project would give a shot in the arm to the poor sister province of the plains. It is the only province which lost population in the 1941-'51 period, dropping 7.2% to 831,228 persons in an area almost as big as Texas. Part of this is due, of course, to greater farm mechanization, but Saskatchewan has not boomed as have other parts of the country. The development, which will be in the vicinity of Saskatoon, will provide power worth several million dollars, in addition to flood control. „It is one of the few remaining areas for agricultural development in Canada," the Saskatchewan government said in a recent report. „If a growing urban industrial population is to be fed, more intensive use must be made of the land."

The province foresees 160 acre farms being staked out in an area which is now chiefly big wheat ranch country. Specialty crops would eventually replace wheat, and the basic agriculture in the area would be forage crops and live stock, the report added. This „on the drawing board" project and the other irrigation works under way recall the recommendation made in 1863 by Capt. John Palliser, commander of a British expedition which explored the southern prairie from the Red river to the Rockies. His report to the British government, which then ruled Canada as a colony, was that the country should never be settled. Ignoring his advice, early pioneers broke the land and set up their own crude irrigation systems, but it wasn't until the provincial and later the federal governments stepped in to give the farmers a helping hand that the land really bloomed. It is in what became known as the „Palliser triangle" - the area that the pessimistic captain described as worthless - that much of the transformation is taking place.«

Cuba

BATISTA'S BRUTAL GOVERNMENT

Joseph G. Martin/Philip J. Santora, *New York Daily News*

When the International Reporting jurors in their report of March 12, 1959, placed an exhibit by the *New York Daily News* on second rank, they did not say a word about the contents of the newspaper's articles submitted for the Pulitzer competition. The Board declared the entry as the winner and gave the award to two journalists of the newspaper, Joseph G. Martin and Philip J. Santora, „for their exclusive series of articles disclosing the brutality of the Batista government in Cuba". The newspaper's entry consisted exclusively of their collective articles.

The two reporters began their search for the truth behind the Batista regime early in March 1958. They sought out underground contacts in Washington, Miami and New York. They spent weeks sifting fact from propaganda in Havana, Guanavo Beach and elsewhere in Cuba. During their stay in Havana they were followed by Security Intelligence Police, their rooms were searched, their telephones tapped. Atrocity pictures, more than 200 of them, were obtained from secret sources and these had to be smuggled out. Martin and Santora were forced to memorize names, addresses and telephone numbers so if they were stopped and searched, the lives of these contacts would not be forfeited. The articles evoked wide-spread interest at the time they were published although in some quarters they were believed too incredible to be true. It was the first time that the real story behind the Batista dictatorship was made known to the American people.

Joseph George Martin was born on May 9, 1915, in New York City. In the depths of the depression, he quit high school in Queens and roamed the town looking for jobs in warehouses, factories and on the docks. He never got a job as a laborer, but somebody was able to place him on the *New York Daily News* as a copyboy in 1933. Within a year he was advanced to reporter, working out of Brooklyn police headquarters and on general assignment until he entered the Army Air Force in 1943; he was discharged early in 1946. Back to work at the *News*, Martin shortly uncovered a large scalebuilding racket on Long Island which defrauded hundreds of ex-GIs and developed other stories that won him awards from veterans' groups. - Philip Joseph Santora, born on July 29, 1911, in New York City, was educated at Syracuse University (1929) and received a B.A. degree from New York University in 1933; then he was a graduate student at the Sorbonne, Paris. During World War II, Santora was assigned to Military Intelligence with Patton's Third Army. Before he took up newspaper work on the *New York Daily Mirror* (1936-1943, 1946-1954),

Santora had a varied career: boxing instructor, clerk at Bellevue Hospital, etc. In 1954 he came to the *New York Daily News* as a special feature writer. Following now are several of their award-winning articles, published between April 7 and 17, 1958:

REIGN OF TERROR

»Tortured, enslaved Cuba is teetering on the brink of the bloodiest revolution in its strife-ripped history, with most of the crocodile-shaped island's population awaiting the call to death or liberation with almost cheerful fatalism. The Cubans hope the outside world will understand. They want others to understand, for instance, that when a young girl is raped by a police chief while his grinning cops hold back the heartbroken father, the day of reckoning can include no mercy. That the police official who produced a bullet-riddled body and sneered, There's the answer to your habeas corpus cannot be dealt with in the ordinary legal way. These are merely random samples of atrocities committed in the name of president Fulgencio Batista. Murder, rape, corruption in low and high places, the torture methods employed by police, the systematic plundering of a rich country, the reduction to enslavement of what was once a gay, happy people - these are merely a few of the scores Cubans must settle. Is this a one-sided picture? It might seem so. But it's the picture we-found - and we went to Cuba to get both sides of the story.

During the past six years, over 4,000 anti-Batista Cubans have met death by violence - victims of a reign of terror that ranks with Heinrich Himmler's Gestapo in Nazi Germany, the OGPU in Soviet Russia and even the Spanish Inquisition. Friends and relatives of the victims have not forgotten. They want the slate wiped clean, and if it can be wiped clean only with blood - well, that's the way they want it. „We won't even try to hold them back for the first three days," said a responsible member of the underground. It would be like trying to hold back the ocean. They have waited a long time - and a blood bath is the only way to make a fresh start." The present reign of terror is taking place less than 100 miles from the mainland of the greatest democracy in the world. It is being conducted with ruthless efficiency and the people of Havana - no matter what their sympathies - don't go out at night unless it's absolutely necessary. The dreaded SIM, the Security Police, patrol the streets in their olive-colored cars and uniforms and shove machine guns under the chins of citizens. They're merely asking for identity cards, but the machine guns are always present. More than any other weapon, the machine gun is the symbol of Cuban rule. There are two types of censorship in Cuba. There is the ridiculous, arbitrary type imposed by the government. And there is the self-censorship imposed by the newsmen, both domestic and foreign, who have sold out to the Batista govemment. Except in rare cases, the things that filter through this palmetto curtain are thoroughly distorted. „Please tell the rest of the world what's going on here," begged a Cuban lawyer.

Our trail began with the underground in New York and led to Miami, where more than 2,000 exiles are fighting to extricate their beloved Cuba from the grasp of its oppressors. It led to Havana, where foreigners who carry typewriters and cameras are viewed with suspicion and kept under constant police surveillance. What really goes on in Havana? At night, for one thing, strange things happen in cemeteries. A woman who went out one morning to pray at the tomb of her husband, thought the slab on the above-ground mausoleum seemed off-center. Her son investigated and found three bodies had been dropped in during the past two nights. The wife of an important banker was sent out of the country by her husband because a police official became smitten with her - and what the police want in Cuba, they take. Rumors have spread that the Communists have been supporting Fidel Castro, military leader of the revolutionaries in Oriente Province. One report states that Russian submarines have been landing arms in the Santiago sector. The insurgents deny these reports. Even though the Communist Party last week announced its support, they say, it is neither needed nor wanted. They add that the Reds are a weak party in Cuba, without resources to buy munitions. They further point out that Batista was on the Red ballot and legalized the party out of gratitude. Since then, however, Batista has outlawed the Reds.

These is a great deal to be said for the rebel argument. The great middle class of Cuba is anti-Red and extremely powerful and respected. There is a saying that when Cuba's middle class takes a hand in politics something happens. More than that - they are completely selfless. Many of these doctors, lawyers, teachers and accountants could find employment in the U.S. if they chose to emigrate. They could bow to Batista and their fortunes would be intact and their families safe from the SIM. But to them this is unthinkable. They are Cubans and they would rather stay and fight - even at the risk of having their families annihilated. Chivatos - spies - are everywhere. The bootblack may be selling information. Taxi drivers keep their ears open. The room boys at the hotel. Waiters. For a few pesos the spies sell their neighbors to the secret police. Phones are not to be trusted even when used by non-political U.S. tourists and businessmen. Cables and mail are subject to censorship. There are 6,000,000 people in Cuba. They are a proud race and they are being held captive by a brutal minority that rules by atrocities, murders, and plunder. Batista is reputed by the revolutionaries to have $300 million in

Swiss banks. Gen. Francisco Tabemilla, head of the Cuban army, is the man behind a chain of discount houses. His son, Gen. Francisco Tabemilla Jr., by sheerest coincidence head of the Air Force, flies in electric appliances and household goods in military planes, avoids the customs inspectors and thus undersells legitimate dealers. Eusebio Mujal rules Cuba's workers with an iron hand and an elastic conscience. He's one of Cuba's most feared and hated men. He even outranks Batista as a man to be eliminated. He is slated for execution at the first opportunity.

The last six years have been a nightmare for those Cubans who do not belong to the Batista group. „The island smells of death," said a Cuban doctor, „the earth is soaked with the blood of Cuban martyrs. We cannot leave it. We must win - whether it is tomorrow or next week or next year. With Castro or with someone else." Batista would like to impose martial law, he said, but this would wreck the already badly-hit tourist trade and ruin the business at the gangster-operated casinos. Schools are closed. Children are kept off the streets. Sugar cane workers are taking lessons in sabotaging the crops - they would rather go hungry than have the profits filter into the pockets of Batista and his insatiable followers. Batista's informers operate widely in Miami and Mexico. They spy for pay, giving the time and place of arms shipments destined for Castro's forces in the Sierra Maestra mounor for Faure Chomon's insurgents in the Sierra Escambray or for the Directorio Revolucionario. Or for other, smaller groups. „If all of these groups could be placed under one command," said a rebel wistfully, „we could take over the government within a matter of days. Much of the army would come over to us." But there is no unified command. Nevertheless, there is help for Castro's forces. Arms are hidden everywhere in Havana. Occasionally, through torture, a captive rebel discloses the hiding place of a cache of grenades or machine guns or carbines, rifles and dynamite. But there is more where those came from. Rich men are behind the movement. Even middle-class Cubans give until it hurts.

And there is sabotage. Cuba's rich sugar cane fields, the backbone of her economy, are particularly vulnerable. The rebels distribute pamphlets showing workers how to tie phosphorous to the rats which infest the fields and thus start fires. There are the bombs that set oil storage tanks afire. Rails are ripped from the railroads that penetrate the interior of the island. Could bloodshed be avoided if Batista consented to free elections? Batista, say the rebels, would merely put up his usual straw men and knock them over and retain power.There can be no solution, they insist, while Batista is in power. Cubans who had been hurt and puzzled by the U.S. policy of sending arms to Batista, are a bit mollified by the recent embargo on munitions shipments to the Cuban dictator.

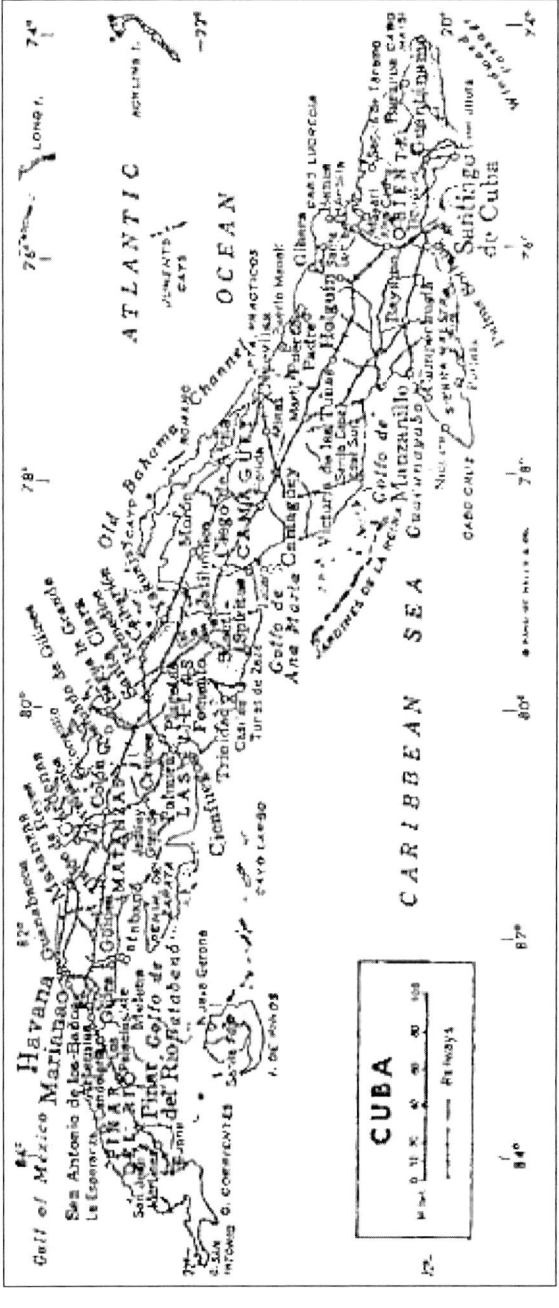

The embargo became known only when the U.S. suspended shipment two weeks ago of 1,950 Garand riffles ordered by the Cuban government in 1956. „We hope that this action will continue," said an insurgent, „and that your country will not give Batista more arms with which to fight us. We cannot fight your country and our oppressor. Give us only the chance to resolve our differences by ourselves. We Cubans emulate you Americans in every way. We try to imitate your dress, your manners. We go to watch your movies. We try to learn your language. Our homes and our lives and even our schools are patterned after yours. Don't force us to cast aside our respect and admiration for you."

Havana has a population of 1,200,000. But only in the dirty side-streets and alleys do the people venture out in numbers after dark. Because these are the people who have nothing more to lose - except their lives. And lives aren't held too dearly by those who have to beg for a living, by those who have to walk the streets selling themselves into prostitution or by the wispy women who hold infants in their arms and beg coins from the dwindling tourist population. The one thing all seem to have is boundless courage. It takes courage for an underground contact to walk through a crowded hotel lobby and telephone the room of visiting newspapermen. For he doesn't know if the elevator man has decided to sell out. Or if the telephone operator is a chivato working for the SIM. A few weeks back, a spy in Miami sold the sons of a Cuban patriot to the secret police. The Cuban had asked the secret Batista agent for the best way of sending his sons to Cuba to take part in the fight for freedom. He was told that the boys could go by plane directly to Havana and that they would be well taken care of there. The father said he didn't want the boys to go, but that they were insisting and he could not forbid them. He wanted them safe. Was the agent sure this was the best way? The agent assured him that was the ticket. The contact would be made in a Havana restaurant, he said. The boys were greeted by the SIM when they landed. They were missing for several days. Then their bullet-riddled bodies were found in a Havana suburb. Back in Miami, the informer was badly beaten. He wasn't killed. „We didn't want a major crime on our hands," said a rebel. „No international incident to undo the work we're doing. But some day the deaths of those boys will be avenged." One more score to be wiped off that slate.

A general strike is the greatest weapon of the men who follow Castro and his insurgents. In every revolution in Cuba's history, the organized force of workers has been a decisive factor in the fall of the regime. The second weapon is the power held by the great middle class - the lawyers, doctors, small bankers and students. The students of Havana University - 18,000 strong - have a history of fighting tyranny that goes back over 80 years. Hundreds of these have been arrested recently. Hundreds of others have disappeared. American gamblers and hoods who took over the casinos at the Riviera, Hilton and Capri are trying to laugh off a revolution. They insist that „Castro is a nut" and that Batista is too strong to be overthrown. They are whistling past the graveyard. It is well known that Castro and other insurgent leaders are against gambling, particularly gambling controlled by shady characters from the U.S. Castro is quoted as saying: „Gambling is the cancer that has been eating at my country; it must be cut out." „But that's a secondary item," said one of our contacts. „The regime must go. We must have free elections. We must have our real plight described to the world by journalists who can't be subsidized or bought. Just tell the true story, that's all we ask."

OFFICIAL SADISM

This is a grim rollcall of Fulgencio Batista's chief terrorists - killers so brutal and ruthless that even the man who helped create the monsters seems afraid of trying to control them. These are the men whose names are whispered with fear and hate, whose incredibly sadistic deeds read like pages torn from the records at Dachau. Maj. Estaban Ventura Nobo dislikes dull evenings. When one comes along, he sends his police out to pick up unfortunates who stray into one of the three police districts technically under his control - actually, he operates throughout Havana. Then he beats a selected victim into insensibility just for the kicks. Ventura's name has become a lewd epithet throughout Cuba. He is an avid student of torture, having been tutored in the fine points by Angel Borlenghi, who was minister of the interior in Argentina under ex-dictator Juan Perón. Recently, Ventura used a Borlenghi invention - putting two electrodes on the genitals of a 16-year-old boy and shocking him into what he hoped would be a confession of „his crimes against the state." The electrodes touched and the boy was electrocuted, cutting short Ventura's fun for the day. Another Ventura gimmick is a basket made of piano wire which is fastend about the genitals. Two wires draw the basket shut, causing indescribable pain. He has been known to rip the ear off a subject when a beating with fists failed to get results.

Ventura goes under psychiatric care at intervals. But in between treatments he roams the streets of Havana with up to a dozen heavily armed bodyguards, looking for victims to assuage his thirst for torture. He loves expensive white suits and keeps one or two in each of the precincts under his command. He's also nuts about publicity and when the photographers show up, Ventura dons a fresh white suit, sprinkles a bit of cologne on his hair and pencil-thin moustache and holds a press conference. Lean, about 160 pounds, 40 years old, married and the father of two young daughters he was born in Pinar del Rio Province in the western part of Cuba. Those are the so-called vital statistics. Ventura has mistresses throughout the area of his command. He can well afford them with the money he gets from business men who either get up the monthly assessment or find themselves answering questions in the cellar of a station-house. Batista turns a deaf ear to pleas - and some of these come from his top aids - to remove Ventura from his post. Even the Gerardo Abreu incident failed to away him from loyalty to the terrorist who swaggers through Havana instilling fear in the most innocent of Cubans. Gerardo Abreu's death resulted in the only indictment ever handed up against Ventura. Abreu was a 20-year-old pianist-student who was socially popular among young people in Havana. Ventura ordered him arrested on charges of terrorism - an ironie touch - and sentenced him to jail. He was released on a writ of habeas corpus. Less than a week after his release, he was again arrested by Ventura.

Immediately, there were cries for „justice" from social and student groups. A witness gives the conclusion of the grim story: „I heard noises on the street in front of the Palace of Justice. Guards from the palace were there and they were discussing something in loud tones with other men. It was about 11 P. M. A few minutes later, I heard the chatter of a machine gun. I saw three men get into a car and drive off." Abreu's body was found there the next morning. No one dared approach the spot during the night. Ventura was quoted later as saying: „They wanted justice - and I gave them justice, with interest." The dreaded, dapper killer is also the author of the phrase, „Here's your habeas corpus." It was uttered when the lifeless body of a suspected terrorist was dumped at the feet of the lawyer who had obtained the writ. Ventura was an obscure lieutenant in charge of the 5th Precinct five years ago, before he distinguished himself by working over a priest, the Rev. Ramon O'Farril, who had plotted to have President Batista ambushed on one of his infrequent visits to church. Father O'Farril was so badly beaten that he suffered fractures of two ribs, internal injuries and is permanently deaf in one ear. In Miami, the exiled priest admitted his part in the plot to have Batista assassinated. „It is high time," he said, „that the UN stepped into the Cuban case. They should step in if for no other reasons than the reasons of humanity. The bloodiest drama in the gory history of Latin America is now taking place in Cuba. There have been thousands of deaths - murders by the Batista regime. There are the countless tortures and humiliations. These and the exiles who have been ousted from their homeland are more than sufficient reason for international intervention in the Cuban problem. Not even the highest prelates of the Roman Catholic Church have escaped terrorist action under the Batista regime. The Cuban people are in immediate need of the help of all the Catholics of the world and also of the moral and physical support of all the upright and wholesome people of the free world."

Ventura's closes rival in the brutality sweepstakes is Capt. Julio Laurent, in charge of naval intelligence. Laurent was an unknown bush-leaguer before he murdered his first Cuban. The victim was a supporter of ex-President Carlos Prio Socarras. He was arrested in a house in the swank Vedado section, dragged out into the street where Laurent, then a lieutenant, was waiting with a submachine gun in hand. While two men held the suspected terrorist, Laurent pressed the tommygun against his body and cut him almost in half with three long bursts. Then he turned to the crowd of horrified spectators and shouted: „And anyone who accuses me will die a similar death." He was charged with murder, but no witnesses would appear against him. Along with Ventura, he was accused of the murder of a captain involved in the Cienfuegos uprising last Sept. 5. The captain, Alfredo Gonzales Brito, was brought to Havana after his arrest in Cienfuegos. In the home of the second ranking commander of the Cuban navy, he was beaten and kicked into unconsciousness. Revived, he was tortured with cigars and cigarets that burned hole over more than half of his body. The finale came when Laurent and Ventura ordered the captain and a close friend taken to a castle tower overlooking the sea. There, the two were gagged, trussed and thrown into the sea.

An incident that has caused the greatest indignation concerns a 50-year-old schoolteacher, Mrs. Esther Milanes. Mrs. Milanes was a teacher in a Catholic school and had a minor part in the underground movement. She was picked up, along with a student from Colombia, South America, by men under the command of Capt. Jose Sosa, another of the sadists who pretend to administer justice in Havana. The woman was beaten with fists and the flat feet of Sosa and his henchmen in an attempt to make her talk. They threatened to have her raped by a particularly repulsive-looking member of the precinct force. When threats and heatings failed, they took an iron bar and inserted it forcibly into her body. Mrs. Milanes' might never have been released alive had it not been for the Colombian ambassador, who went looking for the student. She and the boy were released in his custody and she was rushed to the hospital. She revealed that they tortured the boy in front of her in an attempt to break her down. Then there is Col. Manuel Uglade Carrillo, who likes to sit in the third degree room and watch prisoners being given a working over. Uglade, who was the first chief of the SIM (secret police) when Batista came into power, laughs heartily while the girsly torture goes on. The new chief of police in Havana is Pilar Garcia, who got his reputation by quelling a riot at Matanzas two years ago this month. After the uprising had been put down Garcia made „examples" of 11 rioters. He had them shot. There is, in Santiago de Cuba, a lieutenant colonel named Jose Maria Salas Canizares who, along with his brother; gained notoriety throughout the island for violence. Canizares, 6-foot, 200-pound thug, likes to lead his men into battle with the visor of his legion-style cap tumed up. Sort of a trade mark. He carries an ox goad with which he strikes people during demonstrations. When he was assigned to Santiago, he promptly ordered a blackout and then riddled a few houses with machine gun bullets so that the „people in this city will know who's boss." Then he went out to pick up the local leader of Castro's July 26 movement. He picked up two young men. He had an idea that one of them was the real thing but didri't know which one. So he killed them both to make sure. When the weeping widow of one remonstrated, Canizares laughed and volunteered that he and his men could take care of her sexual wants.

These are the chiefs. But the men under them can be equally brutal. In some instances, they surpass their leaders because they feel that is the way to success and recognition under Batista. Another killer was Col. Fennin Cowley, who won his spurs in Holguin, in the northern port of Oriente Province on Christmas Day, 1956. On that day, Cowley hanged 14 students, supporters of the Castro movement. One of the victims was the brother of Rep. Eugenio Cusido, who is still in office. On the day the victims were being buried, Cowley showed up and said he didn't like the way the ceremonies were being conducted. He ordered the funerals suspended. Early last year, rebels stopped a bus on the main road into Oriente. They ordered the passengers out - with their luggage - and then set fire to the bus. Cowley demanded that the passengers and driver identify the rebels. They said they couldn't. When four suspects were brought in, Cowley asked the driver to identify them. He said he couldn't because he hadn't seen their faces. Cowley hanged all four, „just in case they were all guilty."

A year ago this month, a World War II paratrooper went to Oriente Province with 27 men. The veteran, Calixto Sanchez, was one of those suspected of having taken part in the March 1957 attack on the presidential palace in Havana. In mid-April, he was surrounded by government forces and surrendered to a lieutenant who offered him the guarantee of a formal trial. When Cowley leamed of the surrender he personally machine-gunned all 28 to death. The „mad colonel" was married seven times. He had no children, but he collected German-rnade toys with a sort of psychopathic intensity. His career came to an abrupt halt several weeks later when Fidel Castro sent two men out of the Sierra Maestra with orders to liquidate the colonel. Cowley - traveling con-fidently with a small bodyguard - showed up at a store one day to buy light bulbs. The clerk said he didn't have the type on hand and suggested Cowley return the next day. Cowley came back the following day and was shot to death by the Castro executioners waiting in ambush. On March 24 - two weeks ago - a woman was arrested in a Havana hospital only two days after bearing a child. The charge was not made clear and she hasn't been seen since. The baby is still in the hospital. In the little town of San Juan Martinez, a local magistrate sent his sons off to the movies. The boys, Luis Saiz, 16, and Sergio Saiz, 14, got into an argument with a soldier. He shot them to death. When the funeral was held the next day, the angry towns-people had words with soldiers and police. The police opened fire and killed eight with machine-gun fire. These are but a few of the incidents sworn to by Cubans of highest integrity but smothered by the Cuban press, which is firmly under Batista's thumb. And with such things taking place less than an hour's plane ride from Miami - less than 100 miles from United States soil - these Cubans want their democratic neighbors to know.

FRUITS OF TEMPTATION

Swarthy, solidly-built Gen. Jorge Garcia Tunon is a man who - through an error in judgment - helped write one of the bloodiest chapters in Cuban history. Today, in Miami, he's a bitter, disillusioned man, reluctant to talk about it. For Gen. Tunon is the man who engineered the coup d' etat that put President Fulgencio Batista into power six bloody years ago. It is something that the general, a completely honest man living in poverty, will always have on his conscience. „You must understand the reasoning behind the coup," he said. „Batista just 80 days before the June 1 elections of 1952, was a beaten man. He was being backed by the Partido Accion Unitaria, the PAU, or United Action Party. Less than 10% of the votes were his." Dr. Roberto Agramonte was the candidate of the Orthodox Party, or Partido del Pueblo Cubano. He had about 60% of the votes, according to a straw poll. Carlos Hevia was the choice of the Authentie Party, Partido Revolucionario Cubano. Carlos Prio Socorras was president and high-ranking army officers were unhappy with his corrupt regime.

„The army has always been strong in politics," said Gen. Tunon, „and we were concerned with the fact that those around Prio were weak, that our country needed a group of honest men in office. We had no ambitions for ourselves -

or at least at that time, I believed this was so. We felt that Batista was the best man of the three. We wanted a strong man who would clean up the situation and begin a new, better period of history with liberty and order. I was a captain at the time, in charge of a company in Columbia barracks at Military City. We remembered that when Batista had been president eight years earlier, he had wielded real authority. We talked to him and he told us in many beautiful phrases of his love for Cuba, that he could do many things now that he could not do in the past when so much confusion had been present in his regime. He told me that he was penitent about the reforms he could not carry out in his previous term. The talk took place in the house of his mother-in-law. He told me that he had some young officers already on his side. You must understand that when people spoke of him in those days, they did so with respect. People said that the killings in the streets would be eliminated if Batista were in power - that he would bring peace to our Cuba. What an irony! Originally, the plan was to make Batista prime minister. The president, at that time, was scheduled to be Alonso Pujol. He headed a military junta. But Pujol was too intelligent to be under the thumb of Batista. Pujol backed out. He not only refused to be part of the scheme but he denied he had been in on early conferences. Batista spoke of the main problems facing the new government: (1) an honest administration free as much as possible of corruption; (2) getting rid of the gangster element supported by the civilian government, and (3) to respect all the institutions of the country, such as civil guarantees, free speech, free elections, etc."

The climax of the coup was a thing out of a play. The coup was almost ruined because Batista ordered his car out of line en route to the Columbia barracks so that he could meet a friend and put on his good-luck leather jacket, one which he had worn as an army sergeant. „We prepared a plan," Gen. Tunon continued, whereby 11 officers in Columbia barracks, eight in La Cabana, three in the air force and eight in the navy prepared the men under them. No one else knew of the plot. Early on the morning of March 10, four officers went to the Batista farm, Kuquine, on the outskirts of Havana, I was to bring him to the garrison, where he would take over in a bloodless coup. There were seven cars by this time - with army officers and police. I was in the first car. Batista didn't cooperate. He told us to go on ahead and he would come along later. He wasn't afraid, he was being cautious. He finally consented to take his place in the motorcade. Then he did something that almost ruined our chances. When we neared the garrison his car cut out from the caravan. I ordered the rest of the cars to stop because I thought he might have changed his mind. We looked for him and found that he was changing his civilian jacket for a leather

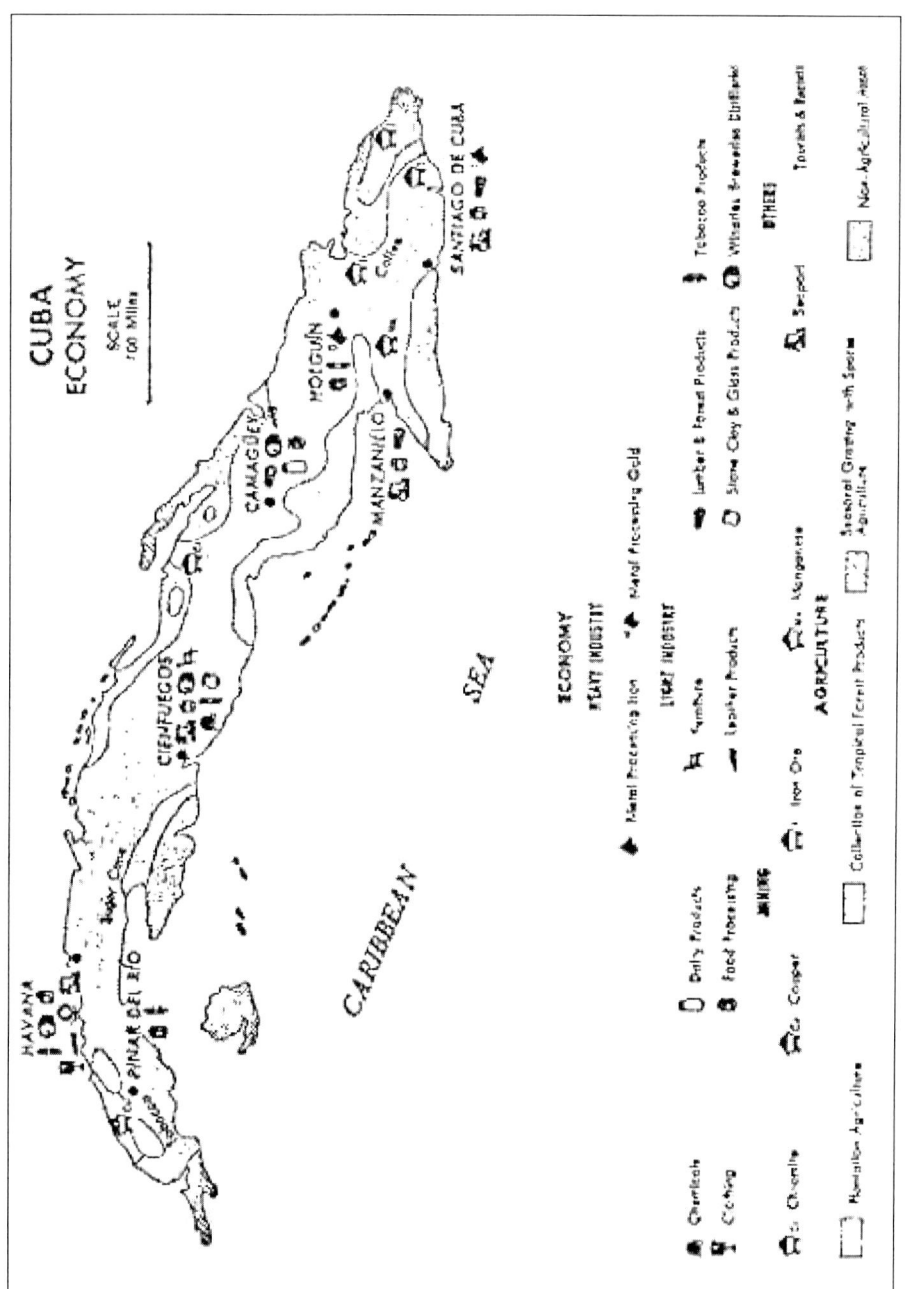

windbreaker he had worn as a sergeant. It was either superstition or ego - or a combination of both. The brown jacket was brought to him by an officer who should not have even known of our mission and moreover, an officer I did not trust. Batista even changed cars, going the rest of the way with that officer. We were supposed to be at the garrison at 2:40 A. M. sharp. The stop made us three minutes late and those three minutes almost cost us our coup, for when we arrived the officer we had expected to be in charge of the gate had gone to another part of the garrison and a new one was confronting us. An alarm could have been sounded but fortunately, the trusted officer returned and talked briefly to the sentinel and we passed through the gates. I had taken the precaution of posting the men of my own company as security guards. A driver and two men went to the home of Gen. Ruperto Cabrera, chief of the army. He lived on the post and was routed out of bed and taken to Batista's farm as hostage. Batista had given his wife a sleeping pill earlier, so that she would not awaken during the night and worry about his absence - one of the few considerate things I have ever known him to do."

There were 4,000 men in the Columbia garrison, but so complete was the coup that not a drop of blood was shed. As each new shift reported for duty, they either joined the movement or were disarmed and put into cells. Batista called newspaper friends with the scoop. He took over completely that first day. „His old friends began appearing," said Gen. Tunon. „He had his claque and our group was being eased out of the picture." An accused embezzler, Marino' Lopez Blanco, was made secretary of the treasury. He had been trying to buy his way into the previous Prio government. Gen. Francisco Tabernilla, who had been kicked out by President Grau San Martin eight years earlier, was put in charge of the army. Juan Rojas, then a captain, became a general in the Batista government. The members of the junta went over to him. Today all of the officers who took part in the coup - with the exception of Gen. Tunon - are rich and powerful members of the Cuban hierarchy. „I came from an old army family," said Tunon, „and the men under me liked me. I was made a brigadier general earlier because I was head of the junta. This was a popular decision with the men. I didn't realize that this didn't set well with Batista, but he reasoned that anyone who could organize one coup might be tempted to create another. I was put under constant surveillance. The men under me were told to disregard my orders. A captain was assigned to my section to countermand any orders I might give. Then guards were put around my house - one was a gardener whom I never hired and the other a sort of handyman. I went to Batista's home to protest and ended up by resigning."

No action is too petty for Batista. Gen. Tunon was retired - and exiled to Miami - with a pension of $331 per month. Charges of conspiracy were made after he left the country and the pension was declared forfelt. What does Gen. Tunon think of Batista? „I think that he cannot remain in power too much longer," he said hopefully. „He has hurt too many people and revoked too many institutions dear to the people of Cuba. His principal support comes from the repressive groups. But his spies are everywhere. The morale of the army is at a new low despite what you hear about salaries and other inducements. „The only way to unseat him is either through the army or through the church. The U.S. government could help by acting as an interested third party - or by just sitting on the sidelines and alowing Cubans to settle their own quarrels." Whether you hear it from the general who helped Batista to power or from a waitress now working in Miami or from a real estate man, the story of Batista's reign is an unlovely thing. Batista is not the first to plunder Cuba. Virtually every government head since Cuba gained its independence has lined his pockets and then gone off the live in sumptuous exile. Those in power cannot resist the temptation of easy money. Batista's brother-in-law has charge of the slot machine racket. A close friend said that the right contractors get the road and building construction jobs and that the proper kickback comes back to the palace. There are the atrocities and the loot and the prostitution and the censorship. These are the things that Batista stands for, no matter how he attempts to disguise them. And an hour's flight from the palace in Havana, the man who helped create Cuba's Frankenstein monster cringes beneath the weight of his conscience. The fact that he has a conscience automatically disqualifies him as a Batista man.

SUBSIDIZED PRESS

Dictator Fulgencio Batista, who likes to call himself an old newspaperman, maintains iron control over virtually all of the Cuban press through a feudal system of subsidies without which most of the major newspapers would cease to exist. This is a normal procedure even when insurgent forces aren't creating little incidents. Now that civil guarantees have been tossed down the drain and censorship has been imposed, control of the press is complete. Not a dissident whisper filters into Cuba's newspapers. And newsmen aren't as indignant - at least not openly - as they would be in this country because they, too, are subsidized and without the added money they would scarcely be able to subsist. The result is darkness and ignorance of the true state of affairs for the great majority of the 6,000,000 people of Cuba as well as a fuzzy picture for the outside world. Censorship, enforced by economic necessity, is the great weapon in Batista's arsenal. No atrocity picture is printed. The press doesn't dare to criticize the inhuman Maj. Esteban Ventura Nobo or the other psychopathic characters who enforce Batista's decrees.

Technically, Batista has imposed official censorship some eight times since 1953. Before that, censorship had been imposed only once, by Machado back in 1931 to 1933. Chief of his censors is Evangelina de las Lleras, a member of the underground movement that ousted Machado in 1933. She's a shade over 50 and, purposely or not, unable to see any point of view but her own. Her decisions, however devoid of reason, are final. There are 40 censors in all, one for each of the 16 newspapers in Havana and the others for telephone, magazines, radio stations and the island's four TV stations. Subsidizing began in 1933, when people within the newspapers were bought. Presidents Grau San Martin and Carlos Prio Socorras followed suit when they came to power. But it was found that a general subsidy was more effective. Batista's tab for purchasing the integrity of newspapers and newsmen runs into millions of dollars each year. The subsidies run from $4,000 per month to as high as $1,000 per day and many of Havana's newspapers could not possibly make ends meet without this largesse from Batista, the boy who wears a button describing him as Newspaperman No. 1. The button entitles him to hold a job with a guild minimum wage of $22.08 per week, despite or because of which he has managed to accumulate what revolutionaries estimate as $300,000,000. Any sparks of rebellion among editors are quickly extinguished. Luis Ortega Sierra, a veteran Cuban newsman, was baldly beaten and exiled to Miami and his newspaper, Pueblo, was sold for peanuts. Five papers are controlled or owned directly by the government. One of these is Pueblo, operated by Andres Domingo Morales, a close friend to Batista. On the rolls of Pueblo appears the name of Fulgencio Batista as a reporter. It's an evening paper with a circulation of about 2,000.

Tiempo en Cuba is operated by the strong-armed Sen. Rolando Masferrer. A brilliant lawyer. Masferrer has distinguished himself by his services to the present regime. He commanded a battalion in the Spanish Civil War and is an extreme liberal, though not a Red. He has organized his own police force. He carries a gun and is known as a rough customer. Tiempo en Cuba is the Pravda of the Batista government. Masferrer constantly harasses those around Batista, making them feel insecure and thus keeping them on their toes. The censors don't bother him because they have no need. Alerta is an evening paper with a circulation of 3,000. It was formerly the property of Minister of Communication Ramon Vasconcelos, a Batista supporter who fell from grace and is now living in Spain. No more patriotic newspaper exists in Cuba than Ataja. It features blue and yellow headlines on white newsprint. The colors of the national police are blue, those of the army yellow, and the Navy, white, and Ataja, which

PRODUCTION OF MAIN CROPS
(Thousands of metric tons)

	1958	1959	Percent change
Sugar	5,778.6	5,964.2	+ 3
Tobacco	41.6	41.2	− 1
Coffee	29.1	49.2	+68
Rice (unpolished)	222.7	295.5	+32
Cotton	0	1.4	—
Black and red beans	30.0	35.0	+16
Corn	147.0	190.0	+29
Peanuts	7.0	11.0	+42
Potatoes	101.0	113.0	+11
Pineapples	100.0	98.0	− 2
Oranges	73.0	81.0	+11
Cucumbers	18.0	18.0	0
Tomatoes	69.3	73.1	+ 5

CUBA'S CURRENT ACCOUNT
(Millions of dollars)
Aggregates for seven years, 1952-1958

	Receipts	Expenditures	Balance
1. Merchandise	4,818.1	4,636.4	181.7
2. Tourism	247.7	232.9	14.8
3. Transportation	49.7	480.7	−431.0
4. Insurance	5.5	11.8	− 6.3
5. Dividends & interest	51.7	369.1	−317.4
6. Gov't transactions	12.0	9.7	2.3
7. Other services	138.5	33.8	104.7
8. Gifts	17.1	36.5	− 19.4
9. Total (1 through 8)	5,340.3	5,810.9	−470.6

The Cuban Economy in 1958

means attack, is circulated in barracks all over the island. Even then, its circulation is only 12,000. It is operated by a pompous little man, Alberto Salas Maro, who stretches out to a height office feet and has a habit of chinning himself on casino roulette tables for hours at a time.

Republica is owned by Julia Elisa Consuegra, in her fifties and an old friend of Batista. The newspaper has a circulation of 1,000 and was started by former police chief Rafael Salas Canizares - who is a better story than Republica. Canizares clubbed a student to death in 1951 and was indicted in Havana. He was to face the court the same week Batista took power in 1952. Batista had the case taken care of and made Canizares a general in charge of the national police. At the time Canizares was poor. But he took control of gambling until 1956 and upon his death left $14,000,000 to his widow. His death was almost accidental. After the March 13, 1957, attack on Batista's palace, four rebels of the Directorio Revolucionario were executed. Out of retaliation, they shot to death Security Police Chief Blanco Rieo in a cabaret, the Montmarte, of which hoodlum Meyer Lansky owned a sizable portion. Canizares heard the killers were at the Haitian embassy and raeed off to intercept them. There were a dozen refugees there, but none of them was involved in the Rico killing. Canizares was hunting for them out in the garage when he was met by a young man with a gun. They both opened fire but Canizares fell, mortally wounded. lrindido Martinez, the boy who fired the fatal shot, is still in hiding.

There are the „independent" newspapers that get money and other favors from the government. The 125-year-old Diario de la Marina, once the voice of the church and the Spanish colony, is a morning paper with a circulation of 35,000. Today it gives Batista no cause for worry. Informacion is run by the Claret family, which is close to Batista. El Munda was born with the republic 57 years ago and once had a great tradition as an independent liberal newspaper. The owner of record is Amadeo Barletta, an italian who went to Cuba 20 years ago and - in between visits to other countries and deals with other dictators - has done very well indeed under the Batista regime, Former President Prio is reported to have put up more than half of the purehase price for El Mundo. Barletta was once Mussolini's consul to the Dominican Republic. When Barletta was thrown into jail there, Mussolini threatened to send his fleet to free him. Barletta has also done business with Peron, as well as with Prio and Grau San Martin. He has had a hectic life. On one occasion, Batista assigned SIM men to guard him and the El Mundo plant, which didn't do much to help the newspaper's reputation. Another morning newspaper, Excelsior, has a circulation of 28,000 with the help of a plan whereby they print lottery numbers. The owner is Alfredo Homedo, almost 80 now, a man with a Texas complex. He has the world's largest theater in the Miramar section of Havana, so big that it's rarely opened because of the expense of operating it. Homedo also owns El Pais, a lottery paper with a circulation of 40,000. The Havana Post is owned by Clara Park, 55, ofNew Orleans. It is Havana's only English daily and during the Little Rock, Ark., incident, heavily played up the cause of Gov. Faubus and attacked the stand of President Eisenhower. Mafiana is owned by

Jose Lopez Viloboy, president of Cubana Airlines, in which Batista is deeply interested.

The great Cuban newspaper, Prensa Libre - Free Press - is not subsidized. It has a circulation of over 85,000 and is headed by Sergio Carbo, a newsman with an excellent reputation. The censorship is evident when you pick up a copy of the usually fearless Prensa Libre. With incidents breaking loose all over the place, with threats of total war by Castro, seizure of arms shipments, the front page heavily played up a chit-chat column which wanted to congratulate one Jose Sierra on his birthday. Reporters are poorly paid. Scale is $22.08 per week, but there is something called the botella. The botella is a government job of doing nothing as a rule. A reporter can have several of these, bringing his salary up to $1,000 per month for the man covering the palace, and somewhat less for those on less important beats. Stories of U.S. mobsters allied with Batista in the gambling racket were so muffled by the purchased press in Havana that the news of the alliance wasn't exposed until THE NEWS uncovered the story last January. Not only does the subsidized press suppress the news, but reporters working for Batista don't hesitate to attempt to slander legitimate newsmen coming into the country to do an honest job.

COUNTERPART CASTRO

There are more than 2,000 Cuban exiles in Miami, which has been called the Siberia for Latin-America, and the reason most of them are battling the Batista regime is simple - they want to go home. They want to go back, however, with the guarantee they won't be dragged out of their beds during the night by the dreaded SIM (Security Police) and forced to submit to torture and worse. There's the pianist who says: „Even here, I can feel the hand of Batista. His spies are everywhere in this city - even in New York and other places where Cubans have gone for refuge. I listen to the shortwave broadcasts from Fidel Castro's headquarters in the Sierra Maestra two or three times a week and they give me hope - even though I am not 100% for Castro, either." You hear that often - Cubans who hate Batista are not necessarily in love with Castro. There is a mistaken idea that if you talk or write about the regime's terrorism you have to be for Castro. A large share of the exiles in Miami are for Cuba only. The insurgents, be they Castro's or Faure Chomon's or followers of other rebel leaders, are merely the weapons by which the anti-Red middle class hopes to free its homeland. There's the exiled newspaperman who says: „Batista is a murderer, but Castro is an ambitious man, and who knows if things will be any better when and if he takes over? Our best hope is a third party - preferably the army - under a non-political man like Gen. Jorge Garcia Tunon, also exiled by Batista." Revolutionaries are common in Miami. They seem to collect in the same places night after night. „I have a family in Havana," said one, „and my sole aim is to go there to live with them again. I saw them eight months ago, but it's too risky for me to make frequent trips. I can only fight against those who keep me from my mother and two brothers."

Portly Dr. Roberto Agramonte, a former sociology professor, his wife, daughter and son - who fought with Castro in the Sierra - are exiles living in a cramped „efficiency apartment." Suitcases are scattered about the place and there is little furniture - the mark of the transient who hopes this is only a temporary stop. Agramonte, Dr. Manuel Bisbe and others in the „26th of July Movement" spoke March 16 at a commemorative meeting at the Flagler Theater in Miami. It was a Sunday moming, but there were about 300 present to pay tribute to the memory of Dr. Pelayo Cuervo, slain as a suspect in the March 13, 1957, attack on the Presidential Palace. Cuervo had no part in the uprising, but he had been a marked man because he couldn't be bought. He was taken from the home of a friend, pushed into a car and shot to death in a Havana suburb. The people at the Flagler were middle class. Some of them arrived late, making excuses to friends that they had to attend church first. Batista likes to call them Communists, but Reds aren't in the habit of putting church services before revolutionary meetings. Inside, there was emotion-drenched oratory. Batista, say these sober, welleducated people, „has drunk the blood of the Cuban people." The current theme - Liberty or death." Cuba's martyrs are remembered in Miami - and there are many martyrs, with new ones created by each abortive uprising. But it's like a chain letter," said a Cuban attorney, „Each person who dies for Cuba inspires a dozen others to take his place in the movement against Batista. Some day - be it this month or this year - we will return to our homes in Cuba." The revolutionaries and exiles don't always find jobs. But they seem to get along - mostly from the bounty of those who have plenty of money and are willing to share it.

Castro has his followers. So does ex-President Carlos Prio Socarras. So do others. Curiously, Batista and Castro profess the same aims for Cuba. They don't want to run the country personally, they say, they merely want a strong, honest group to take over - with free elections, civil rights and all the other benefits the Cubans don't have. Batista turns on his ever-ready charm and tells the world he would like nothing better than to turn over the reins to some deserving characters. In the next breath, he indicates he would like to retain control of the army in case anything goes wrong. Castro has said he doesn' t want to be president of Cuba, not even a high officer of the govemment. He wants to sit on a park bench in the background and make like an elder statesman. „I would act only as the conscience of the administration," he said. The consensus among the more highly-educated exiles is that Cuba would be better off if neither Castro nor Batista ruled the island. „There are many rnisconceptions," said an exile. „There is, for instance, a popular belief in the U.S. that if Batista relents in his reign of terror, takes it easy on his enernies, there will be peace. This is not so. There can be no peace while he directs any phase of the government. But on the other hand, I do not believe that Fidel Castro is statesman enough to rule Cuba as it should be governed."

Batista has ruled Cuba for 17 of the last 25 years. The past six years have been the goriest in Cuba's history. How did he get started? Fulgencio Batista y Zaldivar was born of humble parents and was a laborer in a sugar mill, a farm worker, a tailor and eventuallya stenographer. He joined the army at the age of 20 and attained the rank of staff sergeant because of his knowledge of shorthand. He came into power through a coup in Sept. 4, 1933, ending the reign of tyrannical President Gerardo Machado. But, though he was now Cuba's strong man, Batista didn't become president until 1940 when a coalition - including the Communist Party he now denounces - elected hirn. When he was barred by the Cuban constitution from running for a second term in 1944, he put up his own candidate - who was defeated. Batista retired to Daytona Beach to lick his wounds and plan a comeback. When he regained control in 1952 through a coup d'etat, he was hailed as the savior of the people. But the people were soon to find out that this was a different Batista than the one they had known. This one was out to make a fortune and a place in history. He has done both. Castro is now 32. He is a brilliant lawyer, has three university degrees and comes from a wealthy family in the sugarcane business. However, he has a reputation as a young man who likes to run off in the direction of a revolution. In 1946, he was a member of an expedition against President Rafael Trujillo, of the Dominican Republic. The invasion fell through and Castro escaped by leaping into the sea from a ship. He also took part in a revolt in Colombia. Is he Communist? One of his severest critics says: „Castro may have used Reds to gain the ends he seeks, but he's not a Red. He may have associated with them but I'm sure that he was not aware of the political inferences. He has suffered from nothing more serious than adolescent political growing-pains." The Castro „26th of July Movement" originates from his attack on the army barracks in Oriente Province. From that day on, even though Castros losses were heavy and he had to flee for his life, his name became synonymous with Superman and Robin Hood. There are those who don't believe that Castro will ever really come out of his beloved mountains - that when he does venture out too far he'll be cut to ribbons.

You have to try to divorce the distortions from the realities in any analysis of the Cuban situation. You have to discount the enthusia, some of Castro's followers as well as the propaganda dished out by the Batista regime. The best way is to talk to the solid, substantial men who have never before entered into a revolutionary movement, who refused to go into politics. These men comprise the great middle class of Cuba. They speak with wisdom and authority. They had made great sacrifices - leaving their beautiful homes in Havana: to live in airless little rooms in Miami, New York and Chicago. Dr. Manuelo Urrutia, who will head the provisional government if Castro wins out, is in New York. He was an honored magistrate for 31 years before he was exiled for daring to indict a police official for murder. Men who have known violence only through hearsay form the nucleus of the underground that goes from New York to Miami and Cuba. It is work to which they have become accustomed. They don't complain - they mercly keep the guns going over to the Sierra Maestra and the Sierra del Escambray. One of them said: „Castro is almost a prisoner in his mountains. Batista is virtually a prisoner in the barracks at Columbia Military City. But the Cuban people are the real prisoners.«

CASTRO'S SOVIET POLICY

Harold V. Hendrix, *Miami News*

When the jurors of the International Reporting category in 1963 started their selection process, among the exhibits was one of the *Miami News* containing six artic1es only about the escalation of a global crisis between the USA and the Soviet Union, the Cuban Missile confrontation. „Each story," it was said by the newspaper, „was published by the *Miami News* before it appeared in any other paper in the country. With a single exception, each story was first denied or at least denied comment by the appropriate authorities in Washington only to be confirmed later by the same authorities in Washington. The sum of the work, represented by these six stories, is impressive not only because of the accuracy, but also the enterprise of Mr. Hendrix." Throughout the year", the background description continued, „reporter Hendrix has been ahead of other United States newsmen in reporting what was going on inside the island of Cuba. Events following his reports testified to an unusual accuracy in a most difficult area of getting the story right, in which the difficulty is made large not only because of the reluctance of usual information sources to speak, but also because of the gossip and rumor." The Pulitzer Prize jurors in their report of March 8, 1963, shared that opinion and declared Hendrix's articles „an outstanding example of international reporting." His articles indicated, the report runs, „that by hard digging he had confirmed the presence of large numbers of MIG-21s in Cuba days before President Kennedy's speech disclosing the extent of the Russian buildup in Cuba." So Hal Hendrix earned the Pulitzer award „for his persistent reporting" on the Cuban missile crisis.

Harold Victor Hendrix was born on February 14,1922, in Kansas City, Missouri. In 1941, he began his studies at the Rockhurst College before he went to the *Kansas City Star* in 1944. He stayed with this newspaper until 1957, treating Latin-American questions as a columnist from 1947 on. When he changed to the *Miami News* afterwards, Hendrix covered this special political field intensively. He took advantage of his membership in the leading joumalistic organization for North- and South-America, the Inter-American Press Association, to the board of directors of which he belonged for a while. His various connections rendered it possible for Hal Hendrix to find out from Miami in the second half of 1962 that Cuba was shipping military weapons to other Latin American states; some months later he was the first American journalist to report that Soviet jets, MIG 21s, had arrived in Cuba. Following now are five of his Pulitzer Prize winning articles, published between October 7 and 31, 1962:

SIX MISSILE BASES

»Construction has begun in Communist Cuba on at least a half dozen launching sites for intermediate range tactical missiles, United States intelligence authorities have advised the White House. Although official U.S. spokesmen have declined to disclose the intelligence reports, the *Miami News* has learned that experts have advised President Kennedy that the ground-to-ground missiles can be operational from inland Cuba within six months. From the type of construction under way it has been determined that the launching pads will have the capability of hurling rockets that could penetrate deeply into the United States in one direction and reach the Panama Canal Zone in the opposite direction. Official observers do not believe that the Soviet Union has yet delivered the intermediate range-type missiles to Cuba. But neither do they now doubt that delivery plans have been made. „The United States has a 'grace period' of about six months insofar as these new missiles are concerned," an official observer commented yesterday. After that, once the installations are complete and the missiles emplaced, any time there is a flare-up in tensions anywhere in the world between this country and the Soviet Union, the Communists in Cuba can rattle the offensive rockets in the Caribbean."

Officials have reported that U.S. plans for a crackdown on free world shipping to Communist Cuba could slow down the launching site construction, but there is no guarantee that the Soviets will not divert their own vessels to this high-priority project. Washington also has been alerted to the fact that Communist Cuba's north coast now is solidly banked with „defensive" short-range surface-to-air missiles, capable of downing an aircraft in a 25-mile range. Officially, the State Department has announced that at least 15 to these SAM bases have been completed - adding that the total may reach 25 or more. Behind the coastal missile emplacements, now manned jointly by Cuban military and Soviet „technicians," are an undisclosed number of ground-to-ground missile bases already operational. These are reported to have a range of about 35 miles, designed for firing on ships at sea and strategic ground installations. According to reports from Cuba, some of these shortrange „defensive" missiles now are installed within easy reach of the U.S. Naval base at Guantanamo Bay. Meanwhile, reports from Moscow and Havana point out that shipments of military materials and personnel still are continuing to pour unchecked into Communist Cuba. The State Department has acknowledged that there are now about 4,500 Soviet „military specialists" in Communist Cuba. Outside the department, observers believe the number is closer to 10,000. Since July, according to late State Department announcements, more than 85 Soviet

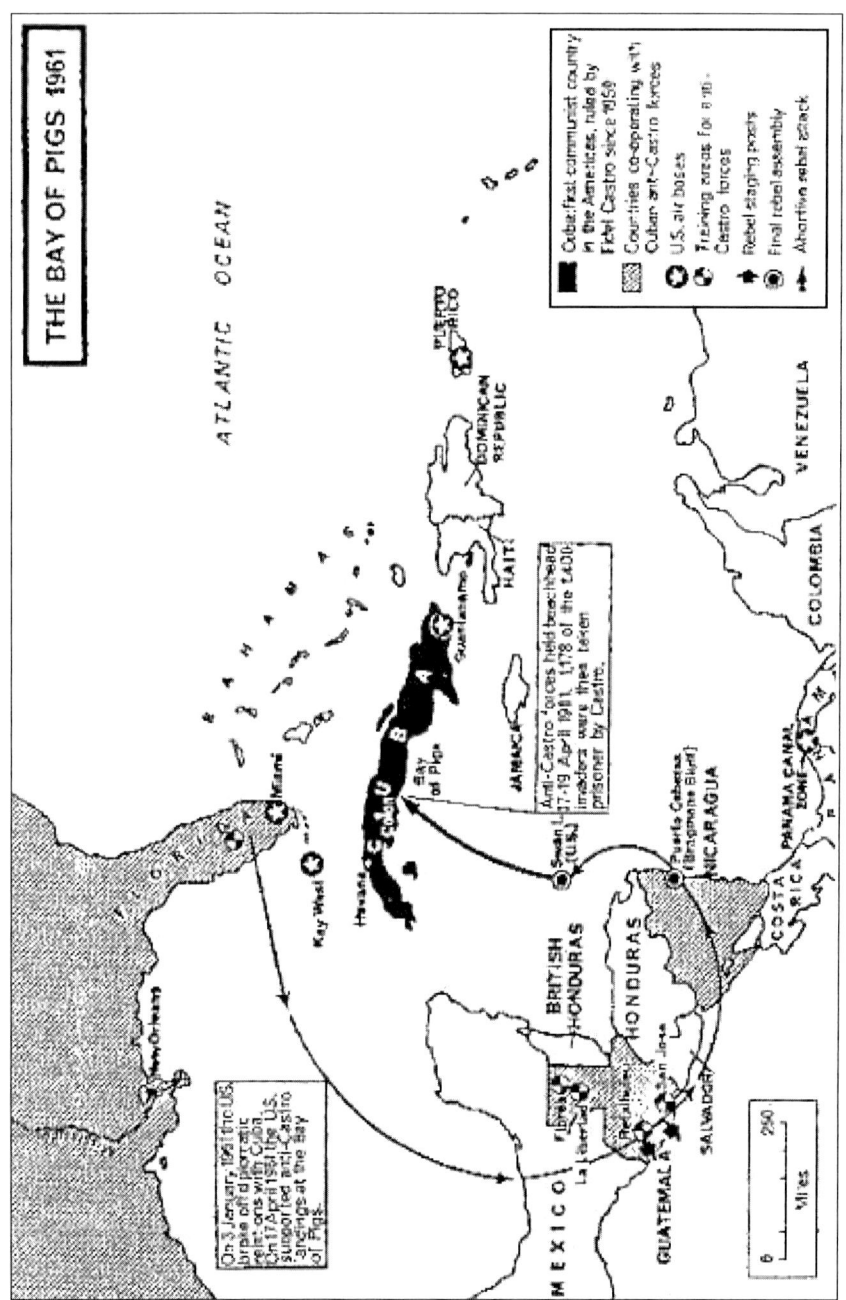

THE BAY OF PIGS 1961

ATLANTIC OCEAN

Cuba: first communist country in the Americas, ruled by Fidel Castro since 1959

Countries co-operating with Cuban anti-Castro forces

U.S. air bases

Training areas for anti-Castro forces

Rebel staging posts

Final rebel assembly

Abortive rebel attack

Anti-Castro forces held beachhead 17-19 April 1961. 1,178 of the 1,400 invaders were then taken prisoner by Castro.

On 3 January 1961 the U.S. broke off diplomatic relations with Cuba. On 17 April 1961 the U.S. supported anti-Castro landings at the Bay of Pigs.

PUERTO RICO

DOMINICAN REPUBLIC

HAITI

JAMAICA

Guantanamo

Bay of Pigs

Havana

Key West

Miami

New Orleans

FLORIDA

BAHAMAS

Swan I. (U.S.)

Puerto Cabezas (Bissingnone Bluff)

NICARAGUA

COSTA RICA

PANAMA CANAL ZONE

COLOMBIA

VENEZUELA

HONDURAS

BRITISH HONDURAS

MEXICO

GUATEMALA

SALVADOR

San José

La Libertad

Retalhuleu

Flores

0   250

Miles

shiploads have arrived in Cuba ports. Red Star, the Soviet military publication, notes that ships „are on the seas daily bound for Cuba with support for our Cuban friends.“

The size of Communist Cuba's air force also continues to swell, as intelligence reports disclose stepped-up Russian supply lines. As first reported by The *Miami News* last month, the Soviets have supplied the Castro regime with at least six supersonic Mig-21 jet fighters. Intelligence sources have reported that there is evidence that at least 25 or 30 more of these most modern Soviet jet fighters will be operational in Cuba soon. Each carries heat-sensing air-to-air missiles and has a maximum speed of 1,685 miles per hour. The Mig-21s are the „frosting on the cake“ for Castro's air force. The backbone of the Cuban air strength, according to published Defense Department figures in the Congressional Record, is about 100 Mig-15, Mig-17 and Mig-19 jet fighters. On the sea, the Communists have delivered to Castro at least 16 „Komar“ class guided missile patrol boats, each carrying two rockets which fire 11 to 17 miles. It has been reported by Western intelligence that the Soviets have earmarked at least two destroyers and two East German submarines for Cuba. Meanwhile, U.S. Under Secretary of State George Ball last week told a special House committee investigating Cuban arms traffic from the Soviet bloc that United States policy on Cuba „still is based on the assessment that Cuba is not a military threat.“

REACTIONS IN AMERICA

The showdown between the United States and Communist Cuba, although long in coming, was inevitable. In retrospect, it began only a few days after Fidel Castro came to power Jan. 1, 1959. Shortly after the bearded revolutionary leader came down from the hills of Cuba's Sierra Maestra mountains when President Fulgencio Batista fled from Havana on New Year's Eve, Castro declared that 200,000 gringos would die if the U.S. Marines ever set foot on Cuban soil. Since that angry declaration in the lobby of the Havana Hilton Hotel early in January 1959, Castro has been screeching about invasions from the U.S. and working overtime to destroy the U.S. image in Cuba and throughout Latin America. Now the United States has moved to liberate Cuba from Castro and his Communist allies - and mend its shuttered image in Latin America. In launehing that decisive last night against Communist Cuba, President Kennedy also has served notice on the world, that the U. S. has drawn a new line on the advance of international communism. „The line is being drawn on the Cuban problems rather than in Berlin or the Far East, because there is more room to move in the Caribbean," commented a U.S. official to the Cuban arena. The most frightening of the apprehensions raised by President Kennedy's address to the nation on the Cuban crisis is that a bearded madman in Havana now has in his hands the dread power to fire missiles or bombs into the U.S. mainland and possibly spark World War III. President Kennedy declared that it shall be the policy of the United States to regard any nuclear attack launched from Cuba against any nation in the Western Hemisphere as an attack by the Soviet Union on the U.S. - requiring full retaliatory response from Russia.

Since the Soviets are cognizant of Castro's history of irrational and unstable behavior, it may be that they would not risk placing any pushbuttons near his itchy trigger finger. Still, it could be difficult even for the Russians in Communist Cuba to keep Castro and his fanatic henchmen away from the pushbuttons. It would still be more difficult to keep them from a capricious attack against the U.S. - if the Castro regime figures it can penetrate U.S. defense. These grim possibilities are certain now to be on the minds of Latin America's heads of state - and they will be a factor in any action taken by the Organization of American States. OAS action to back up President Kennedy's collision with the Castro-Communist combine is expected to develop quickly, although it may not be unanimous. Brazil is likely to maneuver to throw some kind of roadblock up before the OAS action. Such a move could lead to far-reaching repercussions inasmuch as President Kennedy is still planning to visit Brazil Nov. 12. Mexico, who with Brazil has led the „hands off Cuba" fight in Latin America, has shown signs of changing its posture in light of disclosures of Castro's offensive firepower.

In his speech, President Kennedy astutely pointed out that Mexico City could easily be a target for one of Castro's intermediate range ballistic missiles. Mexico's President Adolpho Lopez Mateos, now touring the Far East, declared today in Manila that Mexico would stand by the OAS in meeting the new situation in communist Cuba. „Mexico signed the Rio de Janeiro pact and in that document it was contemplated the possibility of a country being a victim of an aggressor," President Lopez Mateos said. „In case such an event took place, Mexico would duly fulfill her duties contained in that pact." In Central America, the U. S. will find solid support of its new tough and determined policy. This means six voices at the OAS Council table - Guatemala, El Salvador, Honduras, Nicaragua, Costa Rica and Panama. On the huge South American continent, Brazil is likely to abstain rather than fully reverse its pro-Cuba and leftist position. Chile and Ecuador, both with a high incidence of Communist activity and facing threats of strikes, may join Brazil. All the other countries - Colombia, Venezuela, Peru, Bolivia, Argentina, Uruguay and

Paraguay, are expected to line up behind the U.S. program to rid the hemisphere of the Castro regime.

RUSSIA'S INSTALLMENT EFFORT

Temporarily thwarted by the United States' naval blockade around Communist Cuba, the Soviet Union is pressuring desperately for aircraft landing rights in Africa and South America to service an armaments airlift to Havana, The *News* learned today. Authoritative sources in Washington disclosed that Soviet representatives are concentrating heavy pressure on Brazil to give them transit rights for medium-range transport planes en route to Communist Cuba. The squeeze is being applied on Brazilian diplomats in Washington and by the Russian envoys assigned to the Soviet embassy in Brazil. Although Washington sources did not link the Russian pressure on Brazil with President Kennedy's plans to visit there next month, it was reported that the White House has been in touch with the Brazilian government about the projected trip. The expectation now is that the trip, slated to begin Nov. 12 will be canceled. Press Secretary Pierre Salinger said today he probably would have something definite to say on the plans before the day is over. Reports from Brazil say the trip already has been canceled. On the African side of the proposed airlift route, overtures are known to have been made to the government of Algerian Premier Ahmed Ben Bella, who just returned from a visit to Communist Cuba - and the United States. It has been learned that the Russians attempted to obtain transit landing rights at Dakar, but the government of Senegal rejected the proposal.

Soviet affairs specialists interpret the intense airlift pressuring as another indication that the Russians are determined to continue their military buildup in Communist Cuba. It is pointed out that medium-range rockets could be landed in Cuba by the Russian Ilyusyin 11-18 turbo-prop airliners modified for such a mission. The African and South American transit stops are needed for such an operation because of the limited flying range of the Ilyusyin. It is not believed that Russia has sufficient longrange air transports to sustain a nonstop airlift service between the Soviet Union or any of its East European satellites and Communist Cuba. Meanwhile, it was learned that the U. S. intelligence forces have information of additional Soviet supplied firepower in Cuba beyond that which the Defense Department has made public earlier this week. Unofficially, the White House and Defense Department have been alerted to „hard" information that nuclear warheads of the 1-megaton class now are in Cuba under tight control of Soviet military personnel.

It also has been determined that the medium-range missiles already delivered to Communist Cuba include the T-2, T-4 and T-5 models that have

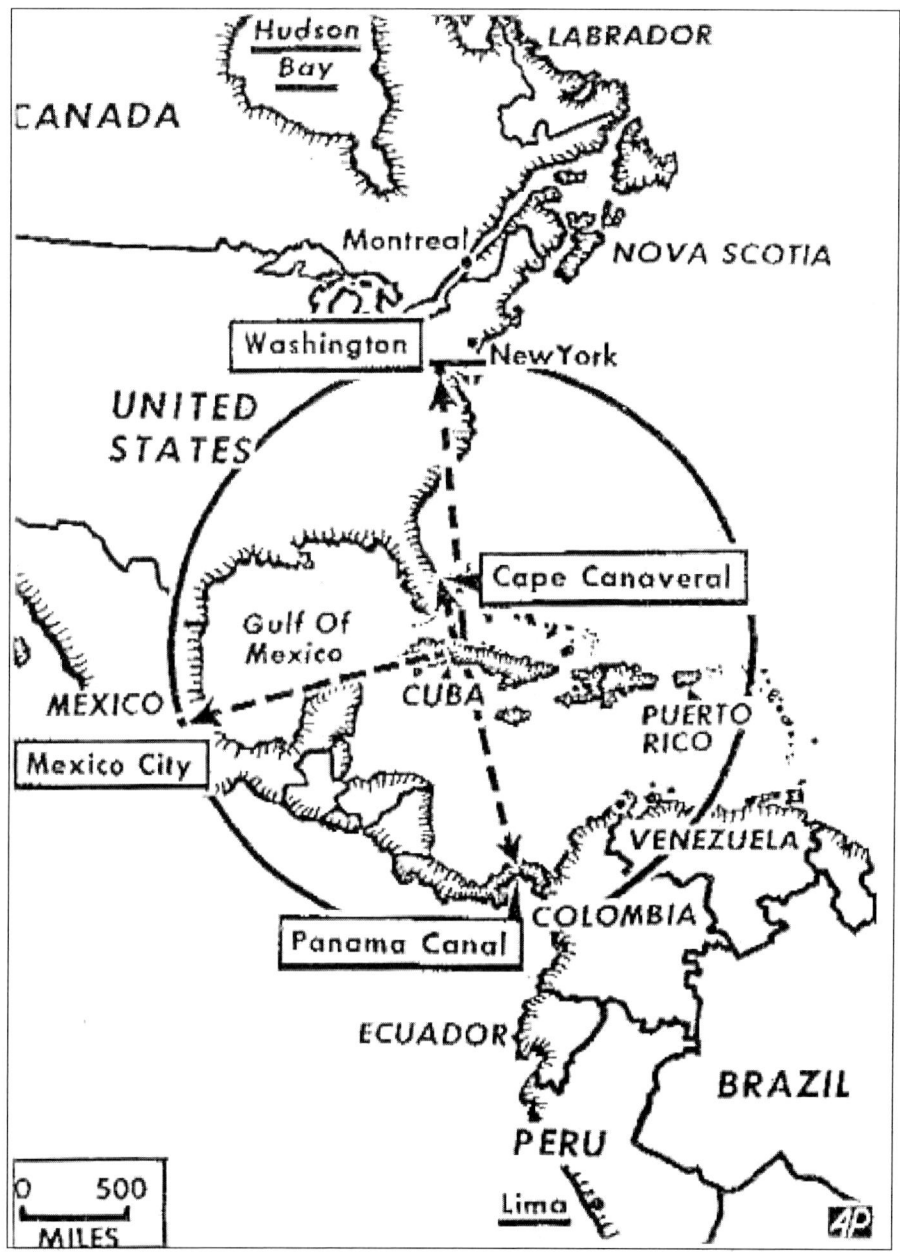

Radius of Cuban Missile Coverage (Arrows Points To Places Within Range)

been observed at Soviet military displays. All are capable of delivering atomic warheads. The T-2 is propelled by liquid fuel and has an operational range of 1,500 to 1,800 miles, with an inertial or self-contained guidance system. It is about 100 feet long and weighs about 60 tons. The T-2 model has appeared in a number of the serial photographs obtained by the United States in flights over Cuba - some at an altitude as low as 500 feet. Shipments of the T-4 and T-5 models are known to have been aboard some of the Soviet vessels that have turned back before encountering the U.S. Atlantic fleet. Photographs of the missiles on the deck of at least one Czechoslovakian ship have been obtained.

EXHIBITION OF POWER

In spite of the wordy correspondence racing back and forth between Moscow and Washington over the explosive Cuban situation, direct military action by the United States is inevitable - and likely to be launched soon with lightning swiftness: Without saying so directly, President Kennedy has in effect given the Castro-Khrushchev axis a 48-hour ultimatum to start dismantling the Soviet missile bases in Communist Cuba or face destruction of them by U.S. force. That was couched carefully in his letter last night to Premier Khrushchev dealing with possible negotiations on the Cuban problem. He commented: „There is no reason why we should not be able to complete these arrangements and announce them to the world within a couple of days." A possible deterrent of significant proportions to quick U.S. direct action is the proposed visit to Havana by Acting U.N. Secretary, General U Thant. Castro late yesterday extended an invitation to the U.N. leader to discuss with him the question of the negotiation proposals sailing between President Kennedy and Premier Khrushchev. The U.N. chieftain said he would announce his decision today.

Apart from the Castro-Thant matter, President Kennedy and his strategy advisers are known to have concluded that last week's strong support from the Organization of American States is clear authority to use force in dismantling the bases - and ultimately destroying the Communist threat to the Western Hemisphere. The U.S. conclusion was quickly backed up by OAS Secretary General Jose A. Mora, who declared that any measures taken by the United States to dismantle the bases would be „multilateral measures with multilateral support." The national and hemispheric impetus to take decisive action is not likely to be slowed down by Khrushchev's letter writing, inasmuch as the United States has demonstrated during the week the Kremlin's penchant for false words, statements and pledges with respect to Cuba and other Cold War

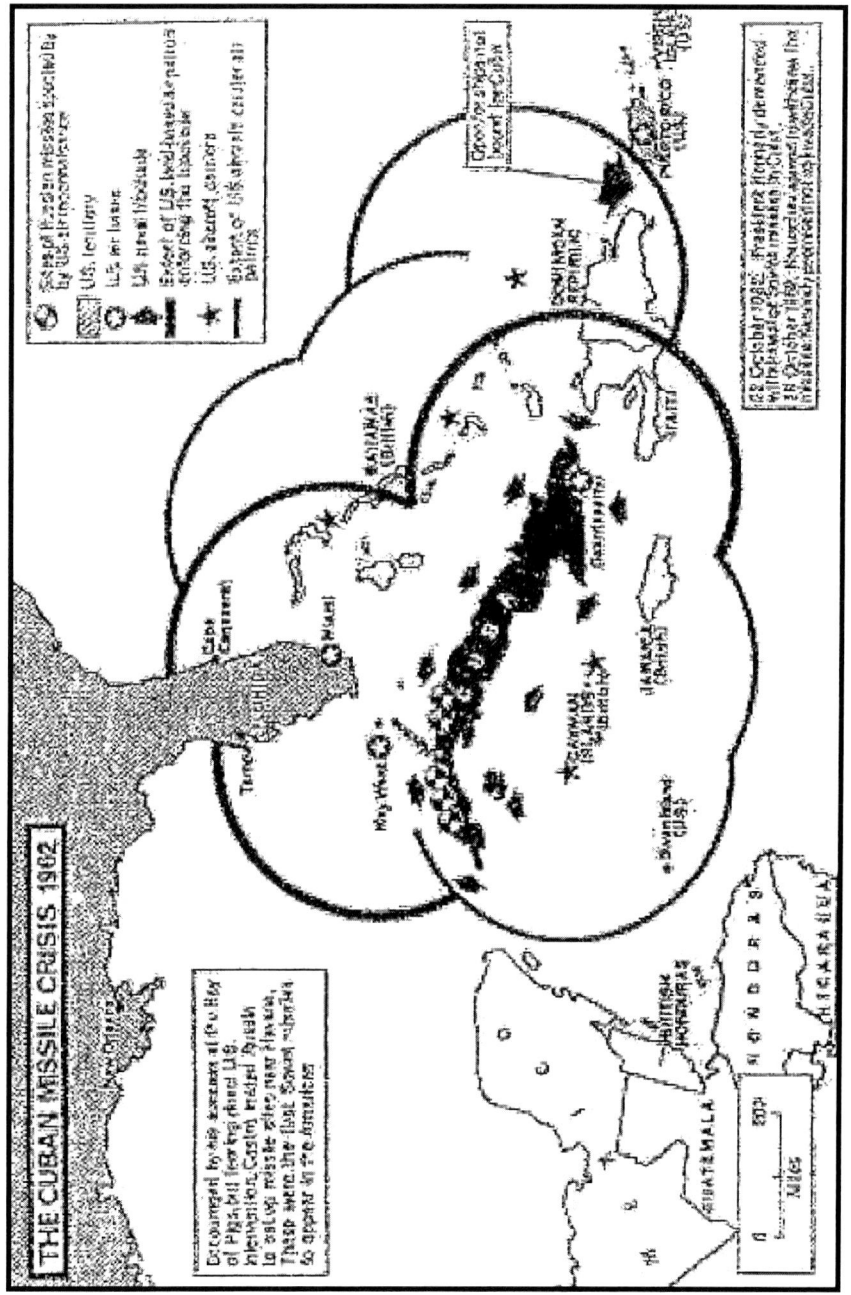

trouble spots. The buildup of U.S. military force in the United States and throughout the Caribbean which began last Monday continued through last night, and Pentagon strategists were working into the morning. Basic blueprints for an invasion of Cuba, an air strike on the missile launehing sites and for numerous other operations in the stack of the Pentagon's „contingency plans" were reported to be under constant review by the Joint Chiefs of Staff and their aides. Meanwhile, in the Caribbean the close surveillance of Russian and Soviet-chartered ships was continuing without interruption. Observers reported that the string of vessels stretched out across the Atlantic and Caribbean was continuing to inch toward Cuba. So far, according to surveillance reports, at least 17 ships, all presumably loaded with weapons, have turned around before encountering the blockade ring around Cuba.

The Defense Department last night added to the already potent potential strike force of the United States by calling 24 troop carrier squadrons to immediate active duty. The units are used to transport paratroopers and other combat forces. When asked if the callup implied that a Cuban invasion was immiment, Assistant Secretary of Defense Arthur Sylvester declined to reply. Observers in the capital last night carefully pointed out that realistically there was little likelihood of the problem of Cuba being resolved by correspondence or negotiation at this stage. It also was emphasized that even if Castro or Khrushchev would agree to „defusing" and removal of the nuclear missiles aimed at the United States, more than 250 million dollars worth of Soviet non-nuclear armaments still would be in Cuba and that an invasion threat to the Western Hemisphere by Soviet international communism still would exist. The United States has publicly announced that its policy with respect to Cuba is „to get rid of the Castro regime and remove the Communists from Cuba." Vice President Johnson, for example, has traveled across the United States with that message, and it has been echoed by dozens of other high officials from Washington in recent weeks.

DELAYED U. S. ACTION

Now that the tensions over Communist Cuba have eased in Washington, a number of nagging questions are being asked from a number of directions. Two puzzlers are foremost: How could the United States have let the situation reach the point it did in Communist Cuba, and why did the Kennedy Administration deliberately mislead the American public by prolonged withholding and denying of intelligence reports on Soviet activities in Communist Cuba? Indecision, which has become the hallmark of both the Eisenhower and

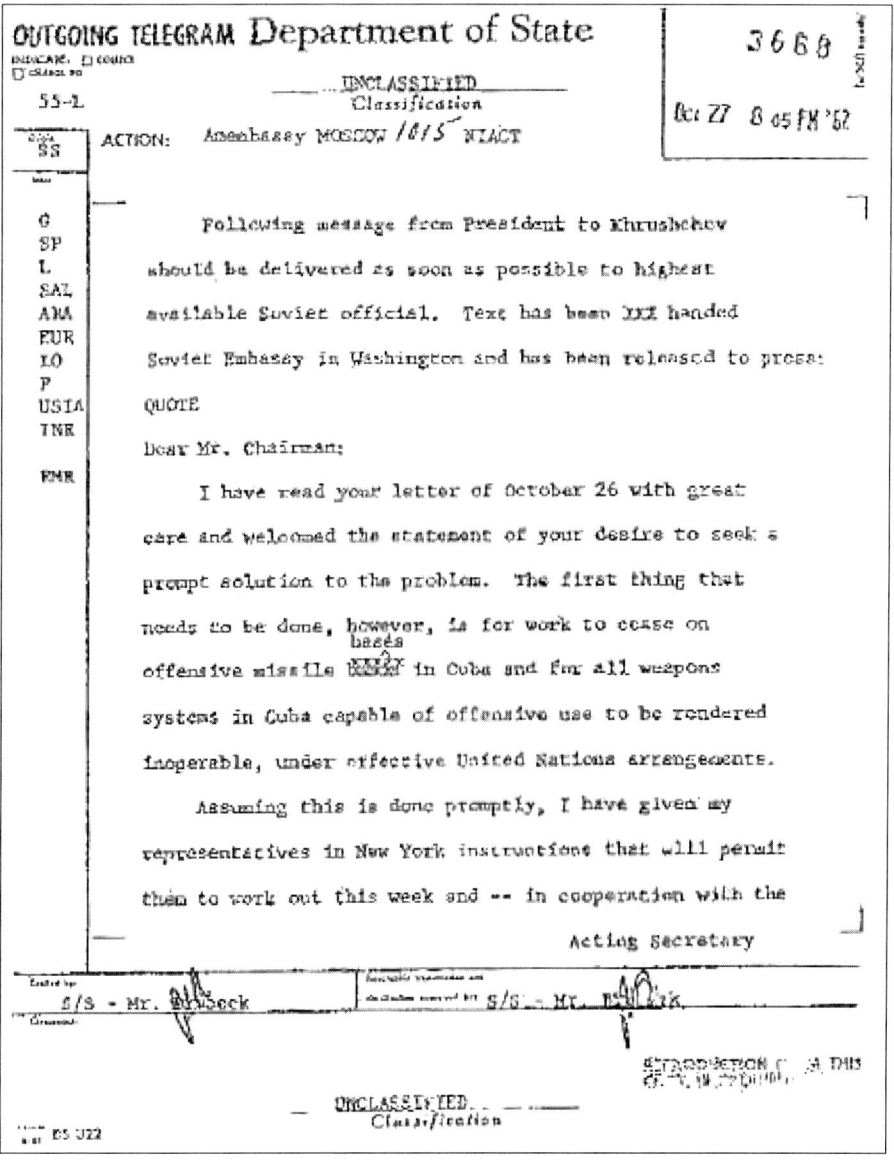

OUTGOING TELEGRAM Department of State

3668

UNCLASSIFIED
Classification

55-1

ACTION: Amembassy MOSCOW 1615 NIACT

Oct 27 8 05 PM '62

Following message from President to Khrushchev should be delivered as soon as possible to highest available Soviet official. Text has been handed Soviet Embassy in Washington and has been released to press:

QUOTE

Dear Mr. Chairman:

I have read your letter of October 26 with great care and welcomed the statement of your desire to seek a prompt solution to the problem. The first thing that needs to be done, however, is for work to cease on offensive missile bases in Cuba and for all weapons systems in Cuba capable of offensive use to be rendered inoperable, under effective United Nations arrangements.

Assuming this is done promptly, I have given my representatives in New York instructions that will permit them to work out this week and -- in cooperation with the Acting Secretary

Kennedy Administrations with respect to Fidel Castro and Communist Cuba, played a tragic role - in connection with the first question. There is no pin-point answer to the second, other than the continuing struggle inside the New Frontier between the „hard action" and „soft action" advisers on Comrnunist

116

UNCLASSIFIED

Acting Secretary General and your representative --

an arrangement for a permanent solution to the Cuban

problem along $ the lines suggested in your letter of

October 26. As I read your letter, the key elements of

your proposals -- which seem generally acceptable as

I understand them -- are as follows:

1. You would agree to remove these weapons systems

from Cuba under appropriate United Nations observation

and supervision; and undertake, with suitable safeguards,

to halt the further introduction of such weapons systems into

Cuba.

2. We, on our part, would agree -- upon the establish-

ment of adequate arrangements through the United Nations to

ensure the carrying out and continuation of these commitments --

(a) to remove promptly the quarantine measures now in effect

and (b) to give assurances against an invasion of Cuba and I

am confident that other nations of the Western Hemisphere would

be prepared to do likewise.

If you will give your representative similar instructions,

there is no reason why we should not MX be able to complete

these

UNCLASSIFIED

these arrangements and announce them to the world within
a couple of days. The effect of such a settlement on easing
world tensions would enable us to work toward a more general
arrangement regarding "other armaments", as proposed in your
second letter which you made public. I would like to say
again that the United States is very much interested in
reducing tensions and halting the arms race; and if your
letter signifies that you are prepared to discuss a
detente affecting NATO and the Warsaw Pact, we are quite
prepared to consider with our allies any useful proposals.

But the first ingredient, let me emphasize, is the
cessation of work on missile sites in Cuba and measures to
render such weapons inoperable, under effective inter-national
guarantees. The continuation of this threat, or a prolonging
of this discussion concerning Cuba by linking these problems
to the broader questions of European and world security, would
surely lead to an intensification of the Cuban crisis and a grave
risk to the peace of the world. For this reason I hope we can
quickly agree along the lines outlined in this letter and in
your letter of October 26.

/S/ John F. Kennedy

END

Cuba. This much in the controversy is certain. The State Department and the White House had accurate intelligence several weeks before President Kennedy finally broke the news in his Oct. 22 television address to the nation. The location of the kink, or where the data was bottled up likely never will be admitted. As late as three days before the President's speech, Under Secretary of State George W. Ball declared Communist Cuba posed no military threat to the United States. But, immediately after the President's address, the Cuban crisis and threat to the United States was being described as the most serious and grave crisis faced by the United States and the world since the explosion of World War II.

Three days before the crisis exploded into global size, the Kennedy Administration was insisting that all the Soviet weapons in Communist Cuba were „defensive." Officials scoffed at month-old reports of IRBM missiles in Cuba. It was repeated often in the previous weeks that possibly as many as 15 surface-to-air missile sites (SAMs) with a slant range of 25 miles had been installed in Cuba. Last week it was announced there were as many as 30. The State Department and White House before last week insisted that Castro had only about 60 older model MIG jet fighters in his air force, and „at least one" advanced jet interceptor (MIG-21) that was operational. But again when the crisis became global, Castro was admitted to have more than 100 operational Soviet supplied jet fighters and at least 39 operational supersonic MIG-21s - plus a number of medium range jet bombers capable of carrying nuclear bombs and striking the United States. Obviously, this jet fighter muscle did not sprout overnight in Communist Cuba. „Hard" intelligence reports placed the planes in Cuba long before last week. Pictures of the Cuban MIG-21s even appeared in this newspaper ... Who was asleep and why?«

Haiti

RICHNESS AND POORNESS

Liz Balmaseda, *Miami Herald*

„In Miami, with more foreign-born citizens than any other city in the nation", the Managing Editor of the *Miami Herald* told the Pulitzer prize jurors, „'local' news often happens far away. A dissident uprising in Cuba is big news in Little Havana. A power shift in Port-au-Prince can send hundreds to the streets of Little Haiti - and to the shores of Miami Beach. Liz Balmaseda's intimacy with South Florida's communities makes her work special ... A Cuban American, she distinguished herself as a foreign correspondent in South and Central America ... There are also the special gifts Balmaseda brings to her craft - a keen eye for detail, an ear for language, compassion and a sense of outrage. Twice each week, Liz reveals, counsels, sometimes scolds. Regularly, through skilled reporting and writing, she breaks news and tells people things they didn't know." When these words, together with samples of her work, reached the Pulitzer Prize jurors they were impressed and stated in their report of March 3, 1993: Balmaseda „did what the entire U.S. government failed to do. She traveled to Haiti and got the truth ... She showed Haiti's elite as well as the poor." The Pulitzer Prize Board shared the praise and gave the award to Liz Balmaseda „for her commentary from Haiti about deteriorating political and social conditions."

Elizabeth R. Balmaseda was born on January 17, 1959, in Puerto Padre, Cuba, admist the Cuban Revolution. Her family emigrated to the United States, and she grew up in Miami, Florida. She received an associate's degree from Miami-Dade Community College, and then a bachelor's degree from Florida International University in communications in 1981. She had been an intern for the *Miami Herald* in 1980, and was hired upon her graduation in 1981 to write for *El Herald*, the *Miami Herald*'s Spanish-language sister paper. She worked in this and several other reporting assignments at the *Herald* until 1985, when she left to become Central America bureau chief, based in El Salvador, for *Newsweek*. She moved to *NBC News* as a field producer based in Honduras before returning to the *Miami Herald* in November 1987 as a feature writer, earning the Pulitzer Prize in 1993. Following now are several of her award-winning articles from Port-au-Prince, published during June, 1992:

BACK TO HOMELAND

»The shame of the new return policy on Haitian refugees is told in a simple number. Only 16 people have been granted political asylum at the U.S.

Embassy in Port-au-Prince since February. Sixteen doesn't begin to reflect the reports of violence and repression in the shanly towns, in the mountain villages, in the coastal slums. I've met people in hiding. I know of villagers arrested, of homes ransacked, of schoolchildren surrounded by security forces. The other day I spoke to a Haitian journalist who was beaten by soldiers when he tried to cover an anti-government student rally. So how on earth can they find only 16?

Josef Paunel is not one of the 16. Most likely, he will be part of the huddled masses, stopped at sea with no opportunity to tell their stories on neutral soil, loaded onto a U.S. Coast Guard cutter and deposited on these docks where cruise ship revelers used to land. On Friday morning, like the masses, Josef is silent as he takes an application from a relief worker before he enters the processing center. The form is in French, a language more likely to be understood by those few who live a world away, in the lush hills above the putrid shanty towns that are home to would-be refugees like Josef. No one explains what is printed on the form, that it is for seeking political asylum.

Last Sunday night, Josef crept aboard a Miami-bound refugee boat after dark in the port of Leogane, just southwest of the capital. He didn't know that several hours earlier the president of the United States had ordered all Haitian boat refugees returned without political asylum hearings. Ifhe had known, Josef tells me, he would have gone anyway, „to save my life." He had left his home in the Carrefour Feuilles slum because armed men had come looking for him several times. „They came in shadows in the night. Afterwards, there was shooting in the neighborhood," he says as he waits in line to receive $15 and a meal card from the Haitian Red Cross.

He didn't know who the gunmen were. Army? Police? Macoutes? Terrorist mobs: known as zenglendo? He wasn't about to stick around to find out. His neighborhood is considered to be one of the most loyal to ousted President Jean Bertrand Aristide, and an area where young men are often harassed by security forces linked to the de facto government. Josef is 19. I stare at his T-shirt. Three white sailors frolicking in 1940s Hollywood style. „Liberty Blues," it says. I ask if he will seek political asylum. He shrugs. He harbors no great hope anyone would believe him anyway. He has no proof. Besides, he doesn't know how much time he has left. „I will be in the street at the will of God," he says. I lose him in the crowd, and, for no reason other than to see his face again, I scour the mob of torsos for his benign sailors. I am terrified for him.

George Bush says people like Josef must apply for political asylum at the U.S. Embassy here. But the reason Josef may never join the lucky 16 is because it could be more dangerous to embark on the feared Haitian magouy, the

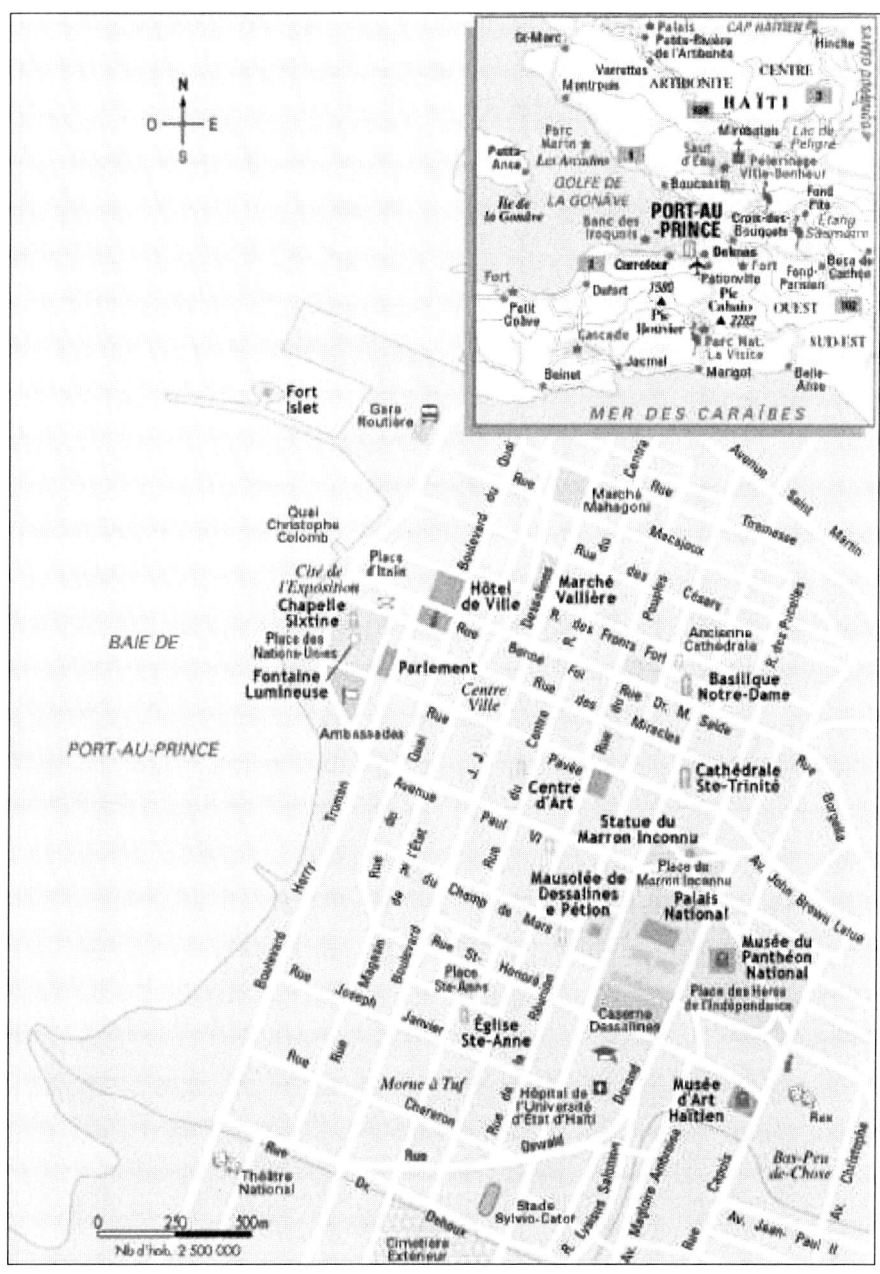

Haiti's Capital Port-au-Prince

labyrinth of red tape and dead ends. Besides, what address would he give? His mother's? She doesn't even know where he went that night when he fled Haiti. All of the would-be refugees in this teeming depot - 740 in several wooden boats - set sail after Bush issued his executive order May 24. None with whom I spoke said they knew about the order when they left. Few understood how to seek protection from what some described as persecution.

„What is this paper? What does it say?"some of the refugees wondered when asked if they would request asylum. There are all kinds of stories here. There are refugees who admit they left because they wanted to make a little more money. Others say they fled their poverty in desperation. I find 22-year-old Edeline Ketelin in a stained pink dress breast-feeding her 2-month-old baby. With no way to support her baby, she sold her bed and kitchen table and bought a $50 seat on a boat to Miami. But had she known how this voyage would turn out, she says she would have stayed home. Her first time on aboat, she had never imagined the power of the sea. As their wooden boat plied the turbulent Windward Passage, its sail ripped and the crew threatened to start tossing passengers overboard. Edeline could not breathe in the cramped quarters. Her baby was burning up with fever. She believes the U.S. Coast Guard saved them. If she had known about Bush's order, she tells me, she wouldn't have tried to leave Haiti.

I watch the refugees jam into the depot, looking much the way they might have looked on their refugee vessels, rib to rib, shoulder to shoulder melting in the tricks of the gwo lame, the „big ocean." Babies on their mothers breasts. Young men waiting to be fingerprinted. A faded sign overhead proclaims, „Welcome to Haiti." At the fringe of this madness, I approach the vice consul of the United States, a good-natured man named Howie Muir. Pointing to the crush of refugees, I ask him if the consulate is prepared to handle it. Yes, he says, there are three to seven windows open to assist asylum-seekers in filling out their forms. The refugees, he says, could either mail their claims or take them in person. If they are fearful, he says, they can give the name of a trusted contact who would be called by the embassy. He's confident this system will be safe for applicants.

But during the week, sources familiar with cases of persecution told me those in hiding are unlikely to take a number at the consulate. Besides, they have little faith that U.S. officials will grant them asylum, no matter how valid their fears may be. They know refugees are presumed economic until proved political, safe until proved dead. They know few in the U.S. government believe the Haitians because it is so difficult to confirm their stories. Too many times in this complex land, their stories are taken as myths. They simply can't be real because they can't be proven beyond a reasonable doubt. And it doesn't help the refugees that in Haiti hunger and politics bleed into each other, muddling claims of persecution. Still, how could the consulate find only 16?

The dramatic contrast between the swelling tide or refugees and the trickle of asylum claims raises crucial questions about the U.S. government's procedure for screening those whose lives could be in danger. So far, in Port-au-Prince only 330 have applied for political asylum, according to an embassy source. Of those, 166 were scheduled for interviews with U.S. immigration representatives here. Of 86 applicants already interviewed, only 16 have been approved for asylum. By contrast, in Guatanamo where 35,000 refugees were interviewed following interdiction, 9,700 have been granted permisssion to pursue asylum claims in the United States. That tells me that on neutral soil frightened Haitians feel safe enough to tell there stories, and be heard.

PRIEST IN HIDING

At first, I don't recognize him, his hunched figure taking purposely brisk steps up a garden path. I remember his electric presence in the diaspora, rustic protest signs in his circumference as he rattled fierce, effcient sound bites, the kind that usually earned him a few seconds on the evening news. But now here he is, eyes fixed upon his feet as they shuffle into a dim room, a safe room. Nine months after a coup toppled popularly elected President Jean-Bertrand Aristide, Miami 's most vocal Haitian political activist is still in hiding. Gerard Jean-Juste, the Roman Catholic priest who spent more than two decades in exile and returned to his homeland after Aristide won, says he wants to stay right here, in the shadows of an increasingly tense, uncertain, violent Haiti. As I watch him enter the darkened room on this recent morning, a watchful companion in his wake, I know his fear is very real. The night before, the brother of a powerful and vocal Aristide supporter was assassinated as he left his business downtown. The three bullets that killed Georges Izmery, relatives believe, were intended for his brother, Antoine, a wealthy merchant who, like Jean-Juste, was vowed to stay and fight the de facto government. The murder confirmed what the Aristide faithful know all too well. „Death is at our doorstep," says Jean- Juste, taking a seat across from me at a friend's table.

For the first time, I find his trademark drama in perfect context. In this safe room he is not an exile barking rhetoric from a fareaway land, as I'm sure many skeptical outsiders saw him years back. He is in Haiti. On the inside. And as we talk, I find he is not afraid to bark just as loud here. It is part of his mandate, even if his president is in exile. When Aristide came to office in early 1991, he named Jean-Juste liaison for the 10th Departrnent, as the exile community is called. After the Sept. 30 coup, Jean-Juste's office was seized, his staff forced to scatter. He was forced into hiding. But he remained quite plugged into the teledio, the rumor mill, the most popular news service in Haiti. And he often broadcasts on Miami's Haitian airwaves what he learns from trusted sources in hiding, in repressed slums, in the city streets.

The other night, for example, he told listeners of Little Haiti's Veye Yo about an army attack against residents of a nearby shanty town several weeks ago. „They raped a 10-year-old girl in front of her mother," he tells me. He tells me about an Aristide militant repatriated from the U.S. Navy base at Guantanamo Bay who was arrested by security forces and disappeared last month. He passes on such reports to human rights groups abroad in hopes of documenting the persecution he hears about every day. His own pursuit of safety has been traumatic. On his trail, security forces have already harassed friends and relatives three times since the coup. One month after Aristide's overthrow, soldiers burst into a safe house and handcuffed his assistant. Weeks later, plainclothes gunmen firing Galil assault rifles in the air surrounded a church rectory where they believed he was hiding. „Where is Jean-Juste?" they demanded. „Bring him down to us!" Claiming to be soldiers, the gunmen beat a seminarian and threw rocks on the roof of the church.

I find it remarkable that he is here. Beyond the risk he lakes, he is away from the politically ignored exile community at a time when it may need him the most. In his exile years, he organized active communities in several American cities and Canada. As executive director for the Haitian Refugee Center in Miami, he needled U.S. authorities for more humane treatment of Haitians, staging rallies and protests. His activism won him a cold shoulder from church authorities in Miami. It is ironic that after 26 years in exile, after so many struggles against Haitian dictatorships, so many press conferences, so many marches, after waiting so long, he savored Haitian democracy for just eight months.

Eight delicious months. That's one month less than the military-backed government has been in power. And now Jean-Juste hides. He rarely sleeps in the same place two nights in a row. His friends and contacts use different names when they call. „A lot of people think I'm in the States," he said, seeming impressed that he could keep a low profile for so long. Frankly, I, too, am impressed. As we say goodbye, he tells me his thoughts are with his „constituens" in the 10th department, the Haitians who listen to Creole radio in the kitchens of Miami restaurants, in the factories, in middle-class offices, in the tiny shops along North Miami Avenue. For them, Jean-Juste, voice of Haitian exiles, has this perfect sound bite: „Don't give up in the struggle for democracy. It's worth giving one's life for Haiti and its peoplc.".

POVERTY AND POLITICS

Those are the neighbor's children dancing in the rain, thrusting their faces skyward, trying to catch the raindrops in their mouths, singing a song that gets lost in the deluge. Those are not the children of Morales Leger. His children are inside, dry, pleased nevertheless to witness the downpour on such a suffocating day. From his house across the alley, he and I watch the neighbor's girls in their euphoric convulsions, drenched, entranced. Morales, a man of 64, has put out large tin pots to catch the clean rainwater, a blessing on this humid Feast of the Ascension. He pulls his young son close to hirn, kissing his cheek, explaining that „he easily gets the flu." The sudden storm caught me as we talked in his home. Entirely by chance. I found myself dropped in the middle of daily life in a squalid shanty strip where a desperate existence churns on endlessly, even on feast days. The rain hammered on the tin roof, veiling doorways and windows in misty curtains. A shower of relief.

To arrive at his house, I crossed the ancient slaughterhouse, walked along the muck-filled canal where pigs slept. The stench of human and animal and vegetable waste clung to my face like a mask. I took quick, shallow breaths through my mouth. A young woman bathed in the pig water, scrubbing her arms with a pink bar of soap, as if the rosy suds could extinguish the film of God-knows-what -is-dumped-in-there. I had passed more than a dozen wooden doorways framing swollen, naked children. Inside, their mothers and sisters and maybe cousins lounged in a darker dimension. Because this was a holiday, no one was working. Normally, this place is alive from 4:30 a.m. with wailing animals and haggling merchants who later seIl the fresh, warm meat at the market.

Then I slipped into the home of Morales Leger. Within dim, green walls there are two beds over which gauze mosquito nets dangle. There is a pink, child-size potty chair where his youngest girl, Philocles, 2, fidgets, naked. We talk about his life. He has not worked steadily in years. He was a sergeant in the military for 26 years, though he says he is not a political man. He left the service 17 years ago and has worked odd jobs since. He married a woman much younger, Margareth Coustan, 28. He delivered their four children in his home, on their matrimonial bed. He writes their names in my notebook in a spidery hand: Gina, 8, Philomene, 5, Philippe, 3. Philocles, 2.

He lifts the youngest from her chamber pot, slides a piece of cardboard over it's seat, and kisses the girl gently. „My consolation," he whispers, kissing her again. Then it begins to rain. I ask him about Haiti, about politics and refugee boats, and the regime du jour. But he shakes his head. „It is a divine presence that guides us. That is all," he says, offering me a seat in his home. The rain is powerful and relentless. In a while, his wife arrives, soaked and shivering. From what I can understand, she brings back what the market ladies don't sell.

A 25-year-old neighbor named Jonny explains that friends sometimes help her buy food. „She has many mouths to feed," he says. „She has plenty babies. And another is on the way. Margareth is five months pregnant." Why so many babies?" I ask. Morales answers for her. „They are my security," he says, clutching his chest. „They are my future." The gray canal outside his window has become a swift river rushing away. After the rain, everything along the alley glistens, and in the distance a rainbow has appeared.

A couple of days later, I watch a storm approach from my hotel balcony high above the capital. The city seems to dissolve gradually into silver sheets of water that sweep inland from the bay, across the slums and markets. I think of the slaughterhouse and the resilient souls who dwell on its fringe. Probably, they're happily getting wet. I know I learned something that afternoon at the house of Morales Leger. I learned that neither poverty nor politics can break the Haitian spirit. I learned that sometimes it can rain on the most putrid of days.

UNDER THE GUN

These are two stories of young men who hide, two stories of cries for help. The first is Michelete Pierre Joseph, a 22-year-old mechanic forced to leave home last fall, when soldiers stormed his house. The second is Paunel Joseph, a 19-year-old student from the same poor neighborhood. He, too, was forced to run away after gunmen burst through his door, shooting in the dark. Both are fervent supporters of ousted president Jean-Bertrand Aristide. Both believe they are hunted by military thugs. Both were returned to Haiti in a U.S. Coast Guard cutter.

Both had families, means of support. Neither had economic reasons for leaving, or any great desire to live outside Haiti - until fear made them run. Their stories illustrate the risks run by young men these days in poor slums like Carrefour Feuilles, the Aristide stronghold where both lived. Even supporters of the de facto government acknowledge that security forces are targeting Aristide loyalists there, searching their homes, arresting them, beating them. Fearing a dechouke, a popular uprising, the military appears to have launched a preemptive strike against members of Lavalas, Aristide's „tidal wave" party.

On Oct. 1, the morning after the military coup that ousted the populist presidentpriest, soldiers invaded Michelete's home, shooting in the air, demanding to see him. While his sister told the gunmen he wasn't there, Michelete scrambled over a wall and made a run for a nearby town. He knew these were men from the police station near his house. They knew him quite well. On election day, in December 1990, Michelete operated a voter registration booth from his house. He also had campaigned for Aristide, sticking posters all over his neighborhood.

The police beat his mother and his young nieces, whom the guards scorned as „lavalas children." Escorted by religious workers, his entire family, including his wife and 2-year-old daughter, went into hiding. They left behind a humble but comfortable home filled with food and clothes and appliances - proof that they did not flee for econornic reasons. Michelete hid for two months with friends, turning his back on a job that paid him up to $500 a month. On the night of Dec. 13, he boarded a small refugee boat. As he and 20 other refugees sailed toward Cuba, they were stopped by a Coast Guard cutter. Michelete wound up at the U.S. Navy base at Guantanamo Bay, Cuba, for two months. In interviews, he told U.S. immigration officials why he left home.

But on Feb. 1, an official told him he would have to go back to Haiti. He wept openly as he stepped onto the docks in Port-au-Prince. An Arnerican television crew spotted him in the crowd and asked where he lived. The crew journalists from Christian Science Monitor television, accompanied him to his home. That same day, military men in civilian clothes came and asked where he had been. Sensing danger, he called the journalists, who helped him into safety. Late that night, soldiers showed up at his house to take him away. The journalists wrote a letter to the U.S. Embassy on Michelete's behalf. „We believe he is in political danger and deserves your attention." Michelete went to the embassy twice. He was interviewed without a lawyer present.

Last rnonth, he received a form letter in French from the U.S. government: „Dear Mr. Pierre: We regret that we cannot approve your request to be admitted into the United States as a refugee." From a list of standard reasons, officials had checked three boxes: First, they said, his claim did not constitute persecution, according to U.S. immigration Iaw, Second, they said, his statements did not support a wellfounded, reasonable fear of persecution. Third, they said his claim of persecution „is not consistent with what is known and accepted as real conditions or practices in your country of origin."

Read: Things like this don't happen in Haiti. „I give up. They beat my mother. They want to kill me. My family is in hiding. 1 can't see my wife and my baby, and still, no one believes me," Michelete told me this week, tears of rage rising in his eyes. The odyssey of Paunel Joseph began two weeks ago, when he says gunmen burst into his house at 3 a.m., firing into the air and demanding that everyone come out. Paunel 's father, a mason, had campaigned for Aristide in the neighborhood during the elections. But that morning, Paunel wasn't sure if the gunmen were from the nearby police station or if they were zenglendo, a gang or common criminals. In fear, he hitched a ride to the port of Leogane and, with the help of a man he met along the way, got on a refugee boat.

It wasn't until last week, after a Coast Guard cutter brought him back from the high seas, that he was told his parents had disappeared that morning and that the men who took them away were police. He has been afraid to go back home, to the house friends say has been vacant since Paunel fled. Friends have warned him to stay away. I met him at the docks on the morning he was repatriated, Several days later, he showed up at my hotel to tell me his parents were missing. From his shirt pocket, he pulled out the application he got at the docks to begin his political asylum process. He would fill it out, he told me.

On Thursday, he returned with an appointment card. He has been given interview No. 417 at 8 a.m. June 11. „But if they ask about proof, I have nothing to offer them," he told me. „What about the fact your parents are missing?" I asked. „Is that enough?" he wondered. I didn 't want to tell him about Michelete, about how his odyssey turned out. I didn't want to tell him what I really thought, that most likely it would make no difference that he is afraid, that he hides, that his parents have vanished. Not in the eyes of those unwilling to accept that in Haiti such things happen every day. No, it probably would make no difference at all.

A DIFFERENT WORLD

„This," says the wealthy factory owner with a sweep of his hand across the restaurant filled with elegant patrons, across the kirs and the five-star rum cocktails, across the trays of delicate canapes, across the smoke rising from Campari lips, across the faces that belong to families with important names, „this is Haiti." He is a man nearing middle age, a handsome man with an acquired distrust of foreign journalists. He, as many here tonight, doesn't like reporters because always, when the conversation turns to Haiti's domestic situation, they talk in comparisons between the very rich and the very poor, comparisons that inevitably leave the elite in a rotten light.

I'm afraid we've fallen into this kind of dreaded conversation tonight. It is Friday night Happy Hour at La Belle Epoch, an upscale nook in the mountain suburb of Petionville. For years, this weekly happy hour has been a ritual of the bourgeoisie on „the hill," one of the few things you can count on - other than blackouts - in this unpredictable land. I ask the wealthy man how he feels about living this way while his compatriots in nearby shanty towns have - sewage dumps for front yards. Must be frustrating. I suggest.

„No, it is not frustrating," he says, putting down his tumbler of scotch to make a point. „You see, I can drink this whiskey with a clean conscience. I know that while I am here, there is a man starving in Cité Soleil. But my consience is clear. I work 18-hour days. I have helped build schools in the slums. I have given jobs to those people. I cannot do anything to stop them from starving." He tells me how he will lay off most of his workers tomorrow morning. The embargo imposed after the coup that ousted President Jean-Bertrand Aristide, he says, is strangling his business.

All through the night, as I mingle with regulars under slow ceiling fans on the terraced cafe. I know this is a Haiti far different than the one I've seen so far. I sit with women who look like they've stepped off the pages of French fashion magazines, shimmery hose, silky scarves, their faces watercolors of perfect shadows and light. This is the world of the MREs, those who are often labeled by outsiders as Haiti's „Morally Repugnant Elites." Haitians who care more about whether their Limoges dishes match their antique tables than the alarming infant mortality rate. Of course this is a stereotype. But it is a fairly accurate label of those who really believe the educated few, the wealthy few, should decide for the impoverished masses because they are too poor and stupid to know any better.

Tonight, I hear such convictions. I sense an intensifying anger toward foreigners. Over and over again. I hear how the wealthy Haitians feel mis-understood, beleaguered, besieged by international pressure to foster demo-cracy, to help create a middleclass, to respect the results of the December 1990 election that brought Aristide to power. Why don't they just leave us alone," they say. „Haiti is our business. Don't force democracy down our throats." In the powerful and healthy sectors of the capital, the fact that Aristide won by a landslide - the fact there was a democratic election to begin with - is almost anecdotal. He is out ofthe picture.

Even though their votes are few, their influence is massive. „You will see Aristide has very little to do with anything in Haiti," one member of the elite told me on my first night in Haiti. „He is nothing." What about what the masses want? I had asked. „Doesn't matter," she responded with a grin. Tonight's happy hour is not a very happy one. It is still uncertain who the next prime minister will be. The word in the clusters of guests is that Marc Bazin, who lost to Aristide 17 months ago by a landslide, is a shooin.

Days later, he was indeed nominated, and Friday he won approval of the Senate. He is likely to be approved within days by the Chamber of Deputies. If any politician exemplifies the Haitian elite, it is Bazin, a man who demanded that his campaign workers wear coats and ties to strategy meetings. Perhaps he is most reflective of the elite in the very fact that although he lost the election, he could still win. Because he has the money. Because he has the education. Because he has the support of the right people. The troubling thing about the Haitian aristocracy is that in too many cases education has not brought awareness. It has brought arrogance.

Despite their exposure to democratic ideals abroad, many haven't a clue what democracy is. „Aristide blew his chance. Now we have to step in and get things done right," one wealthy patron tells me. An elegant woman leans across the table and says: „Democracy cannot happen overnight. You cannot wipe away an entire class, just for the good of democracy." As I get up to leave, the wealthy factory owner reminds me not to write about the fictional Haiti that most journalists write about, the one where people say they are politically persecuted and yearning to be rid of the oppressive forces in their society. „Remember," he says, „this is Haiti." I said goodbye and stepped out of the party into the enormous world that is the other Haiti.«

MILITARY RULE ENDS
Carol Guzy, *Washington Post*

There was absolutely no complication when the five photography jurors of 1995 picked their recommendations as follows: Denis Farrell of the *Associated Press* had documented the first free elections in South Africa after the end of Apartheid. The photographs by Carol Guzy of the *Washington Post* from Haiti, in the words of the jury, had „not only captured the horror of a broken society in chaos, but also a remarkable spirit of survival and hope in a people oppressed for generations." David Leeson of the *Dallas Morning News* was praised for helping lead a Texas family to safety, as he himself had contributed to the rescue of this family from a flooded river. The Board favored the work by Carol Guzy who was announced as winner of the Pulitzer Prize „for her series of photographs illustrating the crisis in Haiti and its aftermath." Guzy had covered Haiti since the early 1980s, returning on her own when she could not convince an editor to send her. It was in September 1994, when U.S. troops landed in Port-au-Prince to help return president Jean-Bertrand Aristide to power. Guzy photographed, she later remembered, a „very joyous democracy march" when someone threw a grenade into the crowd, „so people were killed and wounded. I hit the ground with everybody else ..."

Carol Guzy, born on March 7, 1956, in Bethlehem, Pa., graduated from the North ampton County Area Community College in her hometown with an Associate degree in nursing in 1977 and planned to work as a nurse until a friend gave her a camera. „The nursing program," she later confessed, „gave me more than a degree. It helped me gain an understanding of human suffering and an incredible sensitivity to it. I know that without this background, my photography would have a totally different edge." In 1980, Guzy earned an Associate degree in applied science in photography from the Art Institute of Fort Lauderdale, Florida. Afterward she became an intern, and then a photographer at the *Miami Herald*. In 1986 Carol Guzy gained the spot news photography Pulitzer Prize, shared with Michelangelo E. du Cille for their pictures of the devastation caused by the 1985 eruption of Columbia's volcano Nevado del Ruiz. After having worked for the *Miami Herald* for eight years Guzy switched as a staff photographer to the *Washington Post* in 1988. Carol Guzy won her second Pulitzer Prize in the spot news photography category in 1995 for her series of pictures from the year before illustrating the political crisis in Haiti and its aftermath. Her third Pulitzer Prize followed in 2000 for her images depicting the plight of the Kosovo refugees. In 2011 Guzy was decorated with her fourth Pulitzer award for pictures of a catastrophic earthquake that struck Haiti the year before. Following now are key pictures of her 1995 award-winning Haiti photographs:

ARMY HELICOPTER

Photo, dated September 20, 1994, illustrates the joy with which Haitians welcomed one of the U.S. helicopters that took American troops into the center of Port-au-Prince, Haiti's capital. The helicopters were part of the U.S. peace operation to stabilize the country. Prior to this, the leaders of the military dictatorship had agreed to step down in the middle of October: Lt. Gen. Raoul Cedras, Brid. Gen. Philippe Biamby and Lt. Col. Michel Francois. The Clinton admini-stration had threatened to send in an invasion in order to reestablish former Haitian president Jean-Bertrand Aristide. That the invasion turned into a peace-ful and unbloody operation was due to the successful negotiations of former U.S. president James E. Carter who had convinced the military leaders of Haiti to relinquish power. The operation started on September 19, when the first U.S. troops landed at the Mais Gate International Airport. The deputy commander of the Haitian army, Brig. Gen. Jean-Claude Duperval, met the Americans, an indication how non-aggressive the conflict had turned out to be. The whole day, helicopters were flying troops into town without a single incident. Haitian civilians were watching the operation from hilltops, cheering and jubilating as this was a definite sign that the re-establishment of former president Aristide was on its way - without an U.S. invasion.

AMERICAN SOLDIERS

Photo, dated September 30, 1994, shows two U.S. soldiers shielding a Haitian civilian who had been attacked by the crowd. The civilian was believed to have thrown a grenade into the crowd that had been celebrating the end of the military dictatorship. The attack was believed to have come from pro-military forces. The hand-made grenade had exploded in the midst of people who had been marching in the streets of Port-au-Prince in order to show their support of Jean-Bertrand Aristide. It had killed five people and wounded another 47. This was the bloodiest incident since U.S. troops had arrived in Haiti. Three years earlier, the military leaders, with Lt. Gen. Raoul Cedras, had driven President Jean-Bertrand Aristide from office in a coup d'etat. Since then, the population had suffered under the violent new government which left the country in a desolate state. President Clinton as commander-in-chief of the U.S. forces had threatened an invasion should Cedras not step down voluntarily. Former U.S. president James E. Carter had managed to come to an agreement.

PRESIDENT'S RETURN

Photo, dated October 11, 1994, depicts a crowd of Haitians celebrating the resignation of General Cedras four days before he was scheduled to leave officially, on October 15. On that day, re-established President Jean-Bertrand Aristide was supposed to return to Haiti from his three-year exile. The man on the palm was waving a flag made of the U.S. flag and a portrait of Jean-Bertrand Aristide which indicated his gratitude toward the involvement of the U. S. When Aristide was ousted from office, the U.S. government had issued an embargo and threatened a military invasion in order to restore Aristide's power. Only thirty minutes before the deadline of this invasion did the American government come to an agreement with the top military leader, Gen. Cedras in Haiti. James E. Carter had managed to convince President Bill Clinton that Cedras had not led the coup against Aristide in 1991. Thus he and other military leaders were not forced into exile. Although Cedras left the country on his free will, other militaries decided to stay in Haiti.

Mexico

DRUG CORRUPTION EFFECTS

Sam Dillon/Julia Preston, *New York Times*

In 1998, when the jury of the Pulitzer Prize for International Reporting had to select the entries of this award category, it finally recommended the following exhibits to the Board's consideration: Nicholas D. Kristof of the *New York Times* was chosen „for his ability to offer insight on a wide variety of complicated international topics ... Kristofs work ranges widely from malaria's deadly comeback, to the wounds of war in Japan, to the three overlapping wars in the Congo." Next, the jury report mentions John Pomfret of the *Washington Post* for a series „on Laurent Kabila's rise to power in Zaire and his army's complicity with Rwandan Tutsis in exterminating Hutu refugees ... Pomfret brought to his task a rare ability to master a new part of the world, with impressive investigative acumen and a dogged determination to get a story that the new Congolese government had every reason to keep obscure."

A *New York Times* staff was third on the jury's list. The newspaper's series „on corruption in Mexico and the drug trade provides a powerful application of investigative reporting - inc1uding impressive sourcing and corraborating documentation. Together, the stories make an unassailable case; they are equally revealing of the flaws of U.S. intelligence-gathering on the subject. Uncovering critical facts in the 'drug war' is difficult enough. But to get to the corrupt core in such a secretive and dangerous environment represents a major journalistic achievement." The Pulitzer Board was impressed by the eulogy on the last exhibit and bestowed the 1998 award for International Reporting on the *New York Times* staff „for its revealing series that profiled the corrosive effects of drug corruption in Mexico."

The newspaper was honored for articles written by Sam Dillon and Julia Preston of the *New York Times*'s Mexico City bureau, Tim Golden, a national correspondent, and Craig Pyes, a freelance journalist. Stephen Engelberg served as editor of the award-winning series. These five journalists undertook something almost unheard-of in foreign correspondence: a major investigation of a foreign country, one vital to United States security. Drawing on c1assified intelligence documents and interviews with key officials in both Mexico and the United States, the series of artic1es explored how Mexico's drug barons had acquired the money and power to subvert an entire nation, bribing officials for protection and having Mexican journalists who dared to report on them either prosecuted for criminal libel or killed. The series had a significant effect not only in the United States but also in Mexico, where the press faced legal constraints and the threat of violence in pursuing this kind of investigation. It was mainly the work of Sam Dillon and Julia Preston that earned the *New York Times* team the 1998 Pulitzer Prize for International Reporting. Following are several of their award-winning articles, published between February and December 1977:

HIGH OFFICIALS INVOLVED

»The Governor of the Mexican state that borders Arizona is collaborating with one of the world's most powerful drug traffickers, creating a haven for smugglers who transport vast quantities of narcotics into the United States, according to American officials and intelligence. Officials said this conclusion was based on a wealth of evidence, including „highly reliable" informers' reports that the Governor, Manlio Fabio Beltrones Rivera, took part in meetings in which leading Mexican drug traffickers paid high-level politicians who were protecting their operations. According to the accounts, Raul Salinas de Gortari, the brother of the former President, received suitcases full of cash and was responsible for distributing the money to those attending. Present and former officials said the evidence of Mr. Beltrones' role was so detailed and compelling that the United States had included his name on a confidential document provided to the transition team of President Ernesto Zedillo listing more than a dozen officials suspected of corruption. Another Mexican Governor, Jorge Carrillo Olea, was included on the American blacklist because of reported entanglements with major drug dealers.

While Mr. Zedillo did not name either man to a federal post, both continue to wield considerable power in their states and nationally through their prominence in Mexico's governing party. Both seem to enjoy a tacit immunity from concerted criminal investigation in Mexico and the United States. Although Mexican governors are popularly elected, presidents have the power in practice to force their removal. Mr. Beltrones, in an interview, denied any links to drug traffickers and disputed American law-enforcement officials' assertions that Amado Carrillo Fuentes, one of Mexico's most wanted drug kingpins, was operating with impunity in his state, Sonora. In addition, Mr. Carrillo Olea, who presides over Morelos, the state just south of Mexico City, disputed charges that he had cooperated with traffickers. In a four-month investigation that draws on intelligence documents and interviews in the United States and Mexico, the *New York Times* examined how both governments handled the allegations against the two Governors. The result is a picture of official frustration on both sides of the border and, several officials asserted, a case study of why drug traffickers' political patrons often go unpunished.

Despite the recent disclosures about official corruption, U.S. officials say the Clinton Administration is planning to certify later this month that Mexico is cooperating with anti-drug efforts. Senior administration officials say that decision reflects a belief that Mexico's leadership is doing all it can against staggering odds. But many law-enforcement officials say it also shows that the Clinton Administration considers the narcotics fight less important than fostering commerce with this country's third-largest trading partner. Thus, these officials assert, intelligence reports suggesting corruption among Mexican politicians like Mr. Beltrones receive little attention in Washington. Similarly, agents working in Mexico feel they will get little support if they scrutinize the activities of powerful Mexican officials.

President Clinton praised Mexico last week for arresting the head of its anti-narcotics program on drug charges, citing the act as evidence that corruption, even „at the highest levels," was not being tolerated. Privately, however, American officials acknowledge that Mexican traffickers' political patrons are seldom the targets of law-enforcement officials in either country, even though they play an important role in the drug trade. In a previously undisclosed draft analysis, intelligence officials assert that Mexican traffickers take in as much as $10 billion annually, then spend as much as 60 percent of that money on bribes for officials at all levels. Officials say much of the derogatory information about Mr. Beltrones and Mr. Carrillo Olea, a former director of Mexico's anti-narcotics program, has been gathered through

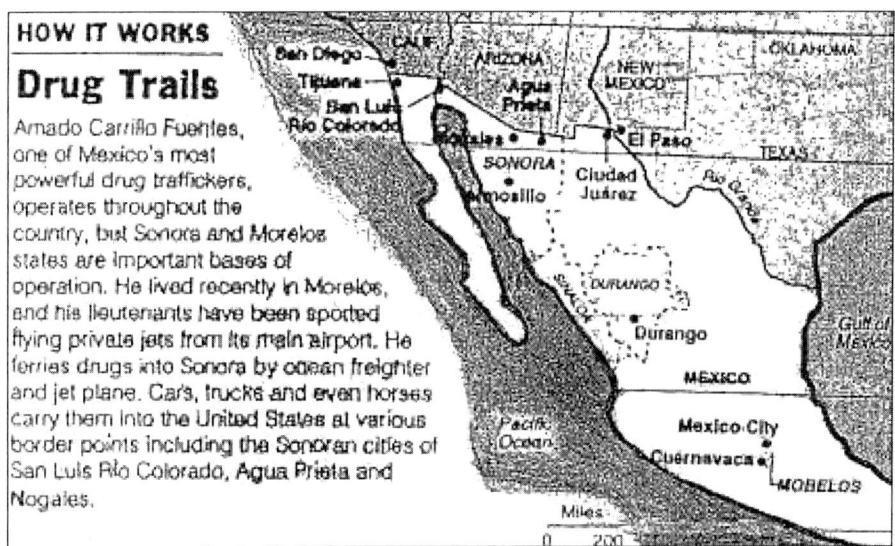

HOW IT WORKS

Drug Trails

Amado Carrillo Fuentes, one of Mexico's most powerful drug traffickers, operates throughout the country, but Sonora and Morelos states are important bases of operation. He lived recently in Morelos, and his lieutenants have been spotted flying private jets from its main airport. He ferries drugs into Sonora by ocean freighter and jet plane. Cars, trucks and even horses carry them into the United States at various border points including the Sonoran cities of San Luis Río Colorado, Agua Prieta and Nogales.

intelligence reports from informers, ranging from inside accounts to raw gossip. Their volume, specificity and persistence over time have persuaded many U.S. officials that the allegations against the Governors are well founded.

But officials said such material was of little use to prosecutors, who build their cases around witnesses willing to testify in American courts. In addition, American law-enforcement officials acknowledge a reluctance to invest time and money in pursuing corrupt foreign officials. „In Mexico," said one American prosecutor in a border state, „political protection is difficult to prove. If we could prove it, we'd have them all under indictment. There's a big difference between knowing something and proving it in a court of law. You have extremely reliable intelligence sources, but unless you can prove it, why burn your sources? You' d have their body parts spread all over Sonora."

Mr. Beltrones, for his part, says the reports collected by American intelligence and drug agents were fabricated by political rivals. „This sounds like a novel, filled with horror and error," he said. „At what time of the day do I govern, if I'm spending my time on all these crimes?" Wilburn Sears, a veteran agent with bulging forearms and a walrus mustache, took charge of the Drug Enforcement Administration's five-person office in Hermosillo, the capital of Sonora, in 1991. He soon came to the realization that the state was overrun by traffickers. Mexico's second-largest state in size, Sonora, was ideal terrain for smugglers, a sprawling region of cattle ranches and desert landing strips etched with raillines and lonely roads leading north to more than 300 miles of remote border. Vast quantities of marijuana were pouring up the highways. Passenger cars were ferrying methamphetamines over the line into Arizona. And the traffickers were traveling in and out of Hermosillo and other Sonoran cities in long convoys or in private jets, under the noses of state and federal police officers.

„The feds were protecting the airports," Sears said in a recent interview. „They were doing everything out there except kick-starting the narcos' airplanes." It was in those years that Mr. Carrillo Fuentes began the ascent that would make him one of Mexico's shrewdest and most influential drug smugglers. The nephew of one of the country's narcotics pioneers, he had been building his organization in the late 1980s, wooing marijuana farmers to the south in Sinaloa, the heroin clans of Durango and especially the cocaine barons of Cali, Colombia. Most of all, he had cultivated the skills of Mexican narcotics diplomacy and knew what it took to buy protection from powerful politicians.

In a lengthy 1994 study, the Drug Enforcement Administration's analysts in El Paso, Texas, painted a detailed picture of how Carrillo Fuentes cultivated

Mexican police officials and political leaders, including Mr. Beltrones and Mr. Carrillo Olea. According to the classified analysis, based on field reports from more than a dozen American agencies, the trafficker has „purchased influence at various key levels in the Mexican government," giving him „powerful connections" that ensure safe passage of his drug loads through Mexico to the United States. In the early 1990s, Mr. Carrillo Fuentes was moving to make Hermosillo a strategic staging area, American officials said. He was living in a pink stucco rnansion down the street from the American consul's residence in a palm- fringed neighborhood. He had begun construction of a much more extravagant, onion-domed house - locals called it a Thousand and One Nights - a few blocks north. And among other properties he or his associates had acquired was a communications center across town.

In August 1991 Mr. Beltrones was elected governor, and in October he moved into the colonial-style governor's palace in Hermosillo. He was a rising star in the governing Institutional Revolutionary Party, one of a handful of ambitious 40-something leaders sometimes called the „babysaurs," to distinguish them from the older „dinosaurs" who have long ruled the party. During his early career, Mr. Beltrones had been the understudy to Fernando Gutierrez Barrios, Mr. Salinas' interior minister and one of the pioneers of Mexico's secret police. Some have seen Mr. Beltrones as a possible presidential candidate.

But about the time that he took the oath of office, American officials began picking up reports from confidential informers documenting his ties to Mr. Carrillo Fuentes. In an interview, Mr. Beltrones raised his voice when reporters described D.E.A. reports alleging that he had accepted payments from Mr. Carrillo Fuentes. „These reports are incredible in every sense, filled with fantasy and lies," Mr. Beltrones said. The D.E.A, he added, „is completely out of focus." As evidence of his hostility to drug trafficking, Mr. Beltrones asserted that he had virtually driven Mr. Carrillo Fuentes from Hermosillo. A high-ranking Mexican official said that Mr. Beltrones learned of Mr. Carrillo Fuentes' residences in Hermosillo shortly after he took office. Months later, the official said, Beltrones ordered aides to videotape Mr. Carrillo Fuentes' arrival at the local airport in a Lear jet, and his travels about the state capital in a convoy guarded by police vehicles. The governor delivered the videotape to President Carlos Salinas de Gortari, the official added, and federal authorities later confiscated four of Mr. Carrillo Fuentes' properties, including the onion-domed mansion. „How would the D.E.A explain that I'm the one who took away this man's houses?" Mr. Beltrones asked.

American officials and reports acknowledge that four of Mr. Carrillo Fuentes' Hermosillo houses were seized. But they said his organization continued to use at least eight other properties, including the communications center. The officials maintain that Sonora remains one of Mr. Carrillo Fuentes' most important operating bases. In the early 1990s, Mr. Carrillo Fuentes set out to increase his air smuggling operations, and for that he needed help at the highest levels of the federal bureaucracy. Under Mexican law the federal government enforces the drug statutes. At the time, Mexican authorities were working with their American counterparts to perfect a radar network that tracked aircraft flying north from Colombia. The system allowed controllers to follow unidentified planes on a walllsized screen in Mexico City and to scramble interceptor aircraft if the planes entered Mexico.

Mr. Carrillo Olea, a former army general whom President Salinas appointed to oversee the drug intelligence center created with American help, was in charge of the radar system. American officials spoke highly of him, and many reacted with disbelief to the first intelligence reports that he was helping the traffickers. But by 1992, additional reports persuaded analysts at El Paso's intelligence center that Mr. Carrillo Olea was helping Mr. Carrillo Fuentes. (The two are not related.) As one intelligence document reads: „Reporting from 1992 indicates that the former Mexican coordinator against narcotics trafficking, Jorge Carrillo Olea, was at that time Amado Carrillo Fuentes' most influential associate in the Mexican government. Carrillo Olea was in charge of controlling the radar detection in Mexico, and by utilizing the information provided to hirn, he was able to ensure safe passage of Carrillo Fuentes' aircraft.“ In an interview last week, Mr. Carrillo Olea, now Governor of Morelos, called these accounts „a oomplete barbarity.“ „What can I say about a thing like this,“ he asked „except that it is a rotund and absolute lie? It has no foundation whatever.“

American officials say that reports about Mr. Beltrones' drug activities have come from nearly two dozen sources inside the Mexican government and its law-enforcement agencies. The 1994 D.E.A study of Mr. Carrillo Fuentes described how his smuggling organization, identified by his initials, A.C.F., expanded „full force“ into Sonora. „Manlio Fabio Beltrones Rivera is well documented as being associated with the A.C.F. organization,“ the report reads. It quotes a commander of the Federal Judicial Police as stating that Mr. Beltrones is „involved in protecting drug traffickers passing through Sonora.“ In 1994, Sears searched the D.E.A.'s computerized intelligence files and found numerous references to Mr. Beltrones and members of his family, according to a memo Mr. Sears wrote: „The Governor,“ the document noted, is mentioned in cases „from San Diego to Tucson.“

Among the most persuasive intelligence reports, officials said, are accounts of regular meetings at a ranch in which Mexico's most notorious traffickers gave cash to Raul Salinas, who in turn distributed it to the senior politicians present. Mr. Salinas, whose brother was President of Mexico at the time, is now awaiting trial in Mexico City on charges of murder and financial wrong-doing, and investigators have found more than $100 million in his overseas bank accounts. He maintains that his fortune has legitimate sources. Mr. Beltrones was said to have attended three meetings at the ranch from 1990 to 1993, and the officials said Mr. Carrillo Fuentes was present for at least one.

In August 1994, the State Department sent William Francisco, a former Army infantry officer, to serve as the senior diplomat at the American Consulate in Hermosillo. Almost immediately he trained his sights on the Governor, raising questions about the reports of corruption and misconduct, which were being ignored by other American officials. Mr. Sears and his D.E.A. staff in Hermo-sillo were busy trying to keep track of the five major mafias operating all across northwest Mexico. They spent much of their time traveling between Hermosillo and the distant border gateways of Tijuana or Cludad Juárez. „They gave me a new car,“ Mr. Sears said, „and I put 35,000 miles on it in seven months. We were just keeping our heads above water. There were so many reports of corruption about everybody that most of the time we didn't even write it up. We just had to accept the fact that corruption exists.“ Mr. Francisco felt otherwise. Shortly after his arrival, he received a briefing from Mr. Sears about the major Mexican traffickers and studied the intelligence report naming Mr. Beltrones as an associate of Mr. Carrillo Fuentes.

Then, Mr. Sears recalled, Mr. Francisco traveled south to the state of Sinaloa and came back with new reports about the pervasive influence of traffickers. At his request, Mr. Sears checked D.E.A.'s computerized intelligence files and found extensive references to Mr. Beltrones. In an unusual step for a State Department official assigned to an obscure consulate, Mr. Francisco began recruiting his own sources about the drug trade and Mr. Beltrones' role in it. When Mr. Francisco heard a report that Mr. Beltrones was being considered for a post in President Zedillo's cabinet as head of Mexico's powered Interior Ministry, he grew downright alarmed. On Nov. 15, 1994, after just 12 weeks as consul, he stalked into his office and fired off an urgent cable to the embassy in Mexico City. „Request for assistance to verify and further develop info of allegations of extensive criminal activities by Sen. Gov. Manlio Fabio Beltrones Rivera, who may be under consideration to become the next Secretary of Gobernacion,“ Mr. Francisco headlined his dispatch, using the Spanish term for Mexico's Interior Ministry.

Mr. Francisco complained that the D.E.A. and customs agents in Hennosillo were too preoccupied with minor traffickers and should instead pursue political figures like Mr. Beltrones, whom he tenned „a truly major kingpin player.“ His cable - which mixed drug, intelligence with lurid tales about the personal lives of Sonoran officials - stunned Mr. Sears and officials at the embassy in Mexico City. Although Mr. Francisco had no direct or specific evidence to document his allegations, he called for a criminal investigation that could lead to Mr. Beltrones' indictment in the United States. The cable reached the desk of the American Ambassador, James Jones, and American officials said he viewed it skeptically. Jones was instinctively cautious about the reliability of law-enforcement intelligence reports. In addition, several officials said, the criminal investigation of a foreign official poses daunting political and practical difficulties. Collecting intelligence on an official like Mr. Beltrones is one thing. But several officials said that building a criminal case against him - linking him to specific drug shipments or conspiracies that violate American law - would be quite another.

Informers willing to whisper an allegation under cloak of confidentiality would have to be persuaded to travel to the United States to testify before a grand jury, and perhaps later at a public trial. That would endanger not only their careers but their lives. Even if all these difficulties were overcome, the accused official would have to be extradited to the United States for trial. Mexico has never before extradited a Mexican citizen accused of narcotics trafficking. (Juan Garda Abrego, a Mexican trafficker, was expelled to the United States a year ago, not extradited, and he holds American citizenship.) „Indicting a public official of a foreign government is cumbersome to say the least,“ the official said. „And then getting them out of Mexico - it never happens.“ Mr. Francisco's recommendation was never seriously considered by the embassy's top officials. Virtually everyone there reportedly regarded it as quixotic, even „goofy,“ as one put it. In fact, officials said, the idea of launching an U.S. criminal inquiry into Mr. Beltrones' dealings was not raised with senior officials in Washington.

As it happened, Mr, Zedillo and his advisers, preparing to take office on Dec. 1, 1994, had already given American officials a less public means of dealing with allegations involving officials like Mr. Beltrones. „The Zedillo administration wanted names of people believed to be corrupt, or possibly in the pay of traffickers, whom the United States would not like to see in the new Government,“ a former American official said. Mr. Jones gave Mr. Zedillo's transition team a list of about 15 current and former Mexican officials. It included Mr. Beltrones and Mr. Carrillo Olea, three officials said. A senior Mexican official said in an interview that neither Mr. Beltrones nor any other of Mexico's 31 active governors was ever considered for a post in Mr. Zedillo's

Cabinet. The Zedillo Government apparently has never followed up on the American warning by investigating either Governor. But embassy officials felt that delivery of the list had shifted all responsibility onto Mexican authorities, where it belonged. Early in 1995 the embassy's No. 2 official, David Beall, telephoned Francisco and lectured him about the cables he had written, American officials said. Mr. Francisco interpreted the call in subsequent conversations with associates as an order to stop reporting on the Governor. A senior American official denied that. „He may have been told, 'For your own safety and forthe integrity of what law enforcement is trying to do, don't be a cowboy,' the official said. „But he was not muzzled."

Still, if he stopped filing cables, Mr. Francisco continued to voice suspicions about Mr, Beltrones' activities. He even shared his opinions of the Governor with Nicolas Escalante Barrett, Mexico's consul general in Phoenix, who reported the incident to Mexico's Foreign Ministry. American officials and Mr. Beltrones said they believed that the Foreign Ministry complained to the American Government about Mr. Francisco's conduct. In September 1995, Mr. Francisco was transferred to Frankfurt. He declined to be interviewed for this article. One senior American official insisted that Mr. Francisco's transfer was a „routine rotation." Others disagreed. „He was a loose cannon," an official said. „He was probably going to get himself killed if we didn't get him out of there." Mr. Carrillo Fuentes has continued to consolidate power. His success at sending cocaine-laden aircraft undetected into Mexican airspace and his largess have led Mexicans to nickname him Lord of the Heavens.

In January, Mexican troops stormed a ranch in Sinaloa during a wedding reception for Mr. Carrillo Fuentes' sister, hoping to capture him. But word leaked, and he slipped away. In the days that followed, authorities acknowledged that three private jets, operating without flight plans, had ferried wedding guests to Sinaloa from the airport in Cuernavaca, the capital of Morelos state, where Mr. Carrillo Olea is governor. American narcotics officials say that Mr. Carrillo Fuentes has been living in Morelos, where he owns many properties, and that his fleet of narcotics jets frequently lands and takes off unchallenged from the Cuernavaca airport. Mr. Carrillo Olea said in an interview that his aides had traced ownership of all residences identified as belonging to the trafficker, without finding his name. Any further investigation, he said, is the responsibility of federal authorities.

Mr. Beltrones is wrapping up his six-year term as one of Mexico's more popular governors. He is working closely with Gov. Fife Symington of Arizona on a plan to improve cross-border commerce and investment. Recent developments have left Mexico's antinarcotics program in chaos. The commander of January's failed wedding raid was Gen. Jesus Gutierrez Rebollo, then the national anti-narcotics coordinator. He was arrested last week and accused of having accepted payments from Carrillo Fuentes for seven years, ever since he was put in a command post in the anti-drug program. Mr. Carrillo Fuentes' capture was intended as a dramatic symbol of progress in the drug war weeks before March 1. By that deadline annually, President Clinton certifies that drug transiting or producing nations are pursuing serious anti-drug efforts. Instead, the trafficker is still at large and still spending his billions. „Money corrupts," said Doug Wankel, who just retired as D.E.A. operations chief, „and in Mexico it's getting to the point where the traffickers can corrupt absolutely."«

DRUGS CONNECT LEADERS

»The owner of a department store in the provincial capital of Culiacan was driving to work one moming last September when three unmarked sedans without license plates surrounded his gray Oldsmobile. As passers-by watched in terror, four men brandishing assault rifles hauled the man, Romulo Rico Urrea, from his car, forced him into one of theirs and sped away. Mr. Rico has not been seen since Sept. 25, 1996. But a notebook dropped in his car by one of the kidnappers, as well as evidence gathered by military investigators, links the abduction to Gen. Jesus Gutierrez Rebollo, the former head of Mexico's anti-drug agency who was arrested last month on charges of collaborating with one of the country's most powerful cocaine barons. Mr. Rico is one of at least 51 Mexicans who have disappeared in the last three years after kidnappings in which there were signs of Government security force involvement, according to lists compiled by relatives, human rights organizations and the press. Now, evidence is emerging to tie many of the abductions to the war against powerful drug traffickers, which has increasingly been under the command of Mexico's military. „We are everyday citizens under attack, caught in the crossfire between narcos, authorities and narcoauthorities," said Lucfa Jurado, whose husband, a semiprecious-stone trader from the border city of Ciudad Juarez, was seized on the front step of his home on Oct. 6, 1996. „It has gotten to the point where it can happen to anyone."

A majority of the victims have no proven ties to drug traffickers or other criminal activities, relatives and human rights leaders contend, although a number have had brushes with the authorities. They tend to be businessmen, students and other citizens who were going about their lives," said Oscar Loza of the Commission for the Defense of Human Rights in the state of Sinaloa, where at least nine people have disappeared. Mexico's military has traditionally played a supporting role in the fight against drug trafficking, mainly eradicating narcotics crops. Shortly after he took office in 1994, President Ernesto Zedillo, facing widespread corruption in the state and federal police, began to place military officers and troops in key positions in the battle against the drug cartels. Gen. Gutierrez was appointed Mexico's chief anti-drug official in December 1996, and army officers were given command of state and municipal police forces in Sinaloa, through which large quantities of drugs flow. Just last week, the army took over narcotics operations in the border state of Baja California.

Since the arrest of General Gutierrez, who was highly decorated, a number of families of missing Mexicans have come forward after enduring their anguish in silence for months and even years. The number of known victims is growing. There is evidence that in addition to Mr. Rico, five men who disappeared since last September in northern Mexico where abducted in operations commanded by General Gutierrez and carried out by his deputies during his two-month tenure as head of the national drug agency or before that, when he was the senior commander of the Fifth Military Region in central Mexico. The abductions in which General Gutierrez appears to have had a role are only a fraction of those reported. The general's lawyers did not respond to requests for comment. The disclosures about the kidnappings raise new questions about General Gutierrez's ascent to the highest position in Mexico's war on drugs, and about Mr. Zedillo's moves to expand the role of the armed forces in the anti-narcotics campaign. Several months before Defense Minister Enrique Cervantes Aguirre recommended General Gutierrez to the President for the top anti-drug job, the Mexican military had substantial evidence implicating the general's two closest aides in the kidnapping of Mr. Rico. Both aides were arrested with their commander on drug charges on Feb. 18. The kidnapping allegations apparently never reached the highest levels.

Mr. Cervantes acknowledged that neither he nor President Zedillo had had any doubts about General Gutierrez until about two weeks before his arrest. Mr. Rico's relatives say they believe that he came under suspicion of drug trafficking because Miguel Angel Rico Urrea, his brother, was falsely accused on drug charges in 1992 and served prison time before he was cleared. A judge ordered his release, but the day he was to leave prison he was murdered. On Sept. 16, 1996, soldiers in Culiacan swarmed into the home of Enrique Rico, another brother. The raid, conducted without a warrant, was led by a brash officer who identified himself with a name that later proved false. Romulo Rico was seized nine days later. At first, federal police agents told his relatives he was in custody at their headquarters. But 24 hours later the same agents denied they had ever seen him, relatives said. At about the same time, Mr. Rico's wife of 33 years, Teresa, received an anonymous telephone call from a man who said her husband had been detained by someone named Horacio Montenegro Ortiz. The caller said he had seen Mr. Montenegro escorting his prisoner onto a military plane at the local airport.

The family did not recognize the name at the time, but it turned out to be significant. Mr. Montenegro, a former army captain, had long worked closely with General Gutierrez. Later that day Mr. Rico's family discovered a notebook that one of his abductors had accidentally dropped between the front seats of his car. The scribbled, sometimes encoded phrases showed that the writer was a military officer who was in Sinaloa pursuing an inquiry into the murder in Mexico City on Sept. 14 of a leading antinarcotics police commander, Ernesto Ibarra Santes. The huge operation to find and capture Mr. Ibarra's killers' was commanded by General Gutierrez, senior army commanders recently confirmed. Unlike many families of the disappeared, the Ricos did not remain silent. They took the notebook to military and police authorities and human rights groups in the state and the capital, raising questions ab out the mysterious Mr. Montenegro. In October, shortly before General Gutierrez was appointed commissioner of the National Institute to Combat Drugs, more than a hundred federal legislators signed a petition calling for a deeper investigation into Mr. Rico's kidnapping.And the military told the family that it was opening its own inquiry.

One man who took up the case was a newly appointed Attorney General, Jorge Madrazo Cuellar, a former human rights lawyer. But the Federal Judicial Police under his command steadfastly denied knowing anything about Mr. Rico, Mr. Madrazo said in an interview. So he sent the Rico family to General Gutierrez, recently appointed to the drug agency at the time, thinking he was „the right man to conduct the investigation." „We were surprised at how pleasant and friendly the general was," Mrs. Rico said bitterly in an interview. „I thought I had finally found the person who was going to give me back my husband." In 10 meetings with her, Mrs. Rico said, General Gutierrez never acknowledged that he had directed the operations in Sinaloa at the time of her husband's kidnapping or that Mr. Montenegro had become his deputy in the drug institute, where the conversations took place. Defense Minister Cervantes confirmed in a speech on Feb. 18 that Mr. Montenegro, „a man with a disastrous reputation," was under military investigation for the Rico kidnapping. He added that last year General Gutierrez had disobeyed „explicit orders" from the high command to dissociate himself from Mr. Montenegro.

Another piece of evidence linking General Gutierrez to the kidnapping became clear after his arrest. Mexican television broadcast film of Capt. Javier

Garcia Hernández, an army intelligence officer and aide to General Gutierrez who was arrested on drug charges the same day as his commander. Relatives who had witnessed the raid at Enrique Rico's home said they recognized Captain Hernández as the brash officer who had commanded the search. In late February, military officials told the Rico family confidentially that the notebook in Romulo Rico's car belonged to Captain Garcia Hernández. In recent days, a half-dozen northern Mexican families, with nine disappeared relatives among them, have come together to somber meetings in the cramped Mexico City apartment where Teresa Rico and her children have taken refuge. They found

A department store owner was kidnapped in the city of Culiacán.

one another through human rights organizations they had approached after General Gutierrez's arrest. As they sadly share photographs of missing loved ones, they worry ab out their own safety. Human rights activists who helped them have received death threats, apparently to stop their publicizing disappearance cases. In interviews the activists confirmed the threats and asked not to be identified.

Gilberto Chaldez, the 22-year-old nephew of two hoteliers who were abducted from the border city of Tijuana, said he had broken down as he watched the televised announcement of General Gutierrez's arrest. Mr. Chaldez, a burly man with a buzz cut, had to stop to control his sorrow once again last week when he recalled his reactions. „We were sure those men participated in kidnapping my uncles," Mr. Chaldez said. „We thought it meant they would finally be released." Rogello Verber Mondaca, 59, is the father of two men who were kidnapped by uniformed army troops from a highway south of Tijuana on Jan. 6. Mr. Verber Mondaca, who until a few years ago was the Deputy Police Chief of Tijuana, called on his friends in local law enforcement to help him mount a statewide search for his sons Rogello and Raul, to no avail. His son Rogello, 28, suffers from advanced Hodgkin's disease and has a catheter in his heart for treatment, Mr. Verber Mondaca said. He produced news photographs and clippings showing that General Gutierrez was conducting anti-drug operations in the area at the time his sons disappeared.

Mrs. Jurado and her family have become outraged about the official response to their quest for her husband, Ruben Guillermo Jurado, 39. A senior official of the state of Chihuahua, where the Jurados live, confirmed in an interview this week that Mr. Jurado had been seized by armed men wearing federal drug police uniforms. Nevertheless the official, who insisted on anonymity, said state investigators believed that Mr. Jurado might have been kidnapped by drug traffickers, because of „narcotics-related wrapping materials" found in his home. The Jurado family indignantly accused the authorities of inventing charges against Mr. Jurado. They point out that the police never searched his residence or workshop, before or since he disappeared. Some relatives have nearly despaired of going through Mexican institutions. Maria de los Angeles de Beltran, whose husband, Manuel, disappeared in 1994, wrote to the United States Secretary of State, Madeleine K. Albright, pleading for help. „Our Govemment doesn't fight drug trafficking," Mrs. Beltran wrote angrily. „It just administers it."«

MISTAKES ABOUT CORRUPTION

»Early last year, a handful of senior American officials in Washington received an alarming secret intelligence report on Mexico. It was on its face, officials said, the sort of document that can force policy makers to change the way they think about a country or a region. In a matter of just weeks, the National Security Agency reported, Mexican drug traffickers had laundered some $6 billion in illicit profits through their country's financial system. The spy agency based its conclusion on an elaborate surveillance of the contacts between drug gangs and their business associates. Almost immediately, State Department officials delivered an angry protest to the Mexican Ambassador over the apparently vast breach in his country's defenses against drug trafficking. Then, however, American officials' outrage gave way to chagrin. The agency, they realized, was asserting that Mexico had taken in a flood of dollars nearly equal to its entire foreign investment that year without any discernible impact on its economy. „It just couldn 't have happened," one official said. And he added, „You have to ask: 'Which reports am I supposed to believe?'"

An examination by the *New York Times*, based on scores of interviews and a review of classified documents, indicates that the agency's discredited assessment was by no means an isolated lapse in the annals of United States intelligence on drugs and corruption in Mexico. Rather, as the United States weighed momentous decisions about Mexico in the 1990s - from the North American Free Trade Agreement to the $12.5-billion bailout of the Mexican economy after a currency crisis - American policy makers were blindsided by some important developments, misinformed about others and inattentive to many more. After insisting for years that Mexican corruption was an old affliction being cured by a new generation of political leaders, senior American officials have begun to acknowledge that the growing power and influence of Mexico's drug traffickers have led to a law-enforcement crisis so deep that it threatens the stability of a country that shares almost 2,000 miles of border with the United States. Yet a good deal of the information upon which that conclusion is based had languished in the files of American law-enforcement agents and intelligence -officers for years, officials said. Only rately did such intelligence command the time of senior policy makers. Even less frequently did it prompt them to take any action.

„A lot of this information has been out there, in the bowels of the system," said Donald F. Ferrarone, who, before his recent retirement as head of the Drug Enforcement Administration's field office in Houston, oversaw investigations that dealt closely with the political protection of Mexican drug traffickers. „But it has been ignored, because people don't want to believe it, the extent and degree of corruption." Allegations over almost two years of drugrelated corruption in the inner circle of former President Carlos Salinas de Gortari have forced American officials to rethink the issue. The governing party's loss of control of the lower house of Congress in mid-term elections last week now raises the possibility that Mexican legislators will examine more closely than ever the misdeeds of the ruling elite. In recent weeks, senior Clinton Administration officials have begun to plot a wholesale reorganization of the Federal Government's drug-intelligence apparatus. Officials said the overhaul will seek to pool some information that is now tightly held by different agencies, disseminate important material more quickly, and thin out a vast intelligence bureaucracy in which different offices perform similar work.

But many officials argued that the failures of American intelligence on Mexico are even deeper and more serious than policy makers have acknowledged. And the problems, by all accounts, have been as much ones of demand as of supply. Law-enforcement agents who worked in and on Mexico while Mr. Salinas was a prized ally of the United States said they were often discouraged by political pressure to keep the drug issue from jeopardizing improvements in the economic relationship between the two countries. At crucial moments, they asserted, intelligence struggled with policy and policy won. For their part, many officials in Washington said they could not help but grow skeptical of the intelligence after being deluged with vague, uncorroborated informants' reports and analysis that was either so thin on evidence or so carefully hedged as to be of little use. At the height of such problems, during the American debate over the free-trade accord that was approved in November, 1993, Mexico's strategic importance to the United States came into focus as never before. The personal reputations and political strength of Mexican leaders became central questions of American foreign policy.

Yet in the case of Mr. Salinas' influential elder brother, Raul, American investigators did little more than file away allegations that he was not only taking kickbacks on government contracts but cutting deals with cocaine traffickers, officials familiar with the reports said. Drug-enforcement agents said they dropped an inquiry into telephone calls by drug traffickers to the Mexican President's offices after they had trouble figuring out whom the traffickers had called. American officials so thoroughly failed to share information on Carlos Salinas' Deputy Attomey General, Mario Ruiz Massieu, that three different agencies raised questions about his conduct without ever hearing of Customs Service reports that suitcase after suitcase of cash had been deposited in Mr. Ruiz Massieu's account in a Texas bank.

Nearly a year after Mr. Salinas left the presidency, a secret Central Intelligence Agency assessment of his own reported misconduct argued that at the least, his hands-on governing style made it „unlikely that he had no knowledge of his brother's affairs or the shady dealings of other close associates." But while a fuller understanding of the drug traffickers' penetration of Mexican politics may await the outcome of criminal investigations that now extend from San Diego to Switzerland, the revelations of wrongdoing have already contributed to a reordering of United States policy. In a recent interview, the newly departed American Ambassador to Mexico, James R. Jones, recalled his arrival here four years ago. His priorities were to manage trade, promote investment and push for more democratic politics. Then, the list began to change. „The majority of my time," he said in May, as he prepared to leave the country, „is now spent on administration-of-justice issues, corruption and narcotics trafficking." As Carlos Salinas took office at the end of 1988, the perspective of United States officials could hardly have been more different.

The Drug Enforcement Agency and the C.I.A. had traced a growing traffic in drugs through Mexico since the mid-1980s, when the United States began to increase pressure on Colombian smuggling routes through the Caribbean.

MOUNTAINS OF DRUGS ARE SEIZED
A Mexican soldier carried cocaine to a pile for incineration in Matamoros in April. The cocaine was part of a shipment of about 10 tons that was found inside a tanker truck

But through the early 1990s, officials said, American experts remained convinced that Mexican traffickers had nothing close to the financial clout or political influence of their Colombian partners. American officials also drew a sharp distinction between the young, American-trained technocrats whom Mr. Salinas brought to power and the more experienced, conservative - and corrupt - politicians whom he appointed in areas like law enforcement, national security and the ruling Institutional Revolutionary Party.

At the start of his six-year term, Mr. Salinas seemed to attack drug trafficking with a new zeal. Having been told by the Bush Administration that the problem could obstruct closer economic ties, Mr. Salinas ordered the seizure of more drug shipments, the eradication of more drug crops, and the capture of a powered drug trafficker, Miguel Ángel Felix Gallardo. John D. Negroponte, the United States Ambassador to Mexico from 1989 to 1993, gave voice to the prevailing optimism. In a confidential memo-randum to law-enforcement officials at the embassy, Mr. Negroponte hailed Mr. Salinas' early steps as „dear proof that Mexico is interested in meaningful cooperation with the United States to reduce this flow of drugs." In a recent interview, he recalled: „I don't think we ever doubted Salinas' personal integrity. He was a very disciplined guy. He always wore that Casio sports watch. He worked like hell."

Several law-enforcement officials who served at the embassy were more skeptical. But they said they also had trouble making their case at a time when the drug problem, like other sources of friction between the two countries, was supposed to be „managed" so as not to threaten growing investment and trade. As United States law-enforcement officials had untangled a Mexican cover-up of the 1985 assassination of an American drug-enforcement agent, Enrique S. Camarena, many became convinced that drug corruption reached the highest levels of the Mexican Government. They believed that unless that system was dismantled, drug interdiction efforts were condemned to futility. Now, American agents were being told to simply do the best they could. „There was a sense that Mexico was a place that we were just going to have to deal with in the shape that it was in," said Matthew J. Maher, a veteran of the Camarena investigation who served as the Drug Enforcement Administration's international-operations chief until 1994. „The only questions you asked were whom you could deal with and how far you could go. It was a matter of finding a path through the minefield."

Moves toward the trade agreement increased contacts between the two Governments geometrically. But that only reinforced Washington's belief that a new political day had dawned in Mexico. „Every American official who came through there met with the Mexicans involved with Nafta," Mr. Negroponte said. „That was the prism through which the American Government was looking at the Mexican Government. We certainly felt that the reformers were in the ascendancy." Those bright, English-speaking officials seemed to sustain an American faith: that the more Mexico opened up to competition, the more its Government would have to scale back its economic role - and the less chance Mexican officials would have to demand bribes in return for waiving rules or awarding contracts. Drugs figured little in the equation. But just as Mr. Salinas embraced a trade deal with the United States, the scope of Mexican trafficking began to change as well.

Colombian cocaine producers had already made Mexico their main route to the thriving American market. Then Mexican traffickers, who had been working for fees of $1,000 or $2,000 for every kilogram of cocaine they smuggled, began to demand their cut in kind. The economics were simple: by taking their payment in cocaine and greatly expanding their distribution network, especially in the western United States, the Mexicans began to increase their profits between 5 and 10 times, officials said. And as the value of their smuggling routes rose, so did their payments for protection to politicians, judges, prosecutors and the police. New trade regulations began opening the already porous border even more. But drug-intelligence officials said it would still take several years before the implications of this change - and the threat it posed to Mexican security - were fully grasped by American policy makers. While Carlos Salinas was being celebrated in Washington and on Wall Street as the man who might lead Mexico into the developed world, American officials began hearing a very different picture of his inner circle from a source they knew well.

In 1991, a Mexican Federal Police commander who had carried out sensitive operations for both Salinas brothers came forward with some startling, specific allegations. The commander, Guillenno González Calderoni, spoke to officials from the Drug Enforcement Administration, the Federal Bureau of Investigation and a United States Attomey's office in Texas. And he told of drug payoffs and dirty political tricks at the highest levels of Government. By 1993 at the latest, American officials said, Mr. González Calderoni had told them that Luis Medrano, a close associate of one of Mexico's biggest drug traffickers, had told him of paying Raul Salinas two years earlier to help their trafficking group acquire two seaports that the Government was planning to sell to private investors. American officials who dealt with the case said Mr. González Calderoni's claims were strongly debated within federal law-enforcernent agencies because he was widely thought to have had his own corrupt ties to Mr. Medrano's boss, Juan Garcia Abrego, and because Mexico had unsuccessfully sought his extradition.

None of what Mr. González Calderoni had to say fit readily into any active drug investigations, the officials said. None of it, without further confirrnation, was enough to open a new inquiry into drug-related corruption. So in the end, they said, his reports were simply filed away. „1 don't think he was ever looked at as being a serious witness in corruption cases," one former official familiar with the debriefings said. „Back in 1993, it was very unpopular to say anything against Mexico, basically because of Nafta. Who was going to go and do a direct investigation against the President's brother? You just put it away, and it goes into the batter." Eventually, Mr. González Calderoni's allegations circulated throughout the Government. The C.I.A., in particular, viewed him as a less than compelling source. He came to personify, one official says, „the difficulty of getting hard, reasonably credible „information on these kinds of allegations." Several other knowledgeable officials put the C.I.A.'s struggle with Mexican corruption in a different light. Throughout the first half of the decade, they said, the agency that is supposed to be the primary source of information for American policy makers about internal workings of foreign governments spent relatively little time trying to verify the sort of charges that people like Mr. González Calderoni made.

The C.I.A. station in Mexico City has generally been the agency's most important in Latin America. But former American intelligence officials said that during the latter half of the cold war - when the city was a hub of Soviet espionage, a crucial base for Cuban agents and the common sanctuary for leftist Central American guerrilla groups - turning a blind eye to the drug-related corruption in the Mexican internal-security apparatus was often a condition for securing its assistance. The quid pro quo became evident as early as 1982, after federal prosecutors in San Diego indicted the chief of Mexico's internal-security force on charges of helping to run a huge cartheft ring. The prosecutors promptly received a cable from the United Stares Embassy in Mexico City telling them to desist; the Mexican official, Miguel Nazar Haro, was an „essential contact" of the C.I.A. station there. Mr. Nazar Haro remains a fugitive from prosecution in the United States and his whereabouts are unknown.

Mexico is one of two dozen foreign nations where the agency is authorized by a 1986 Presidential decision directive to conduct covert anti-drug operations, intelligence officials said. One official said it is also among the handful of nations where the C.I.A. has even broader authority under a top-secret appendix to the Presidential order. Yet until recently, several officials said, C.I.A. officers in Mexico have been far less active against the drug and corruption problems than their counterparts in Colombia, who trained elite anti-drug forces and guided operations against the leaders of the Medellin and Cali cocaine cartels. „In Colombia, you had the agency pushing and clamoring and trying to get in on it," said a retired American official who worked in both countries. „In Mexico, you had to go down there and try to get them jump-started. They were not focused on drugs. And a lot of the D.E.A. guys there didn't want them involved anyway." Mexico has also been something of a stepchild to the secret coordinating group that has orchestrated the increasingly cooperative efforts of United States law-enforcement, intelligence and military agencies in the Andes, officials said.

The existence of the panel, called the Linear Committee, has not been previously disclosed. But officials describe it as an unusually successful collaboration directed by the C.I.A.'s Counternarcotics Center and the Drug Enforcement Administration to find weak points in the linear chain of cocaine production and distribution. Until late 1995, several officials who have sat in on its deliberations said, the Linear Committee's priorities were very much in the Andes. Only after most of the main Cali cartelleaders had surrendered or been arrested did it turn more intently to the major Mexican traffickers. Some officials said that shift has already shown some results. Last year, the committee helped coordinate the pursuit of Jose Luis Pereira, the principal contact between the jailed Cali cocaine baron Miguel Rodriguez Orejuela and a powerful Mexican drug trafficker, Amado Carrillo Fuentes, whom Mexican officials confirmed today had died after plastic surgery last week to change his appearance. Mr. Pereira, a Bolivian known by the code name Jota, was captured by the MexicanArmy after a lengthy surveillance of his safe houses by the C.I.A., officials said. He was then deported home on a plane that stopped in Miami, where federal agents were waiting for him. He pleaded not guilty and is now standing trial on federal drug charges.

United States officials explain some of the lapses of intelligence efforts in Mexico by noting that probably nowhere else abroad do American officials deal with a more complicated mesh of economic interests, national-security concerns, law-enforcement problems and domestic political considerations. But many officials also attributed some of the shortcomings to a chronic inattention by American policy makers. In the months surrounding the agreement's approval in November 1993, officials said, few policy makers even noted reports by the Defense Intelligence Agency indicating that a shadowy armed group appeared to be active in the southern Mexican state of Chiapas. Similarly, though some finance and intelligence officials were concerned in late 1994 about the overvaluation of Mexico's peso, C.I.A. analysts decided not to issue a warning about the problem just a few days before the currency collapsed, according to intelligence officials. At the State Department, copies of an intelligence report titled „A Peso Problem" sat mostly unread on the shelves. „We have had, historically, a great deal of information from down there, but nobody wanted to look at it, because they didn't know what to do," said former Senator Dennis DeConcini, the Arizona Democrat who was chairman of the Senate Select Committee on Intelligence until the end of 1994. „They were afraid of how bad it might be, and how they would be able to justify the economic policies," said DeConcini, who, at his own request, received regular briefings on Mexico from the C.I.A.

Senior officials who dealt with Mexico under the Bush and Clinton Administrations said it was far easier to get the National Security Adviser or Secretary of State to focus on a shortterm problem like Haiti's elections than to devote 20 minutes to a question of Mexico's longterm stability. In early 1995, for instance, a powered group of Deputy Secretaries ordered a far-reaching assessment of Mexico's turmoil and its implications for American policy. It was typical, officials said, that this effort was eventually forgotten, and the study never completed. Nor have United States officials had much success in acting to stop Mexican corruption, even in the rare instances when they have had information they considered solid enough to act on. One such case, in 1992, began when American drug-enforcement agents in El Paso raided the home of amid-level cocaine trafficker and happened upon a fascinating video cassette. Several officials who saw it said the tape showed the trafficker, his wife or girlfriend and several associates cheerfully shooting off automatic weapons with a friend in military fatigues. The friend turned out to be a Mexican Army general, Javier Escobedo.

When the video cassette reached the United States Embassy in Mexico City, Mr. Negroponte, the Ambassador, saw it as an unusual opportunity and he immediately delivered a copy to Mexico's Defense Minister. After being confronted with the evidence by his superiors, however, General Escobedo chose neither to turn informant nor face a court martial. Instead, the officials said, he drove to the grave of his father, who had also been an army general, and shot himself to death. The circumstances of his suicide were never disclosed. In the fall of 1994, as Washington's Mexico specialists tried to make sense of a guerrilla uprising, a tumultuous presidential election campaign and the assassination of two major ruling-party political figures, many of them began to take the corruption problem more seriously. So did many Mexicans. Ernesto Zedillo, who was elected President that August, pledged to clean up the country's judicial system, and Mr. Jones, the Ambassador, offered information that he said might help the new Government keep out corrupt officials.

Diplomats at the embassy saw the exchange of information as a unique opportunity to deal with the problem. But by the way it was handled, the episode seemed to demonstrate American ambivalence about the issue once again. Mr. Jones asked several of the embassy's senior law-enforcement and intelligence officials to draw up a list of current and former Mexican officials who they thought should have no place in the upper ranks of an honest new regime. The list they produced - a copy of which was obtained by a reporter and confirmed in its contents by three knowledgeable American officials - catalogues a much wider presumption of corruption at the senior levels of the Salinas Administration than United States officials have ever acknowledged publicly. Among its 18 names are those of a former Interior Minister, a former Defense Secretary, and a former Attorney General; three officials who had been in charge of anti-drug efforts, Mr. Salinas' former national security chief, and his former drug intelligence chief. It also includes several veterans of the Federal Security Directorate, the state-security force that collaborated closely with the C.I.A. until it was disbanded in 1985.

Those officials who could be contacted by a reporter uniformly denied having ever done anything wrong and said they had no idea that they had been included on the American blacklist. In any case, United States officials did not press the point. Mr. Jones sent the list without first clearing the action with the State Department or White House. He later described it as a mere „exchange of information." A second list of about 30 lower-ranking Mexicans, against whom the embassy officials felt they had weaker evidence, was never sent at all. A senior American official said at the time that the list had been a great success because none of those it named were allowed into Mr. Zedillo's government. But that does not appear to be true. Among those on the list is Wilfredo Robledo, the senior operations official at Mexico's national-security agency, the Center for Investigations and National Security. Mexican officials who work with Mr. Robledo said he remains on the job and in good standing. Officials at the center and Interior Ministry, which controls the center, did not respond to telephone calls asking for comment.

American law-enforcement and intelligence officials said one of their basic problems in understanding the growing political influence of Mexican drug traffickers stemmed from the failure of government agencies to share information. While law-enforcement agents are building their cases, their practice is to guard what they know as closely as possible. After it comes out in court, they say, they generally have little time to try to evaluate the strategic significance of the information they have gathered. C.I.A. analysts who want to borrow such files often have to go to another agency's offices to read them.

Often as not, policy makers are the last to find out what law-enforcement officials already know. „There is an impenetrable firewall," one State Department official said, „between what U.S. attorneys are doing and what the policy side of the house knows." Rarely, however, has the system appeared so uncommunicative as in the case of Mr. Ruiz Massieu, a Deputy Attorney General who was both a close aide to Carlos Salinas and a brother of a leading politician said to have been killed on the orders of Raul Salinas. American officials began to suspect Mr. Ruiz Massieu of corruption after Mr. Garda Abrego, the trafficker, escaped just ahead of a 1993 raid to which he was apparently tipped off. That December, Mr. Ruiz Massieu opened a bank account in Houston. A few months later, his closest aide began arriving there with suitcases and boxes stuffed with hundreds of thousands of dollars in cash.

Customs agents in Texas recorded shipments that would eventually leave more than $9 million in the bank. But even after a suspicious bank officer called them to inquire about the money, Customs officials said, the agents did not investigate further. „Their sense was that there was something wrong there," the head of the Customs Service's financial investigations division, Alan Doody, said of the agents in Houston. But the realization came pretty quickly that this guy was part of the ruling elite. There was a whiff that something wasn't right. But in order to do something about it, you need more than a whiff." In Mexico City and Washington, other American law-enforcement officials were getting more. Some informants told of large gifts to Mr. Ruiz Massieu and his wife. Others described a huge smuggling case in which Mr. Ruiz Massieu and his deputy exonerated corrupt Mexican police agents. The success of Mexican anti-drug operations plummetted. Even then, officials said, Customs, F.B.I. and drug-enforcement officials shared little information about the case. Senior officials in Washington and Mexico learned of Mr. Ruiz Massieu's Texas deposits only after he was arrested at Newark International Airport as he tried to flee to Europe in March 1995.

When word of Mr. Ruiz Massieu's fortune reached the American Embassy in Mexico City, Jones assembled law-enforcement and intelligence officers in „the bubble," a secure room adjoining his office. He asked what evidence they might contribute to the case on Mr. Ruiz Massieu's apparent corruption. „All of our great minds said they didn't have any evidence against him," one official at the meeting recalled. In explaining their belated apprehension of the traffickers' connections to the Salinas Administration, law-enforcement and intelligence officials make an insistent point: Mexican political tradition dictates absolute loyalty until a president steps down. The airing of corruption allegations almost always comes later. Mr. Zedillo appeared to underscore that point as he began his term. Within little more than three months after he took office, Raul Salinas was arrested on murder charges, Mario Ruiz Massieu was accused of taking bribes from drug traffickers, and Carlos Salinas was forced into exile, his reputation in shreds.

As Mexico was being rocked by those tremors, American officials took inventory of the corruption allegations they had against leading members of the Mexican elite. Perhaps the most comprehensive such search was ordered by senior law-enforcement officials in March 1995, as Republicans in Congress fought Mr. Clinton's plan to rescue the Mexican economy. The review turned up all kinds of accusations, officials said, none of them entirely convincing. There was just no smoking gun," said Robert Nieves, who joined the search as the Drug Enforcement Administration's chief of international operations. „That doesn't mean that it wasn't meaningful. But you couldn't go to court with that information." How deeply American agencies dug into such matters is unclear. Several officials who read much of the C.I.A.'s reporting on Mexican corruption between 1992 and 1995 said the reports rarely indicated that intelligence officers had done any significant investigation of the claims of their informants.

United States law-enforcement officials who were stationed in Mexico City said they had little choice but to look skeptically at the allegations they heard. Within the Mexican police and security apparatus, they said, leaking negative information about one's political enemies to American officials was a basic weapon of bureaucratic struggle. „Now, all of that information is almost 100 percent," said a former law-enforcement official who processed some of the most explosive accusations against Mexican officials, politicians and business-men. But at the time, we had to ask ourselves, 'Is it possible that it goes this high up?' We were afraid to write it up sometimes because we thought people would say we were crazy." More recently, even as events in Mexico have forced the Clinton Administration to reassess drug trafficking and corruption here, American intelligence efforts have continued to run into problems. The fall last February of Mexico's drug-enforcement chief was a case in point. The official, Gen. Jesus Gutierrez Rebollo, was arrested on charges of working for Mr. Carrillo Fuentes, the powerful cocaine trafficker who apparently died last week at a Mexico City clinic. Eight days earlier, the bald, rockjawed Mexican officer had stood at attention in Washington as the White House drugpolicy chief, Gen. Barry R. McCaffrey, described him as „an honest man and a nononsense field commander."

As commander of a five-state military region that has its headquarters in the western city of Guadalajara, General Gutiérrez Rebollo had been credited with the capture of one major cocaine trafficker in 1995, the arrest of another last August and the seizure of a plane loaded with millions of dollars in drug profits in between. The prevailing view, said a White House official who reviewed background information about the general from the Central Intelligence Agency and the Defense Intelligence Agency, was that he was „a soldier's soldier." That no other army commander had taken remotely so much initiative in the fight against drug trafficking did not stir much doubt among experts who assessed his appointment for the two intelligence agencies and the Drug Enforcement Administration. Rather, according to several officials familiar with their reports and briefings, the intelligence analysts appeared to take their main cues from American drug-enforcement agents stationed in Guadalajara. The agents, who had dealt with the general on several cases, thought he was all business.

Some of the analysts did note that General Gutierrez Rebollo had managed to avoid the regular rotations to which other commanders were subjected. But officials said that their reports and briefings raised no particular alarm that he had remained for more than six years in Guadalajara, the Beirut of Mexico's drug underworld. It is an established pattern of Mexican corruption that successful police commanders sell protection to one trafficking group while attacking others. But it went unnoticed among drugintelligence analysts, officials said, that General Gutierrez Rebollo had been vigorously attacking the Tijuana-based drug gang run by the Arellano Felix brothers while virtually ignoring their rival, Mr. Carrillo Fuentes. Had United States officials queried senior Mexican law-enforcement officials, they might have confirmed that the general had balked at turning over suspected associates of the Arellano Felix gang whom his officers had captured, tortured and held incommunicado. Had they asked officials in Guadalajara, they would have heard about serious allegations of misconduct against a close aide whom General Gutierrez Rebollo had placed as head of the state police. After the state government dismissed the aide, the general hired him back as chief of investigations at Mexico's drug-enforcement agency. „He was showing results," said one American official who dealt with General Gutierrez Rebollo. „His methods were overlooked."

By the time of his arrest in February, American drug-enforcement officials had heard from several informants who questioned the general's honesty. The reports were not vigorously pursued, officials said. Since the Gutierrez Rebollo episode, officials said, the C.I.A. has instituted a new system to warn of such problems. Every biography the agency's analysts produce on a Mexican official now includes a caveat: just because no negative information has turned up does not mean that the official can necessarily be trusted. By late 1995, the new director of Central Intelligence, John M. Deutch, was sufficiently dissatisfied with the agency's reporting on Mexico that he ordered intelligence officers and analysts to redouble their efforts. Mr. Deutch, who lived briefly in the Mexican city of Cuernavaca as a boy, took over the post with the Clinton Administration still feeling the sting of Congressional and public anger over the peso crisis. Officials said he included Mexico for the first time on the list of strategic priorities for the C.I.A. He asked his officers to focus on the stability of Mr. Zedillo's government and the threats it faced from both drug corruption and guerrillas.

Nearly two years later, the White House's drug-policy chief, General McCaffrey, suggested that the problems of intelligence on Mexico are still far from solved. Fresh from his own embarrasment with the fall of General Gutierrez Rebollo, General McCaffrey said in an interview that he has begun an effort to create „a newly defined architecture" for the myriad agencies that collect information to support anti-drug efforts. General McCaffrey said the goal of the redesign will be to establish new „roles and missions and a hierarchy" for such agencies as the Drug Enforcement Administration's El Paso Intelligence Center, the C.I.A.'s Counternarcotics Center in Langley, Va., the Treasury Department's Financial Crimes Enforcement Network outside Washington, and the National Drug Intelligence Center in Johnstown, Pa.

„We need to make sure that this extraordinary amount of information that we've got supports real-world people involved in drug interdiction better than it does now," he said. General McCaffrey said he had briefed the Secretaries of State, Defense, Justice and Treasury on the idea, described it to the Congressional intelligence committees, and gotten the acting Director of Central Intelligence, George J. Tenet, to join him in leading a study group that is design a new structure by this fall. But other officials said there is already strong opposition to the idea, particularly in the Justice and Treasury Depart-ments. Some officials in those agencies said they were concerned about protecting sensitive or confidential information, such as the details of continuing investigations or income-tax returns. Other officials said that to pool any of their information would be to cede power. „Call me when it happens," one senior official said. „Something like that might work in the military, but those guys don't fight like they do in Washington."«

DRUGS, CRIME, TORTURE

»As the man in the videotape begins to spill the inner secrets of Mexico's most violent drug gang, he appears nervous, chewing off pieces of his left thumb-nail and gulping water. Alejandro Enrique Hodoyan had been a minor though well-placed member of the drug organization, running guns and errands. On the tape, he sits center stage, recounting in a soft voice how his brother and a circle of their childhood friends joined a criminal enterprise that killed dozens of police commanders, prosecutors, drug rivals and innocent bystanders. „Killing is a party for them, it's a kick," Mr. Hodoyán tells Mexican investigators. „No remorse at all. They laugh after a murder, and go off and have a lobster dinner." His testimony, which produced eight hours of videotape and more than 200 pages of transcripts, is viewed on both sides of the border as a law-enforcement triumph, a breakthrough in Mexico's flagging fight against drug traffickers. Mexican officials say his disclosures have already prompted the dismissal of „several dozen" detectives and police commanders accused of ties to the Tijuana-based organization, which is led by the Arellano Félix brothers.

But behind the image on the videotape is a tale of a middle-class family torn apart, with brother turned against brother in a violent drug culture. It is also a story of kidnapping and coercion that highlights some of the perils for the United States in working with the secretive Mexican military, which has been given a central role in the drug war despite its lengthening record of corruption and brutality. Mr. Hodoyán, an American citizen who was born in San Diego and lived most of his life just across the border in Tijuana, was abducted and detained illegally for 80 days by Mexican military officers. Soldiers tortured him with cigarette lighters and electric shocks to the eyelids, accordiug to an account he later gave his family. The Mexican military eventually turned Mr. Hodoyán over to American officials who are preparing a major, new indictment against the Arellano Félix organization. Some American officials involved in the case now acknowledge they were too willing to turn a blind eye to the methods used by the Mexican military to secure Mr. Hodoyán's cooperation.

American diplomats in Mexico learned of Mr. Hodoyán's captivity shortly after he was imprisoned, but did nothing to help him. After his family reported him missing to United States officials, a law-enforcement agent assigned to the American Embassy interviewed him at an unused barracks, where he was blindfolded and handcuffed to a steel bed. The embassy official assigned to follow up on the agent's report of a captive American citizen took no action. United States officials later described that as an egregious failure to deliver the basic protections guaranteed citizens in trouble in foreign lands. Donald R. Hamilton, the embassy's spokesman, otherwise defended its handling of the case, saying Mr. Hodoyán did not complain to any American official in Mexico of torture or suggest that he was under duress. The account of Mr.

Hodoyán's experiences was pieced together from interviews with his family, American officials in Mexico, and Mexican justice officials who knew him as an informant. It is also based on confidential Mexican court documents as well as audio tape-recordings, obtained by the *New York Times*, of telephone calls he made to his family in Tijuana last year when he was a military prisoner.

In December 1996, the military officer who supervised his interrogation and handover to the Americans was appointed Mexico's top anti-drug official, in part because of successes he scored in the drug war using information supplied by Mr. Hodoyán. Two months later, that officer, Gen. Jesus Gutiérrez Rebollo, was jailed on charges of collaborating with another drug lord, a bitter rival of the Arellano Félix brothers. Mexican officials now suspect that much of the information the general extracted from Mr. Hodoyán went directly to the rival drug organization. Since then, the military has dismissed and is investigating 33 other officers, including four generals, on corruption and narcotics charges, defense officials said.

In the end, Mr. Hodoyán was not much help to American prosecutors. After 10 days in San Diego, he suffered what family members described as a psychological breakdown. Under pressure to give evidence against his brother, he disappeared across the border to Mexico where he had numerous enemies, including the Arellano Félix gang, which, he was told, had put out a contract on his life. Alejandro Hodoyán known to his family and friends as Alex, seemed an unlikely candidate for a career in crime. His mother Cristina, who is 55, is a prim, devoutly Catholic woman from an upstanding Mexican family. His father, Alejandro Hodoyán Ramirez, 63, is a respected Mexican civil engineer. The Hodoyáns hoped to raise their children with the best of the American and Mexican cultures. Their three boys and a girl were all born in San Diego, but the family lived just across the border in Tijuana, a city where the multibillion-dollar drug trade has in recent years become a lure even for privileged and educated young people.

The Hodoyán children came of age in Tijuana discos where teen-agers experimented with cocaine in the free-wheeling way of wealthy American youth. They also mingled with Mexican gang members who were rising stars in the cocaine business. One of the flashiest was Ramon Arellano, a leader of the gang who met members of the Hodoyán family at a society wedding in Tijuana. It was a sweltering summer day, but Mr. Arellano sported a mink jacket and leather pants. He was wearing a big thick chain with a big gold cross encrusted with emeralds," said a Hodoyán relative, who asked not to be identified, „Everything about him made you turn around and say, who is he?" Mexican court documents describe Mr. Arellano as a compulsive murderer who has killed several times for sport and is implicated in more than 60 homicides. He and his brothers began their careers as provincial drug dealers, but shot and bullied their way to seize control of drug-smuggling along a western swath of the United States-Mexico border. One by one, friends the Hodoyáns had known since childhood were drawn into the Arellanos' circle of riches and violence.

Fabian Martinez González, a grade-school classmate of Alex Hodoyán's younger sister who teased the girls by lifting up their skirts, grew up to become el Tiburón, or the Shark. He is accused of being one of Mr. Arellano's most feared gunmen and is wanted for murder in Mexico. Emilio Valdez Mainero was a boyhood buddy Mr. Hodoyán chose years later to be the godfather at his first daughter's baptism. Mr. Valdez Mainero became a top operative in the organization, arranging drug shipments and assassinations, the Mexican and American police have charged in court. „In Tijuana the Arellanos bought their way into the cream of society," said a Mexican anti-drug prosecutor who asked not to be identified. „In a normal situation, a family like the Hodoyáns would never find themselves involved with traffickers." Mr. Hodoyán, the oldest of the Hodoyán children, is a 35-year old law-school dropout and cocaine addict who never held a steady job. An even-tempered man with an amiable face, he started doing small favors for the Arellanos and eventually helped them import rifles and grenades to arm their hit squads. In return they gave him loads of cocaine and marijuana to move across the border, allowing him to keep the proceeds, he told Mexican prosecutors. Alfredo Hodoyán, 25, the rakish and strong-willed brother who is Alex's youngest sibling, took on a more violent role in the gang, according to his brother and other associates. He joined one of the cartel's hit squads and is wanted on murder charges in Mexico.

On September 10, 1996, the Arellano gang sent Alex Hodoyán to Guadalajara, the central Mexican city that has emerged as a battleground for competing drug gangs. His mission, he later said, was to find a new „safe house," a local base for the group's operations. He was walking straight into a military trap. Seven weeks earlier, gunmen for the Arellano organizaation had bungled a plot to assassinate Amado Carrillo Fuentes, the leader of a rival cartel. Instead they killed two army soldiers who were at the scene. The killings infuriated the soldiers' commander, Gen. Gutiérrez Rebollo, a bulldog of an officer with a shaven head who was in charge from his headquarters in Guadalajara of a vast military region encompassing much of central Mexico. On the afternoon of Sept 11, Alex Hodoyán went to an existing Arellano safe house in a working-class neighborhood. A squad of General Gutiérrez Rebollo's intelligence troops, wearing black uniforms, was watehing the house and seized him. By law, the

Mexican armed forces can hold criminal suspects for no more than 48 hours before turning them over to the civilian authorities. But General Gutiérrez Rebollo kept Mr. Hodoyán incommunicado for the next two months, mainly in a vacant army base on the outskirts of Guadalajara. The troops had no arrest warrant and filed no report to the police.

Mr. Hodoyán's kidnapping and secret detention have been described in separate, mutually corroborating accounts by army officers who are now testifying against General Gutiérrez Rebollo in two trials. Their statements are contained in confidential court records. According to the officers, the windowless bunker where Mr. Hodoyán was shackled hand and foot to a bed was General Gutiérrez Rebollo's private interrogation center, where illegally detained suspects were questioned for days and weeks. After Mr. Hodoyán was released, he said the soldiers had tortured and threatened to kill him. „They told me I had arrived in hell," he said in a statement he dictated to his parents months later. According to Mr. Hodoyán, the soldiers forced soda water spiked with searing hot chile peppers up his nose until he was nearly asphyxiated. He said they had burned the soles of his feet with lighters and had applied electric shocks to his eyelids and toes. Within days, several witnesses said, there was a change in Mr. Hodoyán's demeanor. He began to cooperate, almost too enthusiastically, with his captors. Drawing on his prodigious memory, he poured out what he knew about the Arellanos in manic bursts. Mr. Hodoyan's claims of torture have not been confirmed by independent witnesses, and the statement he gave his family, which he never signed, remains the only record of his first days in captivity. Two Mexicans who saw Mr. Hodoyán in later weeks of his detention say they noticed a fresh scar in the middle of his forehead. He told them that he had been tortured, but said he could not discuss the details. The scar, he said, was where skin peeled away when his duct tape blindfolds were changed.

General Gutiérrez Rebollo played his prisoner with a maestro's touch, according to the officers who testified in the trials against him. He waited 13 days before visiting Mr. Hodoyán. Then he came on as the consummate good cop, pretending to scold his subordinates for treating the prisoner harshly and ordering them to loosen his manacles and upgrade his food. Mr. Hodoyán so on became devoted to his jailer. When allowed, he trailed behind General Gutiérrez Rebollo. A Mexican drug prosecutor who saw the two men together toward the end of Mr. Hodoyán's captivity said they were „like father and son." General Gutiérrez Rebollo had good reason to court Mr. Hodoyán. On Sept. 14, three days after Mr. Hodoyán was abducted by his soldiers, a hit squad linked to the Arellanos assassinated a top Mexican anti-drug prosecutor in Mexico City. Soon after, Mexican officials sent their American counterparts information developed by General Gutiérrez Rebollo indicating that Alfredo Hodoyán, Alex's brother, was a triggerman in the killing. The Mexicans said Alfredo was hiding out near San Diego with Emilio Valdez, the godfather of Alex Hodoyán's daughter, who was wanted in Mexico on another murder charge.

American federal agents arrested Mr. Valdéz and Alfredo Hodoyán on Sept. 30 in San Diego, and at Mexico's request United States prosecutors opened an extradition case to return them to Mexico for trial. General Gutiérrez Rebollo set out to convince Alex Hodoyán to testify against his friend and his brother. In Mexico, where ties of blood and ritual kinship are nearly sacred and the law absolves suspects from incriminating immediate relatives, it was a formidable undertaking. As soon as the Hodoyán family realized Alex was missing, they turned to the American authorities for help. On Sept. 20, Adriana Hodoyán, Alex's sister, called the U.S. consulate in Guadalajara to say she believed that her brother, an American citizen, had vanished there. Five days later, Adriana Hodoyán, who is 30, traveled to Guadalajara and gave the consulate a photo of Alex and a detailed account of the travel route he had planned.

On Oct. 7, when Alex Hodoyán had been missing for nearly a month, his sister called the consulate again. She was frantic. According to American officials, she said there were reports that Alex had been detained on Sept. 11 by the military authorities in Guadalajara. American diplomats in Guadalajara made what they later described as routine phone calls to local police stations and jails to see if he was there. „It was just a usual-suspects thing," a United States official in Guadalajara said, just another of the 71 cases the consulate handled in 1996 of Americans who went missing in that region. No one at the consulate ever spoke with the Mexican military. „We would have no reason to call the military," an American official said, explaining that the armed forces do not usually detain people under Mexico's legal system. But on Oct. 7, the day of Adriana Hodoyán's most urgent appeal for help, one arm of the United States Government learned that the Mexican military knew exactly where to find Mr. Hodoyán. Officers at the Defense Ministry in Mexico City invited an agent from the United States Bureau of Alcohol, Tobacco and Firearms to question an exceptional informant they had about arms smuggling to Mexican drug traffickers. Not long after General Gutiérrez Rebollo had captured Mr. Hodoyán, he had informed his superiors about him.

The A.T.F. bureau declined to make the agent who questioned Mr. Hodoyán available for an interview. His account was relayed by officials in Washington and Mexico who said they had reviewed reports the agent filed at the time.

American officials said the Mexican armed forces had provided an airplane to fly the A.T.F. agent to Guadalajara. Two Mexican officers, in plain clothes, drove the agent to the base where Mr. Hodoyán was held and accompanied him into the meeting. In the bare room, the agent introduced himself to Mr. Hodoyán, blindfolded and cuffed to a bed. The agent later told colleagues that it bothered him that he could not see the prisoner's eyes. Nevertheless, for nearly two hours the American agent probed to find out what the prisoner knew about the traffic of weapons. „The amazing thing is, the guy just doesn't shut up," said a United States official who questioned the A.T.F. agent about Mr. Hodoyán. „He is talking, talking, talking. He immediately implicated his brother and himself in a number of crimes."

Mexican officers told the A.T.F. agent that Mr. Hodoyán had been blindfolded to prevent him from seeing the American's face, since the prisoner, they said, was a „dangerous and violent criminal." The echo-filled room and strangely empty military barracks struck the A.T.F. agent as an „unusual but not inappropriate" place for the meeting. After two hours, the official said, the agent believed that he „had a live one." He began to make mental plans to take Mr. Hodoyán to the United States as a witness in gun-running cases. That was when Mr. Hodoyán, who had spoken throughout the interview in Spanish, announced that he would not need a visa. „I was born in San Diego, „ he said. „I am an American citizen." Mr. Hodoyán volunteered nothing about mistreatment by the soldiers, American officials said, and the statement he later gave his family suggests a reason. General Gutiérrez Rebollo's officers, he said, warned him before the interview that if he told the A.T.F. agent about his torture, „he would be the last person I would ever cross a word with."

The day after the interview, Mexican military officials told the A.T.F. agent that the general had changed his mind and was not ready to release Mr. Hodoyán. The agent remained uneasy about what he had seen. He consulted with the No. 2 official in the embassy, Charles H. Brayshaw, who sent him to the consul general for Mexico City, a senior diplomat who handles problems involving United States citizens. For half an hour, the agent described the American imprisoned in Guadalajara. According to American officials, the consul general, Thomas L. Randall, told the A.T.F. agent he believed that Mr. Hodoyán was probably one more Mexican trying to get out of a jam by claiming to be an American.

Then, several officials said, Mr. Randall did nothing further about Mr. Hodoyán. „He didn't tell anybody above, below or alongside," a diplomat said later, calling Mr. Randall's performance „a clear case of nonfeasance." Had this person done even the minimum which duty, regulation, law and custom indicate, the consular service would not have been ignorant of Mr. Hodoyán's detention," said Mr. Hamilton, the spokesman for the embassy in Mexico City. Mr. Hamilton refused to identify the consul involved in the case by name. A Washington spokesman for the A.T.P. bureau, Patrick D. Hynes, said classified memos showed that the agent had met with the embassy's consul general, which was the position Mr. Randall held at the time. Other officials confirmed that it was Mr. Randall, who was recalled from Mexico to Washington late last year and retired from the Foreign Service in January 1997. Reached by telephone at his southern California residence, Randall said he had no recollection of Mr. Hodoyán's case.

„I'm sure I would have done whatever needed to be done," he said, calling it „convenient" that embassy officials had heaped all of the blame on the one person involved who was no longer in government service. Mr. Brayshaw did not inquire again what had become of Mr. Hodoyán because he assumed that the Consul General had done his job, Hamilton said. In late October, General Gutiérrez Rebollo was sufficiently confident of his new informant's coope-ration that he allowed him to call his family and tell them he was still alive. They were elated but deeply worried. After the first contact, Mr. Hodoyán was allowed to call his parents regularly, and as he talked in guarded language, they realized that he was informing on the Arellano gang and was under pressure to turn on his own brother.

For his parents the conversations were agonizing. Their eldest son was in the custody of powerful Mexican military officers who, Alex hinted, would think nothing of killing him. The officers were trying to pit Alex against their youngest son, who was in jail in San Diego fighting extradition to Mexico on a murder charge that could put him in prison for decades. Mr. Hodoyán's mother and father urged him to remain loyal to the family and his circle of childhood friends. But Mr. Hodoyán was bitter that the Arellano gang had sent him into an ambush. And General Gutiérrez Rebollo was leaning heavily on Mr. Hodo-yán to talk by offering to place him in a Government witness program where his past criminal record would be erased. Tape-recordings of some of Mr. Hodoyán's phone calls to his family were made available to the *New York Times* by participants in the events who requested anonymity. They depict a man overwhelmed by irreconcilable pressures and dominated by a captor who both terrifies him and inspires his devotion. Cooperating with General Gutiérrez Rebollo, he argued, was the only way he could survive to see his two young daughters again. „I love my brother, Mama," Mr. Hodoyán told his mother at one point. „But my daughters come first."

In one conversation his father asked him what he wanted to tell his brother Alfredo and his brother's lawyers. „Tell them I made a deal with the general, and the general is keeping his word to me," Mr. Hodoyán said. „He even bought new clothes for me." „He spared my life and I want to keep my word to him, too," he said later in the conversation. At one point, the elder Mr. Hodoyán told his son that a Mexican lawyer who had defended the Arellanos was offering to help get Alex out of military custody. Alex exploded, saying: „I don't matter to them! I never did. They just want to help me now because they have problems with the military and the police. They see the end coming." „My stomach is starting to hurt," he said as he raged at the Arellanos. Finally he broke down in sobs. „I don't want them using me," he said, cursing the Arellanos.

Mr. Hodoyán made it clear that General Gutiérrez Rebollo had promised him that his statements against Alfredo could not be used in any Mexican or American court because they were brothers. „My son, it's a trap - you're in a trap, try to understand," Cristina Hodoyán entreated in a phone call on Dec. 10. „You are helping the man who is accusing your brother!" „He can't," Mr. Hodoyan insisted. „Alfredo is my brother. He can't." His parents hoped that if Alex was freed he would testify in the effort to block Alfredo's extradition in San Diego. But they warned Alex that he would have to reveal that he had been tortured by the troops. Alex Hodoyán panicked, afraid that General Gutiérrez Rebollo would retaliate if he denounced him. „No! No! They never did anything to me, Mama, please try to understand," he said. „I thought I explained that to you. I can't say anything about that until I finish what I am doing here."

Alex's father suggested to his son that he was suffering from Stockholm syndrome, which occurs when kidnap victims become attached to their kidnappers. Alex rejected the idea with a fervor that suggested he knew it could be true. „Look, Papa, everything they promised me they have done," Alex Hodoyán said of the military. „I don't want trouble. I don't want them to kill me. I don't want that." Mrs. Hodoyán said she felt torn apart by the clashing interests of her two sons. „Alex, above all, we have to be united," Mrs. Hodoyán said, her voice taut with pain. Alex replied: „I am not sure if I can help Alfredo, but at least I am sure I will be free and clear for the rest of my life. But if they hurt me here, who will take care of my little girls? They will be left without a father."

General Gutiérrez Rebollo won the fight for Alex Hodoyán's allegiance. In the last days of November 1996, he summoned Mexican civilian prosecutors to Guadalajara. In three days of declarations, including the sections on videotape, Mr. Hodoyán once again told all he knew about the Arellanos - this time for the legal record. Speaking to the police video camera in measured words and abundant detail, he accused his brother Alfredo of taking part in not one but several killings. „Prior to the murder the witness's brother arrived at the hotel," the record of Mr. Hodoyán's testimony reads, referring to the April 1996 killing of a Mexican boxer said to have encroached on the Arellanos' turf. Alfredo Hodoyán and one other gunman „were responsible for finding the victim, whom they murdered in the hallway that connects the restaurant and the bathrooms of the hotel." In December, after General Gutiérrez Rebollo was promoted to head Mexico's antidrug agency, he offered agents from the United States Drug Enforcement Administration a chance to debrief his informant. The D.E.A. had been told of Mr. Hodoyán's military detention more than a month earlier by the A.T.P. agent who questioned him. Still, the drug-enforcement agents eagerly accepted the offer as a rare chance to cooperate with the Mexican military and improve their relations with the general. „He was showing results," the law-enforcement official said. „He was a very confident guy who projected the sense that 'we're the military - we're going to get the job done.' His methods, frankly, were overlooked."

By February, Mr. Hodoyán had completed his transformation from hostage to informant. He had been given immunity from prosecution in Mexico in exchange for his testimony. He moved about freely at the federal drug agency in the capital, where General Gutiérrez Rebollo had been transferred. On Feb. 10, D.E.A. agents flew Mr. Hodoyán to the United States. They interviewed him, and hoped that he would eventually be a cooperating witness against the Arellanos. The D.E.A. did not allow its Mexico agents to comment about their role. But James J. McGivney, the agency's spokesman, said Mr. Hodoyán had given no indication he had ever been mistreated. „Every time the D.E.A. saw this guy, he was walking around having a good time," Mr. McGivney said. „When we see him, he's not bruised, not beaten, no chili peppers up his nose, no signs of duress." Soon after he arrived in the United States, Mr. Hodoyán, his 32-year-old wife, Bertha Gastelum de Hodoyán, and his mother met with the American prosecutor who was handling the extradition of his brother. The mother said she had prodded Alex to tell the Assistant United States Attorney, Gonzalo P. Curiel, about his torture in Mexico. But according to both women, Mr. Curiel was reluctant to listen. They said he replied, „This is more than I want to hear." Mr. Curiel declined to be interviewed, noting that he is barred from discussing pending cases.

On Feb. 18, the fragile world Mr. Hodoyan built as an informant imploded. Mexican military officials announced the arrest of General Gutiérrez Rebollo. They released photographs showing that as drug czar he had lived in a luxury apartment owned by Amado Carrillo Fuentes, the leading trafficker. Mr.

Hodoyán reeled. His savior was just another drug don. The information he had given to redeem himself had probably just gone to benefit another cartel. Meanwhile, one of the Arellanos top gunmen, Fabian Martinez, „the Shark,“ placed several calls from hiding to the Hodoyáns, saying he knew Alex was an informant. Then the American prosecutor, Mr. Curiel, said he intended to put Mr. Hodoyán before a grand jury investigating Arellano operatives, including his brother and his friend Mr. Valdez, Mr. Hodoyán's family said. He would have to go briefly to jail, but then he, his wife and daughters could join a witness protection program. „I'll never forget what he said,“ recalled his wife. „'You know what?' he said, 'I'd rather have them kill me.'“

Before dawn on the moming of Feb. 20, Mr. Hodoyán committed what a United States official described as a „totally irrational and suicidal act.“ He bolted from San Diego and appeared, wild-eyed and disheveled, at his parents' home in Tijuana. „He was crazy, loco, desperate,“ Bertha Hodoyán said. „He was crying, telling us he was sorry. Completely neurotic. He was just like a little child, crying and crying.“ Thirteen days later, when Mr. Hodoyán was driving in downtown Tijuana with his mother, armed men blocked the path of their vehicle, dragged him out, shoved him into another car and sped away. He has not been heard from since. His brother Alfredo and his friend Mr. Valdez remain in prison in San Diego fighting extradition to Mexico. Their lawyers have asserted that the statements of Alex Hodoyán and other witnesses provided by Mexico were obtained through torture and are thus invalid. Mr. Curiel acknowledged recently at a court hearing in San Diego that the allegations of torture were plausible and serious, but said they should be investigated by the Mexican authorities.«

ANTI-DRUG PARTNERS

»Hoping to build a new bulwark against the flow of illegal drugs from Latin America, the United States is providing the Mexican military with extensive covert intelligence support and training hundreds of its officers to help shape a network of anti-drug troops around the country, United States and Mexican officials say. The officials say the assistance has included training, equipment and advice from the Central Intelligence Agency to establish an elite army intelligence unit that has quietly moved to the forefront of Mexico's anti-drug effort, sometimes ahead of a new civilian police force that the United States is also pledged to support. The effort has proceeded despite growing American concern that it may lead to more serious problems of corruption and human rights in one of Mexico 's most respected institutions, United States officials say. A new United States intelligence analysis of the military's drug ties, for instance, will cite evidence of extensive penetration of the officer corps, two people who have seen draft versions of the assessment said.

Clinton Administration officials have described the American aid as a stopgap. Echoing Mexico's President Ernesto Zedillo, they insist that the military's law-enforcement actions will be limited and temporary, helping to disrupt the country's thriving drug trade only until its badly corrupted federal police forces can be overhauled. But according to many officials, the Pentagon and the C.I.A. have pressed their help partly out of their need to find new tasks after the cold war. They hope to use the aid to expand their roles in the anti-drug campaign in Mexico and to improve their relationships with a secretive, nationalistic neighboring army that has often looked at them with suspicion, the officials said. „They didn't have anybody to play with on the Mexican end of the drug issue, so they went for the military," a former senior official who was involved in American policy in Mexico said, referring to the Defense Department and the C.I.A. „They knew the risks, but they thought they could control the situation."

Some of those risks have resounded in recent news reports: the jailing of army generals on charges of protecting major drug traffickers; allegations that military officers have been linked to the torture and disappearance of criminal suspects; failures of due process and proper legal procedure by soldiers stepping in for the police. Other pitfalls have been less apparent. Some officials, for instance, worry that American intelligence officers may face conflicts in trying to build good relationships with Mexican Army officers to sustain the cooperation, and trying to remain watchful of military corruption at the same time. A few other current and former United States officials date their unease to what they described as a disastrous C.I.A. program in the late 1980s to deploy a Mexican Army strike force against the traffickers. The force was disbanded after several failed operations, one of which resulted in the killing of four Mexican civilians.

Mexico has long stood out in Latin America for the sureness of its civilian control over the military. But American officials said they had been troubled by indications that some officers, detailed to the federal police have operated with considerable independence from the judicial authorities. With the Mexican Army searching for new missions, many American officials doubt that it will limit its participation in law enforcement to the two-year deadline that Mr. Zedillo and his aides set last summer. "The whole thing has snowballed," said a senior American official who, like others, would discuss the matter only on the condition that he not be identified. „We are now seeing two separate anti-drug efforts in Mexico - one by the military and one under the Attorney General. If I were in the Attorney General's office, I would be asking whether it has gone too far." To some degree, the policy debate is fueled by old rivairies between American lawenforcement agencies and their intelligence and military counterparts. But the two sides also have some philosophical differences, which center on the question of whether United States support for the military complements or competes with efforts to transform Mexico's crippled criminal-justice system.

„They have basically to rebuild their entire police force," a senior drug-enforcement official said of the Mexican Government. „You can't do that in a year or two. And the longer the emphasis is put on the military, the longer it is going to take to get the police up and running." The Pentagon spokesman, Kenneth H. Bacon, disputed the idea that the two directions of American anti-drug aid in Mexico were at cross purposes. „There is no conflict," he said. James R. Jones, who left Mexico City this summer after serving for four years as the United States Ambassador there, echoed that view, and denied that American officials had encouraged the Mexican military's new role. „The temporary detailing of military officers to civilian law enforcement was the Mexicans' and Zedillo's decision - we had nothing to do with that," Mr. Jones said. „Our efforts to improve the quality and exchange of intelligence information and our training programs for certain military units had nothing to do with their decision." The C.I.A.'s chiefspokesman, Bill Harlow, declined to comment on the agency's activities in Mexico. Despite a widespread belief in the corruption of Mexico's federal and state police, Mexicans and their political leaders have been wary about seeking the help of the military to enforce civilian laws. In the late 1970s Mexican officials turned to the army to help drive marijuana and heroin-poppy growers from their sanctuaries in the rugged folds of the western Sierra Madre. Their sweep succeeded in temporarily dislodging the traffickers, and it institutionalized a program in which about 20,000 of the army's 150,000 soldiers are detailed to drug-crop eradication campaigns.

For an army that has relatively little to do in securing the country's borders, the drug eradication program has been a source of pride. Yet even while it avoided policetype activities, the military was shaken during the 1980s and early 1990s by public allegations that some senior officers - including a former Defense Minister, a Secretary of the Navy and several senior army commanders - colluded in the drug trade. After Carlos Salinas de Gortari became President in late 1988, American officials said, they gave relatively little thought to the Mexican Army because of their hopes that at least one of the Government's many police-reform campaigns would succeed. Some also harbored cause for concern in the experience of the Mexican Army strike force created years earlier. With anti-drug efforts stalled in 1987, American agents developed information that big traffickers were building nearly impenetrable compounds in the countryside. Working with the military, current and former officials said, C.I.A. officers helped form what they envisioned as an elite team of about 50 soldiers that would strike more effectively and operate more securely than the police. Mexican law-enforcement officials were told nothing of the plan, they said.

The team's first operation, against a stronghold of a cocaine smuggler in Sinaloa state, ended with one soldier's capture by a police agent working for the traffickers, two former officials said. The next foray went considerably worse. On the morning of April 11, 1988, helicopters -swung out of the dawn sky near the northern town of Caborca, a sanctuary of a reputed marijuana smuggler. „The idea was that you could take a well-trained military unit and go in there and boom - take everybody out," a former official said. The soldiers did take everyone out, but they did so at what turned out to be a workshop in a residential neighborhood, killing four apprentice welders. Former officials said the Mexican Attorney General at the time, Sergio Garda Ramirez, was so mystified that he asked whether American agents had carried out the raid themselves. Eventually, the military issued a terse statement taking responsibility for the attack but not disclosing the C.I.A.'s involvement. After a third, unsuccessful raid on another suspected drug base, the program was shut down for good, the officials said.

Mexico was near the same point in its political cycle - the end of a six-year presidential term, a period when corruption has historically flourished among outgoing officials - when United States officials looked to the military again in 1994. The idea of greater army support for the police was raised first by American diplomats and again during a visit by the United States Army Chief of Staff, Gen. Gordon Sullivan, current and former American officials said. But at the time, they said, it was rejected by Mexican justice officials. Mr. Zedillo, who took office on Dec. 1, 1994, has called drug trafficking one of Mexico's most serious problems of national security. United States officials strongly endorsed that view, briefing his aides on such developments as the use of passenger jets to fly cocaine into Mexico from Colombia. „The military was the only trained, disciplined force that you could use to deal with this situation in the short term," one of Mr. Zedillo's closest aides said. „There was no one else." Mr. Zedillo first brought army commanders into the redesign of the Government's drug-control strategy. He then authorized them to work with United States officials in an ultimately abortive effort to deploy its aging

F-5 fighters to chase drugjets. Finally, he began allowing military officers to replace federal police agents in several border cities plagued by smugglers. In October 1995, when William J. Perry made the first official visit to Mexico in memory by an American Secretary of Defense, anti-drug aid was at the center of several cooperative ventures he proposed to Mexican military officials, Mexican and United States military officials said.

„You were looking for general ways to engage, military to military,“ a Pentagon official said. Within months, a first group of young Mexican Army officers were training in anti-drug operations at Fort Bragg, N.C. Of some 3,000 Mexican soldiers who are expected to have passed through Defense Department training courses by next fall, 328 young officers will have completed special 12-and 13-week programs intended to create a corps of anti-drug specialists. Those trainees are being sent in turn to train airmobile special forces units that are now stationed at the headquarters of the 12 regions and 40 zones that make up Mexico's military geography. Defense Department officials said the anti-drug curriculum of the units, called Air-Mobile Special Forces Groups, ranged from air-assault operations and military policing to human rights. The Pentagon has also given Mexico 73 aging UH-1H helicopters to transport those troops. The helicopters may be used only for anti-drug operations. But Mexican and United States military officials said there was nothing to stop the transfer of American-trained army officers to similar special forces units that might be deployed against leftist insurgents in southern states like Guerrero and Chiapas.

American officials said that what is perhaps the most significant United States support for the Mexican military's anti-drug efforts is probably the least visible. It comes, they said, in the training, equipping and operational support of C.I.A. officers for a special force of the army intelligence section called the Center for Anti-Narcotics Investigations. The unit, comprising some 90 carefully chosen young officers, began to come together about three years ago, officials said. Like the civilian intelligence groups the C.I.A. works within Mexico, the military anti-drug force is not supposed to be an „action“ unit like the group trained by the agency in the 1980s. But it does appear to sometimes take the lead in raids as well as surveillance actions. Several American officials compared the program to the C.I.A.'s work in Colombia, where the agency has been credited with critical help in the capture of major drug traffickers. A key difference, they noted, has been Mexico's extreme sensitivity to anything involving the C.I.A. Officials familiar with the operations of the intelligence team said that after a clumsy start - at one point its agents lost track of an important Bolivian drug broker they had under surveillance because they insisted on asking a superior for instructions rather than simply follow him - it has emerged as probably the most active of all Mexican anti-drug units.

Officials said the unit played a central part in the pursuit of Amado Carrillo Fuentes, then Mexico's most important trafficker, before he died during plastic surgery last summer. It also worked closely on the investigation of Mr. Carrillo Fuentes' organization after his death, and on a series of raids against the Tijuana-based drug mafia run by the Arellano Felix brothers. Yet reviews of the unit, which is known by its initials in Spanish as the Clan, have been mixed. Officials said some Mexican prosecutors have complained privately that the unit's officials have demonstrated spotty notions of the law, at times handing captured suspects over to the civilian authorities without ever gathering evidence to hold them. Some Mexican police investigators have also questioned why - if the United States is willing to provide the sort of sophisticated surveillance and intelligence-gathering equipment that it is said to have given to the Clan - it will not offer the same support to new anti-drug units created in the Attorney General's office. American officials said questions had been raised about the unit's integrity after two of its agents were dismissed this year for what one official described as „unprofessional conduct." Some have also wondered about its independence - from both Mexican civilians and American intelligence officers. „It could be a time bomb," a former intelligence official said, „because they have a lot less control over that unit than they think they do."

The Mexican Army's Chief of Staff, Gen. Juan Heriberto Salinas Altes, praised the unit, saying it has gathered important information for both army special-forces troops and the federal police. He denied, however, that the unit has any formal or continuing relations hip with the C.I.A. „There could have been some contact, but it was not any official contact," General Salinas Altes said in an interview, his first since becoming Chief of Staff three years ago. For their part, Clinton Administration officials said the closer military relations-hip of that anti-drug cooperation had already paid dividends for the United States. In recent months, they noted, Mexican officials agreed to streamline procedures by which United States drugsurveillance planes are allowed to fly over Mexican airspace, and those by which Coast Guard ships can dock at Mexican ports. The impact of American support on the Mexican military's anti-drug efforts remains somewhat to be seen. Thus far, Defense Department officials said they knew of no instance in which special forces officers trained in the United States had been sent off on an American-donated helicopter in the pursuit of a drug flight.

But many United States officials said it had already become evident that although the Mexican officer corps may be more resistant to the traffickers' bribes than the police, it faces a more serious threat than most American officials foresaw. Clinton Administration officials were shocked this year when the army commander installed as the Zedillo government's drugenforcement chief, Gen. Jesus Gutierrez Rebollo, was arrested for taking bribes from Mr. Carrillo Fuentes, the trafficker. Since then, though, it has become clear that the episode was not an isolated one. Other high-ranking officers have been implicated in connection with Mr. Carrillo Fuentes' organization, including one retired general who was arrested after the wedding of the trafficker's sister. Several more senior officers have been arrested for their supposed ties to the rival trafficking organization run out of Tijuana by the Arellano Felix brothers; one has been charged with offering $1 million monthly bribes to another army general who serves as the Attomey General's representative there. Still, United States officials are divided between those who see new proof of the military's vulnerability and those who see evidence of an institution fighting aggressively against temptation. Mexican officials, not surprisingly, side strongly with the latter camp. „If there is action, there are going to be people hurt," General Salinas Altes said. „We have people killed. We have people wounded. We have people in jail."

General Salinas Altés has himself been a focus of theAmerican scrutiny. According to officials familiar with American intelligence reports in which the Chief of Staff is mentioned, he first came to the United States attention after he moved from Baja California in 1988 to head the Ninth Military Region headquarters in the city of Acapulco. There, he spent six years in charge of drug-eradication efforts in Guerrero, the state that is Mexico's leading producer of heroin poppies. After he became Chief of Staff in December 1994, two American officials said, General Salinas Altés was again in briefly a subject of scrutiny when intelligence officials intercepted a drug trafficker's telephone call for a „General Salinas." They described the report as disturbing but unclear.

Most recently, United States officials became concerned again this summer when it emerged that General Salinas Altés and several other senior officers had met with a top lieutenant of Mr. Carrillo Fuentes. According to a military document published in the Mexican magazine Proceso that appears to be notes from the Jan. 14 meeting, the lieutenant, Eduardo Gonzalez Quirarte, said the trafficker had offered essentially to clean up his business - halting the sale of drugs in Mexico, eschewing violence, helping the economy - if he was allowed to keep half his fortune and continue operating in peace.

General Salinas Altés was interviewed at his Mexico City offices on the condition that he not be questioned about the allegations against him, but only about the cooperative efforts he oversees as the military's representative to an anti-drug group of senior officials from the two countries. But in a separate interview, Gen. Tomas Angeles Dauahare, a senior aide to Mexico's Defense Minister, Gen. Enrique Cervantes Aguirre, dismissed the allegations against General Salinas Altés vehemently. General Angeles confirmed that Mexican military officials had received an unsigned American report forwarded from the Foreign Ministry. After an extensive investigation, in which United States officials did not answer repeated requests for supplementary information, he said, it was found that the guilty officer was in fact a Gen. Javier Salinas Payares, the commander of a military air base, and that he was eventually imprisoned in the case.

Similarly, General Angeles said there was no evidence that General Salinas Altés had acted inappropriately in meeting with Mr. Gonzalez Quirarte, who he said had posed as a young businessman with information about the Carrillo Fuentes mob. „He spoke about Amado Carrillo," General Angeles said. „He gave information about the drug organization internationally. It was only discovered later that this was Eduardo Gonzalez Quirarte." General Angeles also strongly denied a claim made by General Gutiérrez Rebollo during his trial that Mr. Gonzalez Quirarte had two other meetings and that he paid a $6 million down payment on a promised gratuity of $60 million to Government officials. You can be fully certain that had he done that, he would have been arrested because that is bribery," General Angeles said. Referring to General Gutiérrez Rebollo, he added, „That is characteristic of his accusations - the lies, the infamy, the slander." One current and one former American official said there was credible information that Mr. Gonzalez Quirarte had been to see military officials more than once, and they added that a recent assessment of General Gutiérrez Rebollo's testimony concluded that much of it was true.«

CRIMINAL JUSTICE SYSTEM
Kevin Sullivan / Mary Jordan, *Washington Post*

The two reporters became the *Washington Post*'s correspondents in Mexico City in 2000. According to the newspaper's statement in a letter to the Pulitzer Prize jurors, they „started examining rule of law as a key to the challenges facing the Mexican government after seven decades of authoritarian, one-party rule. They were shocked by the depth and breadth of abuses they uncovered. A painter is falsely imprisoned after police knowingly assigned him the name of another suspect. Two deaf, teenage sisters bear pregnancies resulting from rape, but no police investigation ensues. A man serves a long jail term even though police acknowledge that he was tortured to gain a confession. Kidnapers built their lucrative industry with impunity. Local 'bosses' dominate regions where their word is law. Thousands of children are locked away in 'little jails' unregulated and unexamined by the state. One conclusion common to these stories is that Mexico has two justice systems: one for the rich, another for the poor.“

Sullivan and Jordan's reporting anticipated the emergence of crime and justice as the most explosive public issues in Mexico, their stories were widely followed in the Mexican press and by officials, and had impact. The Pulitzer Prize jurors of the International Reporting award category also were impressed by the two journalists and stated in their report of March 7, 2003: „Mary Jordan and Kevin Sullivan exposed and explored the medieval criminal justice system of Mexico and brought to life horrific injustices that have destroyed lives and warped the values of a country ever more important to the U.S. economic and strategic weIl being. They took readers to lawless places they would have never visited, told the story of victims, and showed how those in power have not only benefited but perpetuated a system that yet shows little sign of change.“ For the Board it was no question that Jordan and Sullivan earned the Pulitzer recognition.

Kevin Sullivan, born on November 5, 1959, in Framingham, Ma., was raised in Brunswick, Maine, and graduated from the University of New Hampshire in 1981. After working for the *Providence Journal* in Rhode Island and the *Gloucester Daily-Times* in Massachusetts, Sullivan joined the *Washington Post* in 1991. On the *Post*, Sullivan reported on six continents from more than 75 countries, including Afghanistan, Pakistan, Iraq, Cuba, Burma, Democratic Republic of the Congo, Sierra Leone and Haiti. In 2000, Sullivan and his wife, Mary Jordan, reported from Mexico; they both earned the 2003 Pulitzer Prize for International Reporting. - Mary Jordan, born on November

10, 1960, in Cleveland, Oh., graduated from Georgetown University in 1983 and earned a master's degree from Columbia University in 1984. Jordan began her career at the *Washington Post* as an intern and moved up to higher positions at the newspaper and finally she became foreign correspondent and reported from nearly 40 countries. With her husband, Kevin Sullivan, Jordan ran the newspaper's bureaus in Tokio, London and Mexico City. In 2003 she became the co-winner of the Pulitzer Prize for International Reporting. Following are several of their award-winning articles, published during the first half of 2002:

INMATES IN „PARADISE"

»Avila Suarez was 8 years old when she arrived by boat on this tiny Pacific island of Isla Maria Madre, coming ashore to be with her father, a convicted murderer. She grew up among the other inmates and their children in one of the world's most unusual prisons, an island with a church, a bakery and a dance hall where convicts are allowed to serve sentences alongside their family members. Then she fell in love with a convicted cocaine trafficker. So when her father was released a few years ago, and her mother and three sisters left with him, Avila Suarez stayed behind with her new husband. She still lives here in the prison where she has spent most of her life. „Sometimes 1 would rather be on the outside. It is always the same here," said Avila Suarez, 25, nuzzling up to her husband, Jesus Lopez, 33, who has 18 years left to serve. „But when I leave, I would like it to be with him."

Isla Maria is a Mexican government prison experiment in the Pacific Ocean 95 miles south of Mazatlan. Started at the turn of the century as a Mexican version of Alcatraz, where the worst of the worst were condemned to a life of hard labor, it has been transformed into a relative paradise for inmates who have shown a willingness to reform. Rehabilitation is a bedrock principle of the Mexican judicial system, so much so that neither the death penalty nor life imprisonment is allowed under law. Proponents say Isla Maria is a logical extension of that idea: If prisoners are going to have to return to life in a normal community one day, why not keep them in a prison that simulates a normal community? There are no cells or bars here. The inmates are called „colonists." They wear no uniforms and live in ordinary housing on streets that look like those in any Mexican town. While navy officers on the perimeter of the 54-square-mile island carry machine guns, the prison guards carry no guns. About 600 children of inmates live in little houses with their parents and attend public schools on pretty, palm-lined streets.

„This prison used to be almost hell. The inmates were treated savagely and humiliated," said the warden, Raul Soto Calderon. Now, he said, „If you didn't know this was a prison, you wouldn't realize it. There is nothing like this in the world." For one thing, it would be expensive to duplicate. With an annual budget of $4 million for 1,600 inmates, the government pays about

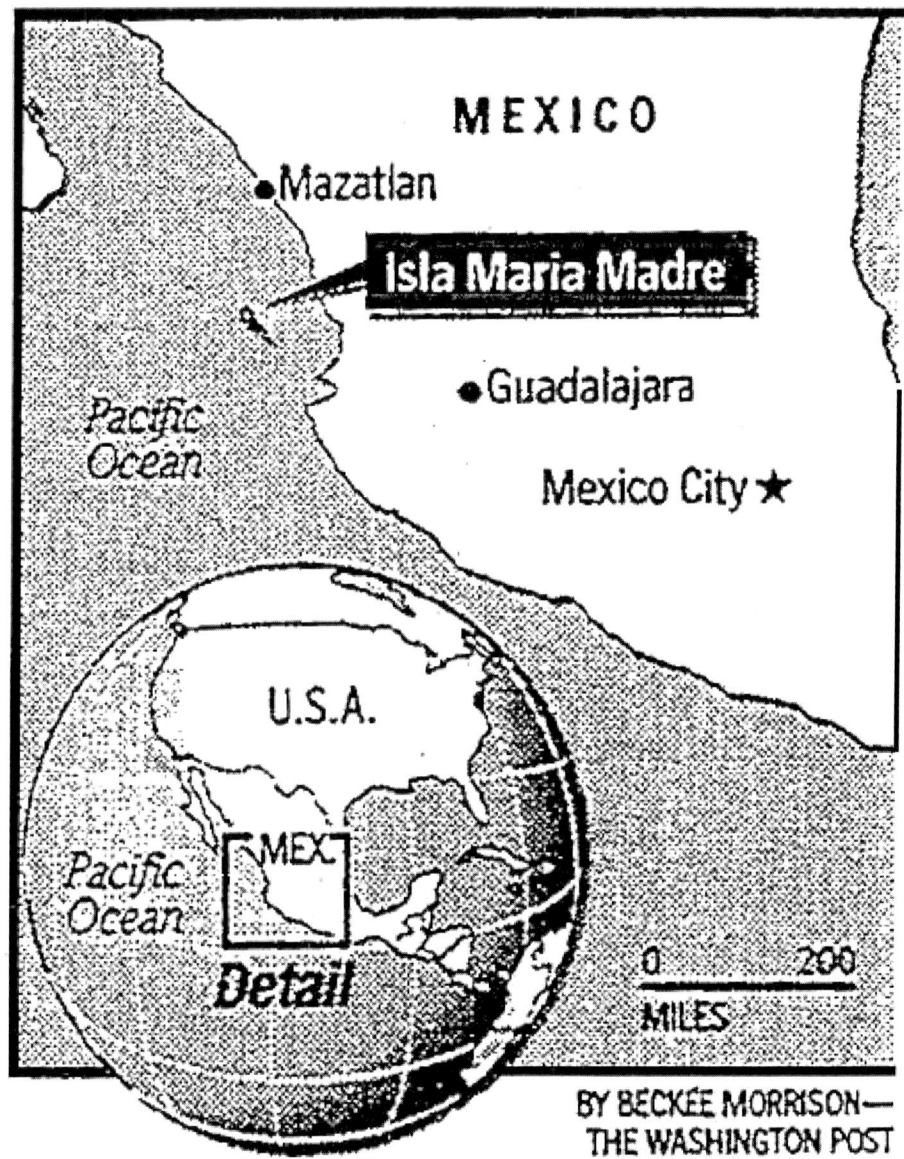

BY BECKEE MORRISON—
THE WASHINGTON POST

three times as much to handle each prisoner here as it does for those at any other prison. Transportation costs for supplies and people are high. The warden, for instance, recently had to rent a small plane to airlift a prisoner with a severe kidney problem. Public Security Minister Alejandro Gertz Manero, whose department runs the prison, questions the wisdom of a cash-strapped government running what he calls a „paradise." He would like all Mexican prisons to focus on making criminals pay restitution for their crimes. Some also question the wisdom of allowing children to grow up in prisson. In several other Mexican prisons, children also live alongside their parents, usually their mothers. Although this practice is lauded for keeping families intact, it is also criticized because it means children are raised in a community of criminals, where everything from freedom to food is limited.

„For some children it can be a little damaging," said Oliva Suarez Ilago, Avila Suarez's mother, who now lives on a peach farm in central Mexico. „They see things they shouldn't. They become aggressive and badly spoken." Avila Suarez, who does not have children, says other parents worry about having to wait for medicine that arrives on a weekly ship. „Some children are exposed to good people on the island who say to them, 'See where 1 am. Learn from me," she said. But other children live among „people who don 't want to change." Yet for some children, living here is far safer than it is in the rough neighborhoods they left behind, and the govemment white-washed housing is often better, too. „I like it here because 1 am here with my dad," Maribel Cisneros, 13, said recently as she sat at her desk in a history class. „My dad is here because of drugs." The inmates clearly like it here. „When I got here I cried. What beauty!" said Guadalupe Rodriquez Quiroz, a convicted heroin-seIler who spent four years in a crowded, violent Tijuana prison before arriving here. There, she said, guards made inmates pay for everything, including use of the bathroom.

A key element of the Isla Maria experiment is to take power away from guards, who have often turned Mexican prisons into sewers of bribery and illegal punishments. Here there are only 36 guards. Most of the inmates are at Isla Maria on drug convictions; the typical sentence here is 10 years for marijuana trafficking. But there are a few who committed robbery, assault or even murder. And the sight of Luis Oscar Mendez Juarez, who killed a man during a robbery in Mexico City, swinging on a hammock by the ocean can be a bit jarring. The new warden said he is still weeding out the prison population. He said some of the inmates who have been sent here do not meet the island's current standards. He is in the midst of a major expansion, nearly doubling the inmate population this year to 3,000. He is also planning to order off the island

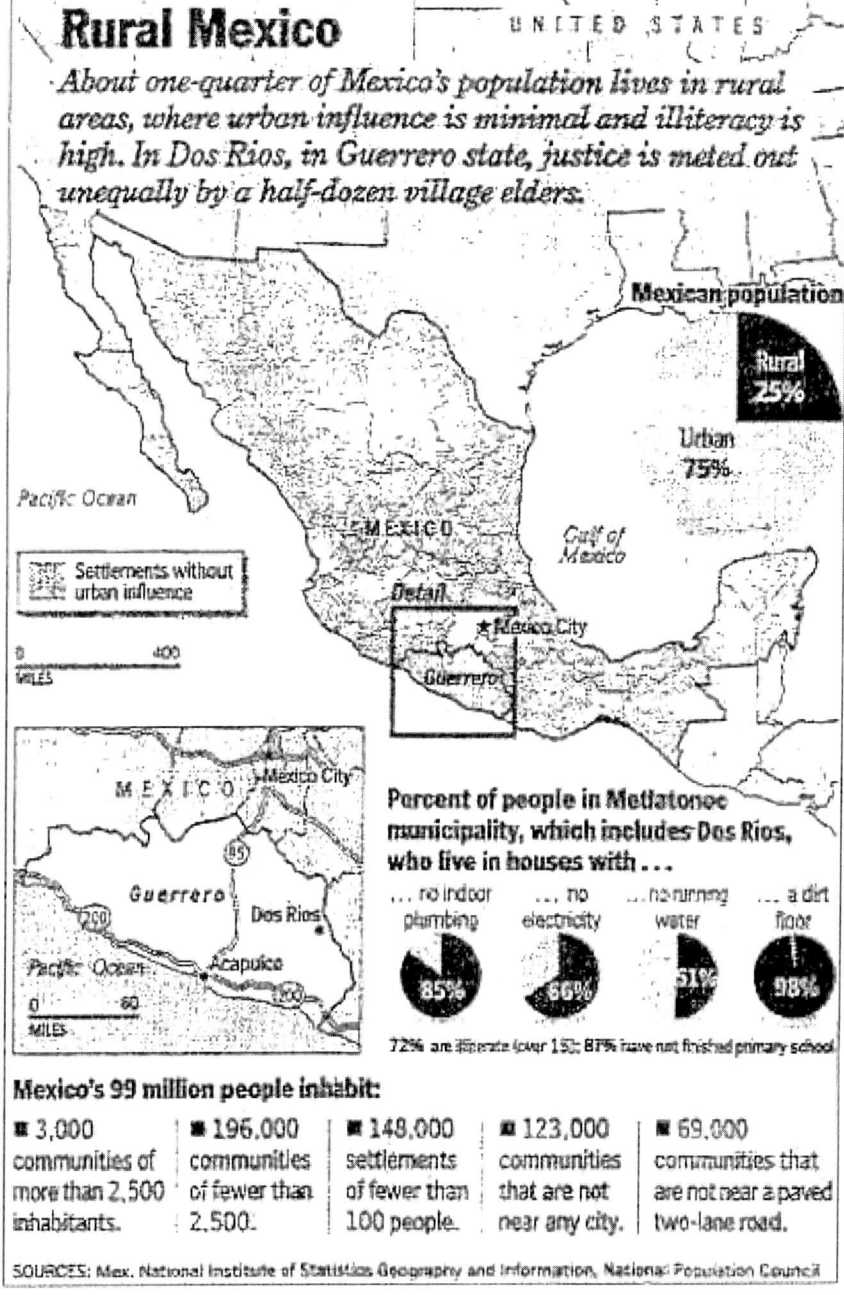

Rural Mexico

About one-quarter of Mexico's population lives in rural areas, where urban influence is minimal and illiteracy is high. In Dos Rios, in Guerrero state, justice is meted out unequally by a half-dozen village elders.

UNITED STATES

Mexican population

Rural **25%**

Urban **75%**

Pacific Ocean

MEXICO

Gulf of Mexico

Settlements without urban influence

0 — 400
MILES

Mexico City

Detail

Guerrero

MEXICO — Mexico City

85

Guerrero

200

Dos Rios

Pacific Ocean — Acapulco

0 — 60
MILES

Percent of people in Metlatonoc municipality, which includes Dos Rios, who live in houses with . . .

. . . no indoor plumbing	. . . no electricity	. . . no running water	. . . a dirt floor
85%	86%	51%	98%

72% are illiterate (over 15); 87% have not finished primary school.

Mexico's 99 million people inhabit:

3,000 communities of more than 2,500 inhabitants.	196,000 communities of fewer than 2,500.	148,000 settlements of fewer than 100 people.	123,000 communities that are not near any city.	69,000 communities that are not near a paved two-lane road.

SOURCES: Mex. National Institute of Statistics Geography and Information, National Population Council

any children over the age of 12. All inmates have the option of bringing their families, but many spouses and children do not want to forfeit their jobs and routines on the mainland. For some, it is prohibitively expensive to get to Mazatlan, where a navy ship shuttles families to the island. Isla Maria has also been unable to completely shed its reputation for harsh treatment, so it has not been much in demand among the main prison population in Mexico. But word is getting out.

Avila Suarez and her husband share a one-bedroom home with a concrete floor and sparse furnishings a double bed, a tiny television and a radio. They eat red snapper and other fresh fish caught by inmates. Their two lime-green parrots, Lino and Gustavo, fly freely about the house. „They have never been caged," Lopez said. Before being moved here, Lopez spent several years in a Guadalajara jail, where, he said, „you are obliged to be aggressive to stay alive." „I would be a different person if I had to stay in Guadalajara," Lopez said. There he learned that „you rob or are robbed, you defend yourself or you are beaten. Here, it is so safe you can leave your bike outside for three days and nobody would take it. Now the chatty Lopez is host of the island radio show, „Window by the Sea." He said people here „are afraid to make mistakes because they will be forced to leave the island." Warden Soto Calderon said that in the nine months that he has been here, he has transferred 93 troublemaking inmates to mainland prisons. A few people have been punished for trying to ferment corn or rice to make moonshine or for smoking marijuana. Punishment is banishment to a camp on the far side of the island where there is no music, television or family life. In the old days, it used to be splitting rocks in the hot sun. Suarez Ilago, Avila Suarez's mother, said there were many good things about Isla Maria. Her husband, who killed a man in a street brawl, had no formal schooling when he arrived, but spent his years on the island finishinng primary school and learning to work a farm. She said he now works hard on their little peach farm no longer drinks and has had no more troubles with the law.

Despite the rehabilitative effect Isla Maria had on her husband, Suarez Ilago said, „I never forgot for a moment that I was in jail." During the decade she spent on the island with her four daughters, she would look out at the endless ocean and see it as invisible bars. „1 feel bad that I brought her to the island and then left her there," she said about her one daughter still in the penal colony. „It was like leaving half of my heart there." But Avila Suarez said she does not feel like someone left behind. She has a job as a telephone operator, takes occasional vacations and lives what she considers a normal life. She said she misses the little comforts that the mainland provides, like variety of food, the sight of a mountain or a highway, the latest magazines. But more important to her are the good times, and the lifetime of memories here. Nearly everyone on the island came to her wedding ceremony seven years ago. She was just 18, stepping lightly into marriage and adulthood in a prison dining hall with an inmate band playing salsa.«

LIFE BEYOND LAW

»Teofilo Gonzales Cano stabbed his cousin to death with two quick jabs to the heart. They had been the best of friends, growing up together in the same mud-brick house in this tiny village of Dos Rios in southern Mexico. But one night they drank themselves nearly blind on homemade grain alcohol. An argument about nothing got out of hand, and soon Vicente Gonzalez Santiago lay dead in the dirt. Teofilo ran. They found him at dawn, sitting in a forest clutching his empty bottle. The local farmer who served as village constable, another cousin of Teofilo's, bound his hands behind his back and brought him in.

The whole village was waiting, more than 300 people. They forced Teofilo to lie facedown next to Vicente's corpse. They shouted at him, called him a murderer. His mother sat in the dirt next to her son, pleading for mercy. The nearest police were more than two hours' drive away and there was no telephone in Dos Rios, hidden in rugged mountains 180 miles southwest of Mexico City. Justice in this backwater belongs to a half-dozen town elders, who stood over the two cousins in their early thirties, one dead and one accused, and debated the punishment that day in 1999. Finally they agreed. „They said the two of them should be buried, together,“ said Catarina Cano Santiago, Teofilo's mother.

According to Cano, other Dos Rios residents and human rights investigators, the elders enlisted villagers to carry out the sentence. Some of the men hacked a grave in the rocky soil of the village cemetery. Someone banged together a flimsy wooden coffin, and the villagers put Vicente's body in it. They hoisted the box and began a procession down a narrow cow path to the graveyard. Others dragged Teofilo by the arms. Women and children followed, marehing under a hot sun past fields of dead corn. They placed Vicente's coffin in the hole, then threw Teofilo in on top, with his arms and legs tied together. He screamed and begged for his life, calling out to his mother. „Please don't let them do this to me!“ She tried to help him, but her neighbors and friends held her back. The law had spoken, and no one would stand in its way. Twenty men started throwing dirt into the hole with shovels and sticks. Teofilo, screaming, tried to climb out. His 14-year-old son, Felipe, ran to him and tried to hug him and pull him up. Someone tossed a lasso around Teofilo's neck and jerked him back into the grave, ripping him from his boy's embrace. They pulled the crying youth away from his father as the dirt piled higher and higher on top of him, until he disappeared into the ground. „When they finished," said his mother, „you could still hear him screaming under the ground."

Dos Rios is a dusty wisp of a village clinging to a mountainside in Guerrero state. It takes 12 hours to drive there from the capital, down a road that turns from pavement to dirt to a harrowing path that drops thousands of feet on either side. Fewer than 400 people live in Dos Rios, in a cluster of soft-brick huts baked by a close, heavy sun. There is no electricity, not a light bulb in town. The only vehicle is an old Ford pickup truck. A priest comes once a year to say Mass in the crumbling Roman Catholic church. It has been months since a police patrol passed through. As Mexico seeks to modernize, setting up a formal justice system in places like this is one of its most difficult challenges.

Mexico has more than 148,000 communities with fewer than 100 residents, many of them isolated in the vast stretches of mountains and deserts that cover much of this country. By comparison, the United States, which has five times more land area, has fewer than 2,000 towns with populations under 100. More than 25 million Mexicans - a quarter of the population - live in communities of 2,500 people or fewer. Government officials say it is simply too expensive to run roads and electric lines to many of them, let alone provide police, pro-secutors and judges. As a result, millions of Mexicans live in places that remain largely beyond the law. „The rule of law is absent in these towns. The level of impunity is extremely high," said Adolfo Aguilar Zinser, Mexico's new ambas-sador to the United Nations, who served until recently as national security adviser.

He said the administration of President Vicente Fox is working to equip rural police with satellite communication systems and create more uniform police coverage around the country. But he said many state and local govemment officials have resisted that idea because they still operate under the practices that dominated during seven decades of rule by the Institutional Revolutionary Party. For years, he said, the PRI encouraged powerful local bosses to handle justice in their own way. Abel Barrera, a human rights activist based in Tlapa, near Dos Rios, called justice in Mexico „unbalanced." „Things have changed in the cities, but in parts of the country like this, here in the countryside, violence is still the accepted mechanism of justice," said Barrera, who investigated the Teofilo Gonzalez Cano case. „It's still the law of the jungle."

There is no formal accounting of how many people are killed in Mexico's rough rural justice every year. But human rights groups estimate that hundreds have been killed and hundreds more beaten over the years in punishments meted out beyond official scrutiny. Barrera said at least 10 people a year are killed in the region around Dos Rios in a form of local justice. „People here have not yet taken notice that Mexico is changing," Barrera said. Equal protection under the law does not exist. Sentences are given out on the judgment of a few men, who often have little education and no legal training. Their decisions are effectively beyond the oversight of federal, state and municipal governments. In some cases, their punishment is far more harsh than the formal legal system requires. For example, Mexico has no death penalty or life sentences, but the Dos Rios villagers buried Teofilo alive.

In other cases, local elders are far more lenient than judges. Town elders in Dos Rios said they would punish a rapist with „a few hours" in the town's small jail cell, plus a restitution payment of perhaps $100 to the victim's family. They recalled one case in which the rapist was forced to pay for a party that the victim's family was planning. Dos Rios is a Mixtec Indian community, governed by traditional practices. Mexico has long debated how far to go in allowing its 10 million Indians to run their own judicial systems. Critics argue that all Mexicans should be governed by the same legal system. But Dos Rios remains one of many places - Indian and non-Indian - set apart from mainstream justice in Mexico.

With each passing decade, roads and other public services creep closer to these self-ruled villages. Ten years ago, the road into Dos Rios was little more than a donkey path used largely by farmers hauling their opium poppies to market. Today, trucks hauling beer and Pepsi lumber down the roads, supplying villages with the syrupy smack of globalization. But the rule of law cannot be loaded on to a delivery truck, and the protection of police and courts still barely exists. „We can't get everywhere," said Isidro Basurto Mendoz, the official in charge of police in Metlatonoc, the municipal seat, which is three hours from Dos Rios by car and 10 on foot. „The distances are too great, and we have no communications. The problem is that when we can't get there, people take justice into their own hands."

Basurto said he has 18 police officers and one pickup truck to cover 30,000 people in 156 small communities spread over an area about the size of Montgomery County. Most are reachable only by four-wheel-drive vehicles. In the rainy season they are cut off by impasssable roads. As Basurto spoke, word filtered in that two men had been killed the night before in a village a couple of hours' drive into the mountains. A dozen of Basurto's officers grabbed their shotguns and hopped into the back of the police pickup. Despite the display of firepower, Basurto said he and his men would almost certainly not solve the crime. „I'm going to get the information, give the bodies to the families for burial, then I'll come back to do the paperwork," he said. Basurto said it was unlikely that any suspect would ever be convicted. He said his officers are not trained to gather or handle evidence. Witnesses would need to drive for hours or walk for days to give testimony before a judge. He said people have no money to make such a trip, and would fear retaliation.

Two suspects were recently arrested and charged with murder in a nearby village. Basurto turned them over to regional prosecutors, but they were free within three months. He suspects they paid a bribe to get the charges dropped. Now, he said, they are back in their village, threatening to kill those who identified them. Basurto said that case is unusual because the suspects were charged and turned over to prosecutors. „Usually by the time we find out about a case, it's already been resolved," he said. „Or we don't find out about it at all." Teofilo and Vicente grew up the way all children do here: poorly nourished, without shoes and with little knowledge of the outside world. They played among the chickens and mango trees, and they were lucky to survive. Elders here say that until a state government doctor began making regular visits a few years ago, many children died for lack of medicine and basic care.

The two boys were reared in one of the village's small red-brown cubes of mud. Together, working the fields of corn and beans, they grew into men. There are no known photos of either cousin in this village, where cameras are rare. Their families describe them as typical in every way, two sturdy farmhands. They both married and had the same kind of families: three sons and a daughter. Then things went sour for Teofilo. His wife died in childbirth. He remarried, but his second wife died of a fever about five years ago. He was raising his children alone. Vicente was building his own house, next to a shady grove of banana trees where he was raised. His uncle lived there, too. It was in his house that Vicente and Teofilo started drinking one afternoon in March 1999. They drank all night. Some here say that Vicente began making jokes about Teofilo's two dead wives. All that is known for sure is that sometime after midnight, Teofilo pulled out a small knife and stabbed Vicenterwice in the chest.

By 8 a.m. Teofilo had been brought in and the two men lay side by side on the dirt floor of Vicente's house, with the six elders standing over them, discussing their fate. Vicente's brother, who declined to give his name in an effort to avoid drawing more attention to the case, said the elders made the decision to bury Teofilo alive. The town elders also wish to avoid attention. Asked about the case one recent moming, Juan Gonzalez Ruiz, the comisario, or head of the local government, switched out of Spanish and consulted with the five other elders, all men in their forties and fifties sitting outside the village hall. They debated for 20 minutes in their Indian language. According to a local schoolteacher who speaks both languages, Gonzalez wanted to tell the truth but the elders instructed him to lie. They said they did not want any more trouble. Following their orders, Gonzalez told a reporter that Vicente had died in an accident and that Teofilo had run away. The elders nodded in agreement.

The comisario is elected by village residents, and the elders are former comisarios. They said their main goal was to find negotiated solutions to crimes and disputes. They have 10 unpaid „community police" officers, whose duties inc1ude helping to keep the peace at festivals and tracking down stolen animals. Justice varies greatly by community. In some villages, stealing an animal has led to hanging. But here, Gonzalez said, the penalty for stealing a cow is a few hours in jail. He said he or the elders go to the cell and ask the thief why he stole. They try to impress on him that stealing is bad.

Education is sorely lacking. Sixty-seven children study in the village school, which goes to the sixth grade. Only a few children finish all six years. If they wanted to continue their schooling, they would have to drive three hours to Metlatonoc. No one can remember anyone ever doing that. The people are accustomed to accepting the punishments meted out by the elders. But Teofilo's case shocked many residents. Guadalupe Martinez Castillo, who said she is about 40, said she still cannot believe what her town did. „It frightens me because I think the same could happen to me, my children, my family," she said. „Everyone lives in fear because they didn't do that to an animal, they killed a person."

Cano, Teofilo's mother, said she lives with fear and regret. From her home, she can just about see the village's hilltop cemetery, where the two cousins are buried in a grave marked by a single anonymous slab of wood jammed into the rocky ground. Sitting in the red dirt at her house, Cano said she wished she had filed some kind of complaint about her son's death. But she is afraid to challenge the men who run Dos Rios. „I don't have the courage to confront them," she said. „If I were a man, it might be different. But people here don't know who to go to for justice." Francisco Estrada Rojas, who teaches at the elementary school, said the elders ordered Teofilo to be buried alive to „teach a big lesson." He said there had been several murders in Dos Rios in the years leading up to Teofilo's execution. He said that, in the absence of police, disputes over land, family matters, a few cattle or other minor issues often ended in bloodshed. He said few of those killers were caught, and when they were, they almost always seemed to be able to bribe police or prosecutors to let them off.

„That's why people take justice into their own hands," Estrada said. „This happened because the community had been beaten down by so many crimes without punishment. Estrada said that when the police arrived a day after the murders, they wanted to dig up the men to see for themselves what had happened, and to put the two men in separate graves. But local officials told the police that no one in town would help them. Estrada said they told the police: „You'll have to pay for the food and drink of the laborers, and no one wants to do that kind of work." Several people in the community said the police stayed only a few rninutes longer. There is a widespread belief here that the officers were paid a bribe to forget about the whole thing. „They didn't arrest anybody," Estrada said. „Because they would have had to arrest the whole community."«

THE TORTURE GHOST

»Alfonso Martin del Campo Dodd stood naked in the basement of a Mexico City police station, where he said cops took turns punching him and slapping him, kicking him in the groin and screaming at him. His sister and her husband had just been murdered in their sleep, stabbed a total of 64 times, and the police wanted Martin del Campo to confess. They waved a typewritten statement in his face and ordered him to sign it. He told them he didn't kill anybody and wasn't going to sign anything. Then came the plastic bag. According to Martin del Campo, whose story was corroborated under oath by an officer who was suspended for torturing him, two cops held him by the arms while another put the bag over his head. „That's one minute," he remembers the officer saying."Next we will do it for two minutes, then three, until you confess." They put the bag over his head again and again. „I was sure they were going to kill me," Martin del Campo said.

So naked, bleeding and gasping for breath, he scratched his name at the bottom of a confession he did not write and had never read, admitting to a crime he said he did not commit. Based on that document and no direct physical evidence - no witnesses, fingerprints, bloodstains, hairs or clothing fibers - a judge convicted him of the double murder and sentenced him to 50 years in prison. That was 10 years ago. Martin del Campo, a U.S. citizen born in Chicago, now sits in prison in this city 40 miles north of Mexico City. His appeals are exhausted. Four different judges ruled that his allegations of torture were irrelevant. Confessions obtained by torture are not necessarily false, they ruled, repeating a conclusion, reached frequently by Mexican judges. The principle that someone charged with a crime is innocent until proven guilty does not exist in Mexico. Until 1984, federal law explicitly said a defendant was guilty until proven innocent. Although the presumption of guilt was later removed, it remains the practice defendants must still prove their innocence. Martin del Campo could not.

He is 37 now, and his hair is tinged with gray. His father moved to this small city to be near him, and he visits every day; his mother, who lives in Mexico City, comes on weekends. They said losing a daughter was devastating enough, and they want their son back. „I have been legally kidnapped here, and I want to be free," Martin del Campo said, sitting in his tiny cell. „The worst of this is losing my sister. But I am dead, too. I am dead in life." Martin del Campo is a ghost in Mexico's closet, haunting this country as it tries to move beyond a history of authoritarian abuses. Even now, Mexico's record on torture is one of the worst in the world, according to the United Nations, Amnesty International and other groups.It is a legacy that built up over generations. For much of the 20th century, Mexico was run by the Institutional Revolutionary Party, or PRI. Under its rigid system, from the president's gilded office to thousands of rural villages run by strongarm political bosses, official power was wielded as a blunt and often brutal tool of control.

In a rule-of-law state, the law is a higher authority than the arbitrary action of any individual, whether a police officer or president. But throughout recent Mexican history, it was the other way around: Party bosses were above the law. Police departments, especially in the countryside, were developed largely as political security forces to support local bosses, and not as investigative law enforcement units to solve crimes. Fists and kicks and plastic bags have long been standard practice for solving cases. The innocent and the guilty have confessed simply to stop the pain. Prosecutors have been neglected. There has been little need to professionalize them when their chief function has been to present confessions to judges. „They just look for a quick, easy solution to a crime, rather than the truth," said Emma Maza of the Miguel Agustin Pro Juarez Human Rights Center in Mexico City.

Mexican judges have also been part of the system that ruled above the law. The goal has been to keep the political bosses satisfied, resolving cases by whatever means necessary. To keep their jobs, they have to do what they are told," said human rights lawyer Pilar Noriega. Defense lawyers also have seen little chance to buck the system. Public defenders have been even more poorly trained and less likely to serve their clients well. The PRI era ended in December 2000 with the swearing-in of President Vicente Fox, who was elected by voters fed up with the abuses and corruption of the PRI system. Fox has promised to clean up Mexico's human rights record, but Amnesty International and even

Fox's top human rights adviser, Mariclaire Acossta, acknowledge that torture continues. Acosta said Fox's government was trying to pass new anti-torture laws, train police and soldiers not to beat confessions out of suspects, and enact reforms to prevent judges from accepting torture-induced confession. But, she said: „Those are still common practices. Its an abomination."

Theoretically, torture is illegal in Mexico. The constitution prohibits „all incommunicado detention, intimidation or torture" and states that confessions made before anyone other than a prosecutor or a judge are not admissible in court. In 1986, Mexico began enacting laws to punish torture, and to make torture-induced confessions inadmisssible in court.In addition, in 1987, Mexico ratified a U.N. convention against torture. Fox has invited U.N. human rights officials to set up an office in Mexico. But Mexico is slow to change, and torture is still a common tool of the authorities. Last month, in Nuevo Leon state, a man suspected of robbing an ATM died of asphyxiation while in police custody. The state attorney general's office said it believed he died as the result of torture, and the case is under investigation. On Wednesday, the Durango state human rights commission concluded that five state police officers had tortured three murder suspects in March. Two weeks ago, the national human rights commission concluded that a suspected kidnapper who died in custody of federal police in March was beaten to death.

The challenge facing Mexico today is not only to enforce the ban on torture but to change the mind-set of a generation of police, prosecutors and judges, whose practices and beliefs were set in an earlier era. Acosta said the government faces enormous obstacles, including decades of official indifference to torture and other abuses. Just as important as preventing torture in the future, she added, is redressing wrongs of the past-including victims of torture locked away in prisons. Sitting in his cell, next to a dirt field where other inmates played soccer, Martin del Campo, who has a round face and a soft voice, recounted the story he has told many times, about the early morning hours of May 30, 1992: He woke to the sound of his sister, Patricia, screaming his name. She and her husband, Gerardo Zamudio Aldaba, slept in another bedroom in the Mexico City apartment they shared. The two men were partners in two businesses: importing carpets, and operating buses for the city. Patricia, 33, worked as a waitress and took care of the couple's three daughters, then 6, 4 and 2, who were sleeping in the next room.

Martin del Campo ran toward the screams. He was met at his bedroom door by two men with stockings over their heads. They called him by his nickname, Chacho, then, he remembers, they beat him. They forced him downstairs and threw him into the trunk of a car. They drove for about 30 minutes, until the car came to a crashing stop. Martin del Campo heard the two men get out and run. He said he found a tire iron, smashed out a brake light and saw that he was on a highway, where the car had crashed into the concrete barrier dividing the road. He fiddled with a lock until the trunk popped open. He flagged down a passing bus and rode it to the first tollbooth, where he ran to some police officers and told them what happened. The police drove him to the crashed car, where they found a bloody knife and started asking questions. They drove him back to his apartment, now surrounded by police cars and ambulances. A neighbor's teenage son told him that his sister and Zamudio were dead. Police drove Martin del Campo to the station, where, he said, he was taken to a basement room and surrounded by a dozen police officers. The officer in charge, later identified to him as Sotero Galvan Gutiérrez, asked him to tell his story. Martin del Campo said he told them everything. They made him tell the same story at least four times. Nobody wrote anything down, he recalled, and there was no tape recorder.

Finally, he said,one officer started hitting him swore at him and said, „Tell us how you did it - how did you kill them?" Martin del Campo said he was shocked. Then all the officers started taking turns hitting and kicking him. They made him strip naked and kept hitting him, some with wet towels wrapped around their fists to leave fewer marks. Eventually, he said, Galvan came to him with a typed statement and demanded he sign. He still refused. Then came the plastic bag. And he finally signed. „That made them very happy," he said. The case against Martin del Campo, who had no previous criminal record, was made largely by Galvan, according to the court file. In Galvan's version, described in his investigative report, Martin del Campo was drunk and killed his sister and her husband because he was angry with his brother-in-law over a $70 car repair bill. He waited until the two were asleep, then stabbed them with kitchen knives. He smashed his own head and face, hard enough to cause deep cuts, and staged a phony kidnapping to cover up his crime, Galvan said in the report.

But hundreds of pages of court documents contain no evidence to support Galvan's version. They don't prove Martin del Campo's innocence either. But the record shows blood tests indicate he was not drunk. Lab tests showed that hairs found in the clenched fist of his sister when she died, presumably from her killer, were not Martin del Campo's. There were no witnesses, no blood-soaked clothes. There was no motive offered for why he would kill his sister. Galvan offered as evidence a reconstruction of the events, based on his theory. Officers brought Martin del Campo back to the apartment, over his objections, and took 85 photos as they made him reach for knives in the kitchen, and forced him to preterid to stab the victims, played by two police officers posing in the bloody bed. Reenactments are a common technique in Mexican crirninal investigations and are often accepted as evidence in trials, although they are based on nothing more than a prosecutor's version of events. The trial judge, and several judges who considered Martin del Campo's appeals, cited the reenactment photos as evidence of his guilt, and an appeals judge called it „convincing" evidence, according to court documents.

Galvan said Martin del Campo was represented by a public defender during the reenactment. But the person listed by Galvan as defender was a police department computer specialist, court documents subsequently showed. The record also shows that a public defender eventually assigned to his case never argued that the confession should be excluded because of torture. An appeals court judge called the confession „the only relevant piece of evidence" against him. During the trial, Martin del Campo was given the opportunity to question Galvan directly. He asked him if he and other officers had stripped him, beaten him, suffocated him with a plastic bag. The court record shows that, under oath, Galvan acknowledged that he had done it. But the judge accepted the confession anyway, noting, as the appellate judges also did, that in Mexico, confessions obtained by torture are often still considered as evidence, despite the laws that say confessions obtained by torture are inadmissible.

In April 1993, Galvan shot and killed an unarmed man while on duty. He was convicted of murder, fired from the police force and sentenced to 10 years in prison. After serving five years, he was released for „health reasons." In October 1994, acting as a result of Galvan's admission in the trial, the Mexico City attorney general's office punished Galvan for violating Martin del Campo's human rights. Although he had already been fired, his punishment was a three-year suspension from the police force. The notice was delivered to him in prison. Galvan, in responsc to a message sent through an intermediary, said he would not comment on the case. Martin del Campo also filed a complaint seeking criminal torture charges against Galvan. But prosecutors closed the case in 2000, saying there wasn't enough evidence, despite Galvan's admission that he bad tortured Martin deI Campo. Enrique Plota, a top official in the prosecutor's office, was asked why Galvan didn't face criminal prosecution. That question has no answer," he said. „It's something that we are going to look into. We are very worried that there were irregularities."

In one sign of the potential for change, the leadership of the city attorney general's office has changed hands since 2000, when a new mayor was elected. In an office that had long been suspected of covering up abuses, several former private sector human rights activists have been hired to high positions. Flota, for example, was previously a private defense lawyer who specialized in human rights cases. Flota, who started his job in January, said he and others in his office were just now beginning to confront abuses from the past. They plan a complete review of Martin del Campo's case. „There was a frequent practice of torture and irregularities by the police, we all know that," Flota said. „In this case, we have to find out exactly what happened. We have many doubts about this case."

Flota also said he planned to review why his predecessors never investigated a 1998 complaint filed by Martin del Campo's relatives in which they offered another version of the case. The complaint alleged that Zamudio's family arranged the murders to collect his inheritance. It also alleged that Patricia was killed to prevent her from inheriting her husband's assets, and Martin del Campo was spared so he would be blamed. The complaint includes documents showing that Zamudio's brother and his mother ended up with all of his assets, as well as Martin del Campo's share of two small businesses in which he and Zamudio were partners. Martin del Campo, speaking in the fluent English he picked up as a child in Chicago, said no one has ever investigated what he said was the obvious line of inquiry: „In murder cases, the first question you ask is, „Who benefited?'" he said. „Look at me. Did I benefit?" With no legal appeals left, Martin del Campo has thrown his fate to the Inter-American Commission on Human Rights in Washington, an arm of the Organization of American States, which is reviewing his case to determine if the Mexican judicial system violated his rights. The commission's report is due by the end of the year. If it recommends his release, Acosta said, Fox would find a way to comply.

Martin del Campo has asked the U.S. government for help, but so far it has given him only vitamins and copies of *Sports Illustrated*, delivered every three months by an embassy official who checks on all U.S. citizens in Mexican prisons. With 40 years left in his sentence, Martin del Campo passes his days working at a little snack shop in the prison. His father, 68, works alongside him during his daily visits. His mother, 67, spends much of her time trying to find her orphaned granddaughters, who are now 16, 14 and 12. A court awarded her custody of the girls in 1995, but she said Zamudio's family has them and she does not know where they are. „This has all been the worst thing anyone could imagine," she said. „It has been hell."

Earlier last month, Martin del Campo married his longtime girlfriend, Janeth, in the prison. They had been dating at the time of the murders. At the ceremony, they stood in a bare prison room before a priest, nuzzling and giggling and pledging to spend their lives together. It was almost normal, except that the photographer was a convicted drug dealer and the honeymoon trip was a walk past the guard tower to a prison cell. „It's not how'd like it to be," Martin del Campo said. „But time is passing. I've had a lot of years of bad news. Now I want to have children, and a life."«

BIBLIOGRAPHY

Unpublished Materials

Media Exhibits

Miami Herald Entry for Liz Balmaseda, 1993
Miami Herald Entry for Bastian Obermayer et al., 2017
Miami News Entry for Harold W. Hendrix, 1963
Milwaukee Journal Entry for Austin C. Wehrwein, 1953
New York Daily News Entry for Martin and Santora, 1959
New York Times Entry for Sam Dillon et al., 1998
Wall Street Journal Entry for Penn and Karmin, 1967
Washington Post Entry for Carol Guzy, 1995
Washington Post Entry for Sullivan and Jordan, 2003

Jury Statements

„Commentary" Jury Report, March 3, 1993, 1 p.
„International Reporting" Jury Report, March 9, 1953, 1 p ,
„International Reporting" Jury Report, March 12, 1959, 1 p.
„International Reporting" Jury Report, March 8, 1963, 2 pp.
„International Reporting" Jury Report, March 4, 1998, 3 pp.
„International Reporting" Jury Report, March 7, 2003, 3 pp ,
„International Reporting" Jury Report, March 2, 2017, 2 pp.
„National Reporting" Jury Report, March 8, 1967, 1 p.
„Spot News Photography" Jury Report, March 7, 1995,3 pp.

Published Materials

Allison, Graham: Conceptual models and the Cuban Missile Crisis, Santa Monica, Calif., 1968.
Barry, Tom/Browne, Harry/Sims, Beth: Crossing the line. Immigrants, economic integration, and drug enforcement on the U.S.-Mexico border, Albuquerque, N.M., 1994.
Bonachea, Rolando E./Valdes, Nelson P. (Eds.): Cuba in revolution, Garden City, N.Y., 1972.
Brunet, Michel: Canadians et Canadiens. Etudes sur l'histoire et la pensée des deux Canadas, Paris 1954.
Callahan, James Morton: American foreign policy in Canadian relations, New York 1967.

202

Clarkson, Stephen (Ed.): An independent foreign policy for Canada?, Toronto 1968.

Conant, Melvin: The long polar watch. Canada and the defence of North America, New York 1962.

Craig, Gerald Marquis: The United States and Canada, Cambridge, Mass., 1968.

Crispo, John H. G. (Ed.): Wages, prices, profits and economic policy, Toronto 1968.

Deutsch, John J. et al. (Eds.): The Canadian economy. Selected readings, rev. ed., Toronto, 1965.

Fischer, Heinz-D.: Outstanding International Press Reporting. Pulitzer Prize Winning Articles in Foreign Correspondence, 5 vols., Berlin - New York 1984-2000.

Fischer, Heinz-D.: Picture Coverage of the World - Pulitzer Prize Winning Photos, Berlin 2011.

Fischer, Heinz-D./Fischer, Erika J.: Der Pulitzer-Preis - Konkurrenten, Kämpfe, Kontroversen, Berlin 2007.

Fischer, Heinz-D./Fischer, Erika J.: The Pulitzer Prize Archive, vol. 4: International Reporting 1928-1985, Munich - London - New York - Oxford - Paris, 1987.

Fernandez, Damian J.: Cuban Studies since the Revolution, Gainesville, Fl., 2005.

Girard, Philippe: Haiti - The Tumuluous History, New York 2010.

Goldenberg, Boris: The Cuban revolution and Latin America, New York 1965.

Hamnett, Brian R.: A Concise History of Mexico, London 1999.

Hohenberg, John: Foreign Correspondence - The Great Reporters and Their Times, New York - London 1964. .

Hohenberg, John: The Pulitzer Prizes - A History of the Awards in Books, Drama, Music, and Journalism, New York - London 1974.

Hohenberg, John: The Pulitzer Prize Story - News Stories, Editorials, Cartoons and Pictures, New York - London 1959.

Hohenberg, John: The Pulitzer Prize Story II - Award-Winning News Stories, Columns, Editorials, Cartoons and News Pictures, 1959-1980, New York 1980.

Jackson D. Bruce: Castro, the Kremlin and communism in Latin America, Baltimore, Md., 1969.

Karol, Kewes S.: Guerillas in power - the course of the Cuban revolution, New York 1970.

Lupsha, Peter A./Schlegel, Kip: The political economy of drug trafficking. The Herrera organization (Mexico & the United States), Albuquerque, N.M., 1980.

Mallin, Jay: Fortress Cuba. Russia's American base, Chicago 1965.

Mills, Charles Wright: Listen, Yankee - the revolution in Cuba, New York 1960.

Morray, Joseph P.: The second revolution in Cuba, New York 1962.

Nelson, Lowry: Cuba - the measure of a revolution, Minneapolis, Minn., 1972.

Pachter, Henry Macimilian: Collision course - the Cuban Missile Crisis and coexistence, New York 1963.

Phillips, Ruby Hart: The Cuban dilemma, New York 19?3.

Plank, John (Ed.): Cuba and the United States - long range perspectives, Washington. D.C., 1967.

Robert, Jean-Claude: Du Canada français au Quebec libre. Histoire d'un mouvement independantiste, Paris 1975.

Russell, Peter (Ed.): Nationalism in Canada, Toronto - New York 1966.

Ruiz, Ramon Eduardo: Cuba - the making of a revolution, Amherst, Mass., 1968.

Seers, Dudley (Ed.): Cuba - the economic and social revolution, Chapel Hill, N.C., 1964.

Smith, Robert Freeman (Ed.): Background to revolution. The development of modern Cuba, New York 1966.

Smith, Robert Freeman: The United States and Cuba - Business and diplomacy, 1917-1960, New Haven, Conn., 1960.

Stovel, John A.: Canada in the world economy, Cambridge 1959.

Thomson, Dale C./Swanson, Roger F.: Canadien foreign policy - options and perspectives, Toronto-New York 1971.

Toro, Maria Celia: Mexico's „war" on drugs. Causes and consequences, Boulder 1995.

Pulitzer Prize Panorama
Prof. Dr. Heinz-Dietrich Fischer (Bochum)

Heinz-Dietrich Fischer
Caricatures on American Historical Phases 1918 – 2018
Pulitzer Prize Winning Editorial Cartoons from Wilson to Trump
This volume covers main phases of United States history over the span of a century, 1918 – 2018. Starting with fights for „Americanism" during World War I until the „America-First" movement of our times, there are, among others, Pulitzer Prize-winning editorial cartoons about these topics: Ku Klux Klan, Foreign Policy, Great Depression, Lynching Practices, Labor Conditions, War Productions, Truman's Administration, Korean War, Racial Integration, Vietnam War, Watergate Scandal, Death Penalty, Ronald Reagan, Clinton's Sex Affair, Terrorist Attacks, Iraq War, Deadly Hurricanes, Financial Crashes, Washington Establishment, Presidents Barack Obama and Donald Trump.
vol. 19, 2019, ca. 208 pp., ca. 29,90 €, br., ISBN-CH 978-3-643-91154-4

Heinz-Dietrich Fischer
Facets of the Vietnam War in American Media
Pulitzer Prize Winning Articles, Books, Cartoons and Photos
This volume assembles Vietnam War-related stories by twenty Pulitzer Prize laureates – reporters, cartoonists, photographers and book authors – about various phases and aspects of the fightings. There are articles about the origins of the conflict, shocking reports from the combat zones or disclosures of American war crimes; there are book portions re President Nixon's war conduct, anti-war demonstrations in Washington or the death of soldiers; there are cartoons expressing U.S. illusions about alleged war successes or the loss of thousands of casualties; and there are pictures showing Vietnamese civilians facing the war: family members fleeing across a river or children escaping from a war zone after napalm bombings.
vol. 18, 2019, ca. 208 pp., ca. 29,90 €, br., ISBN-CH 978-3-643-91074-5

Heinz-Dietrich Fischer
Distinguished Criticism on Theater, Film and Television
Pulitzer Prize Winning Samples
vol. 17, 2019, ca. 256 pp., ca. 29,90 €, br., ISBN-CH 978-3-643-91044-8

LIT Verlag Berlin – Münster – Wien – Zürich – London
Auslieferung Deutschland / Österreich / Schweiz: siehe Impressumsseite

Heinz-Dietrich Fischer
Acclaimed Press Coverage of Latin American Countries
Pulitzer Prize Winning Articles, Cartoons and Photos
This volume contains award-winning articles and pictures from various Latin American countries and tells stories about German Nazi members in Uruguay, the dictatorial Perón régime in Argentina, the brutal Batista Government on Cuba and the upcoming of Fidel Castro, facets of the Civil War in El Salvador, politics and poverty on Haiti and the effects of drug corruption in Mexico.
Bd. 16, 2018, 208 S., 29,90 €, br., ISBN 978-3-643-90988-6

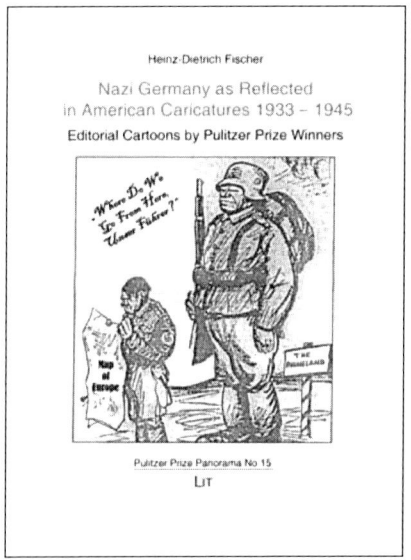

Heinz-Dietrich Fischer
Nazi Germany as Reflected in American Caricatures 1933 – 1945
Editorial Cartoons by Pulitzer Prize Winners
This volume contains about 170 political caricatures about the history of Nazi Germany from the start in 1933 to the collaps in 1945, drawn by sixteen American Pulitzer Prize-winning editorial cartoonists, among them multiple laureates like Rollin Kirby of the 'New York World', Edmund Duffy of the 'Baltimore Sun' or Herbert L. Block of the 'Washington Post'.
Bd. 15, 2017, 244 S., 34,90 €, br., ISBN 978-3-643-90942-8

Heinz-Dietrich Fischer
The Pulitzer Prize Century
All Winners and their Merits 1917 – 2016
This volume presents a synopsis of the 100-Years-History of the prestigious Pulitzer Prizes by listening the winners and samples of their work in all award groups, like Reportage Journalism, Recherche Journalism, Opinion Journalism, Picture Journalism, Nonfictional Books, Belles Lettres, Performing Arts and Honorary Awards.
Bd. 14, 2017, 292 S., 59,90 €, br., ISBN 978-3-643-90882-7

Heinz-Dietrich Fischer
Reports from Middle East Conflict Regions
Pulitzer Prize Winning Articles
Bd. 13, 2016, 196 S., 59,90 €, br., ISBN 978-3-643-90813-1

LIT Verlag Berlin – Münster – Wien – Zürich – London
Auslieferung Deutschland / Österreich / Schweiz: siehe Impressumsseite

Heinz-Dietrich Fischer
Outstanding Caricatures on World Politics
Pulitzer Prize Winning Editorial Cartoons
Bd. 12, 2016, 180 S., 59,90 €, br., ISBN 978-3-643-90762-2

Heinz-Dietrich Fischer
American Historians Describe the European Past
Bd. 11, 2016, 216 S., 89,90 €, br., ISBN 978-3-643-90717-2

Heinz-Dietrich Fischer
Coverage of Political Occurrences in Asia
Pulitzer Prize Winning Articles, Cartoons and Photos
Bd. 10, 2015, 234 S., 89,90 €, br., ISBN 978-3-643-90592-5

Heinz-Dietrich Fischer
Key Images of American Life
Pulitzer Prize Winning Pictures
Bd. 9, 2014, 232 S., 59,90 €, br., ISBN 978-3-643-90518-5

Heinz-Dietrich Fischer
Foreign Correspondents Report From Africa
Pulitzer Prize Winning Articles and Pictures
Bd. 8, 2013, 168 S., 69,90 €, br., ISBN 978-3-643-90441-6

Heinz-Dietrich Fischer
Main Achievements of American Presidents
Pulitzer Prize Winning Books' Excerpts
Bd. 7, 2013, 240 S., 89,90 €, br., ISBN 978-3-643-90362-4

Heinz-Dietrich Fischer
Outstanding Broadway Dramas and Comedies
Pulitzer Prize Winning Theater Productions
Bd. 6, 2013, 232 S., 89,90 €, br., ISBN 978-3-643-90341-9

Heinz-Dietrich Fischer
American Top Journalists Analyse Russia
Pulitzer Prize Winning Articles and Cartoons
Bd. 5, 2012, 256 S., 89,90 €, br., ISBN 978-3-643-90243-6

Heinz-Dietrich Fischer
Political Caricatures on Global Issues
Pulitzer Prize Winning Editorial Cartoons
Bd. 4, 2012, 224 S., 89,90 €, br., ISBN 978-3-643-90222-1

Heinz-Dietrich Fischer
Reporting on International Political Conflicts
Pulitzer Prize Winning War Coverage
Bd. 3, 2012, 224 S., 89,90 €, br., ISBN 978-3-643-90173-6

Heinz-Dietrich Fischer
Picture Coverage of the World
Pulitzer Prize Winning Photos
Bd. 2, 2011, 264 S., 89,90 €, br., ISBN 978-3-643-10844-9

Heinz-Dietrich Fischer
Germany Through American Eyes
Pulitzer Prize Winning Reports
Bd. 1, 2010, 176 S., 89,90 €, br., ISBN 978-3-643-10719-0

LIT Verlag Berlin – Münster – Wien – Zürich – London
Auslieferung Deutschland / Österreich / Schweiz: siehe Impressumsseite